Springer Series on Ethics, Law, and Aging

Series Editor

Marshall B. Kapp, JD, MPH
Director, Wright State University
Office of Geriatric Medicine
and Gerontology
Wright State University,
Dayton, OH

Michael A. Smyer, PhD, is Dean of the Graduate School of Arts & Sciences at Boston College. He has published extensively on a broad range of research interests and policy concerns, which include the effects of mental health interventions in nursing homes, notions of health and well-being for older adults and families, the problems of workers in long-term care, and the effects of pharmaceutical assistance programs for elders. He is the recent recipient of Penn State's Pattishall Award for Outstanding Research Achievement and numerous other professional honors. Dr. Smyer received an American Council on Education Fellowship in Academic Administration and served as Associate Chairman of Penn State's Gerontology Center and Professor-in-Charge of the University's Department of Individual and Family Studies.

K. Warner Schaie, PhD, is the Evan Pugh Professor of Human Development and Psychology and Director of the Gerontology Center at the Pennsylvania State University. He has previously held professional appointments at the University of Nebraska, West Virginia University, and the University of Southern California. Dr. Schaie received his BA from the University of California-Berkeley, and his MS and PhD degrees from the University of Washington, all in psychology. He is the author or editor of 22 books and over 150 journal articles and chapters related to the study of human aging. Dr. Schaie is the recipient of the Distinguished Scientific Contributions Award of the American Psychological Association and of the Robert W. Kleemeier Award for Distinguished Research Contributions from the Gerontological Society of America.

Marshall B. Kapp, JD, MPH, was educated at Johns Hopkins University (BA), George Washington University (JD with Honors), and Harvard University (MPH). Since August 1980, he has been a faculty member in the School of Medicine at Wright State University, Dayton, Ohio, where he is a Professor in the Department of Community Health and Director of the WSU Office of Geriatric Medicine and Gerontology. He holds an adjunct faculty appointment at the University of Dayton School of Law. In addition to being admitted to practice law in a number of state and federal courts, he is also licensed as a Nursing Home Administrator in the District of Columbia. He is the author of a substantial number of published books, articles, and reviews. Dr. Kapp is a Fellow of the Gerontological Society of America.

Older Adults' Decision-Making and the Law

Michael Smyer, PhD

K. Warner Schaie, PhD

Marshall B. Kapp, JD, MPH

Editors

SPRINGER PUBLISHING COMPANY

Springer Publishing Company, Inc.
536 Broadway
New York, NY 10012-3955

Cover design by Tom Yabut
Production Editor: Pam Lankas

96 97 98 99 2000 / 5 4 3 2 1

Library of Congress Cataloging-in-Publication Data

Older adults' decision-making and the law / Michael Smyer, K. Warner
 Schaie, Marshall Kapp, editors.
     p. cm.
   Includes bibliographical references and indexes.
   ISBN 0-8261-8990-3
   1. Aged—Legal status, laws, etc.—United States. 2. Capacity and
 disability—United States. I. Smyer, Michael A. II. Schaie, K. Warner
 (Klaus Warner), 1928- III. Kapp, Marshall B. KF390.A4063 1995
 346.7301'3—dc20   95-24250
 [347.30613]   CIP

Printed in the United States of America

Contents

Contributors

Alison P. Barnes, Esq.
Marquette University Law School
Milwaukee, WI

Gay Becker, PhD
School of Nursing
University of California
San Francisco, CA

Rae Brown, RN, MS
School of Nursing
The Pennsylvania State University
University Park, PA

Elias S. Cohen, MPA, JD
136 Farwood Road
Wynnewood, PA

Gene Cohen, MD, PhD
Washington, DC Center
  on Aging
1915 Biltmore Street, NW
Washington, DC

Cheryl Dellasega, GNP, PhD
The Pennsylvania State University
University Park, PA

Lori Frank, MA
The Pennsylvania State University
University Park, PA

Lawrence A. Frolik, PhD
University of Pittsburgh
School of Law
Pittsburgh, PA

Penelope A. Hommel, MSc
Center for Social
  Gerontology, Inc.
Ann Arbor, MI

Sharon R. Kaufman, PhD
School of Nursing
University of California
San Francisco, CA

Mrs. A.B. Macfarlane
Master Court of Protection
London, England

Mary Joy Quinn, Director
Probate Court Services
San Francisco Superior Court
San Francisco, CA

John J. Regan, JD, JSD
Hofstra School of Law
Hempstead, NY

Charles P. Sabatino, JD
American Bar Association
Commission on Legal Problems of
  the Elderly
Washington, DC

Timothy A. Salthouse, PhD
School of Psychology
Georgia Institute of Technology
Atlanta, GA

Winsor C. Schmidt, JD, LLM
Center for Health Services
  Research
Memphis State University
Memphis, TN

Lori A. Stiegel, JD
American Bar Association
Commission on Legal Problems of
  the Elderly
Washington, DC

Kathleen H. Wilbur, PhD
Andrus Gerontology Center
University of Southern California
Los Angeles, CA

Sherry L. Willis, PhD
The Pennsylvania State University
University Park, PA

Preface

This is the eighth volume in a series on the broad topic of "Societal Impact on Aging." The first five volumes of this series were published by Erlbaum Associates under the series title of "Social Structure and Aging." The present volume is the third published under the Springer Publishing Company imprint. It is the edited proceedings of a conference held at the Pennsylvania State University, October 10–12, 1993.

The series of conferences originated from the deliberations of a subcommittee of the Committee on Life Course Perspectives of the Social Science Research Council chaired by Matilda White Riley in the early 1980s. That subcommittee was charged with developing an agenda and mechanisms that would serve to encourage communication between scientists who study societal structures that might affect the aging of individuals and those scientists who are concerned with the possible effects of contextual influences on individual aging. The committee proposed a series of conferences that would systematically explore the interfaces between social structures and behavior, and in particular to identify mechanisms through which society influences adult development. When the third editor was named director of the Penn State Gerontology Center, he was able to implement this conference program as one of the center's major activities.

The previous seven volumes in this series have dealt with the societal impact on aging in psychological processes (Schaie & Schooler, 1989); age structuring in comparative perspective (Kertzer & Schaie, 1989); self-directedness and efficacy over the life span (Rodin, Schooler, & Schaie, 1990); aging, health behaviors, and health outcomes (Schaie, Blazer, & House, 1992); caregiving in families (Zarit, Pearlin, & Schaie, 1993); aging in historical perspective (Schaie & Achenbaum, 1993); and adult intergenerational relations (Bengtson, Schaie, & Burton, 1995). The present volume was designed to examine how social, behavioral, legal, and ethical perspectives impact the law on older adults' decision-making capacity.

The strategy for each of these volumes has been to commission six reviews on three major topics by established subject-matter specialists who have credibility in aging research. We then invited two formal discussants for each chapter—usually one drawn from the writer's discipline and one from a neighboring discipline. This format seems to provide a suitable antidote against the perpetuation of parochial orthodoxies as well as to make certain that questions are raised with respect to the validity of iconoclastic departures in new directions.

To focus the conference, the editors chose three topics of broad interest to gerontologists. Social and behavioral scientists with a demonstrated track record were then selected and asked to interact with those interested in theory-building within a multidisciplinary context.

The volume begins with an examination of the alternative approaches taken by different disciplines in defining the concept of competence. The first chapter provides a review of legal perspectives on competence, and how the law views the impact of aging on an individual's competence. Next we consider older adults' involvement in health-care decision making, their understanding of the issues, and their ability and willingness to grapple with their options and potential outcomes.

The second topic in this volume deals with methodological and ethical issues in assessing decisional capacity. An assessment battery is described that can be applied to measure the significant impairments in instrumental activities of daily living often associated with Alzheimer's disease and that reduce the capacity of individuals to live independently. This is followed by a focus on the ethical dilemmas faced by clinicians and family members in trying to assess the changing capacity for decision making in an impaired older person.

The third topic deals with alternative processes and mechanisms for addressing the consequences of decisional incapacity. Once an individual has been determined to have impaired decisional capacity, social strategies must be developed and implemented to protect that person from harm without excessively intruding on his or her autonomy. The continuum of alternatives to guardianship mechanisms presently available are therefore reviewed in some detail, followed by an account of the important substantive and procedural reforms that have occurred over the past decade. The practice and policy ramifications of these legislative reforms are discussed from the point of view of an action agency administrator.

We are grateful for the financial support of the conference that led to this volume, which was provided by conference grant AG 09787-03 from the National Institute on Aging, and by additional support from the Vice-President for Research and Dean of the Graduate School of the Pennsylvania State University. We are also grateful to Judy Hall and Alvin Hall for handling the conference logistics, to Anna Shuey for coordinating the manuscript preparation, and to Audrey Shadek for preparing the indexes.

K. WARNER SCHAIE

REFERENCES

Bengtson, V. L., Schaie, K. W., & Burton, L. (1995). *Adult intergenerational relations: Effects of societal changes*. New York: Springer Publishing Co.

Kertzer, D., & Schaie, K. W. (1989). *Age structuring in comparative perspective*. Hillsdale, NJ: Erlbaum.

Rodin, J., Schooler, C., & Schaie, K. W. (1991). *Self-directedness and efficacy: Causes and effects throughout the life course*. Hillsdale, NJ: Erlbaum.

Schaie, K. W., & Achenbaum, W. A. (1993). *Societal impact on aging: Historical perspectives*. New York: Springer Publishing Co.

Schaie, K. W., House, J., & Blazer, D. (1992). *Aging, health behaviors, and health outcomes*. Hillsdale, NJ: Erlbaum.

Schaie, K. W., & Schooler, C. (1989). *Social structure and aging: Psychological processes*. Hillsdale, NJ: Erlbaum.

Zarit, S. H., Pearlin, L., & Schaie, K. W. (1993). *Social structure and caregiving: Family and cross-national perspectives*. Hillsdale, NJ: Erlbaum.

CHAPTER 1

Competency: Refining Our Legal Fictions

Charles P. Sabatino

In Western jurisprudence, the concept of competency is a legal presumption. It rests upon the assumption that each of us, at adulthood, is best able to decide what is in our best interest, and that we ought to be left alone to pursue our own choices (Meisel, 1989).

Incompetency, or incapacity, is a term that defines, or attempts to define, when a state may take actions to shatter this assumption and limit the individual's right to make decisions about his or her person or property based on disability (Parry, 1985a). In truth, incompetency is a legal fiction. This means that it is a construct treated as a fact, whether or not it is it really so, because it is recognized as having utility. Here I am referring to legal incompetency, or more accurately, legal incapacity, and not clinical or *de facto* incompetency.

There is great confusion in both legal and clinical practice over terminology with respect to mental capacity (Meisel, 1989). In this chapter, I will use the terms *incompetency* and *incapacity* interchangeably, although *incapacity* is the preferred term, increasingly used in both case law and legislation. It avoids the "all or nothing" connotation of the *incompetency* label as well as other historical baggage of the term.

The analysis below traces certain core themes in the statutory evolution of incapacity in the context of guardianship proceedings. The term *guardianship* is used here to refer to the judicial process for appointing a manager or decision maker over the personal and/or financial affairs of an incapacitated person, regardless of the particular term or terms used in any specific jurisdiction. An aim of this analysis is to bring into focus the historical, value-driven subjectivity of the law, even as contemporary statutes have attempted to refine criteria for determining capacity to more scientifically justifiable standards. The conclusion proffered at the end of this review suggests that, no matter how articulate, detailed, or comprehensive the legislative definitions or substantive standards, incapacity determinations for all but the most clear cases will depend on a malleable weighing process—that is, the judicial task, ultimately, is to weigh medical variables, social variables, and a constellation of very practical variables, relating to the need for state intervention in a unique human situation.

Judicial discretion will not easily be contained by more elaborate statutory definitions of incapacity. Instead, because the determination unavoidably remains a weighing of multiple variables, the more vital protector of individual rights in the context of guardianship is the procedural component—what we call *due process*. We can and must require that determinations of incapacity in judicial proceedings be premised on a thorough fleshing out of all perspectives, especially the perspective of the putative ward, and a thorough assessment that considers the interplay of these perspectives. This chapter does not address the nature or utility of particular assessment instruments or theories. Kapp (1990) and others such as Anderer (1990), Grisso (1986), and Nolan (1984) have accomplished that task. The goal here is to shine a clear light on the legal basis of state intervention and its search for objectivity.

INCAPACITY AS LEGAL FICTION

First, let us consider the nature of the legal concept of incapacity. The title of this chapter refers to it as a legal fiction. Labeling the concept a legal fiction does not mean that the concept lacks reality, legitimacy or consequence. To the contrary, legal fictions exist to meet sometimes very powerful social needs and values, and such fictions can have far-reaching consequences. One of the most notorious and consequential legal fictions was incorporated into our country's Constitution. The concept of slaves as chattel was a legal fiction with painfully real consequences until the passage of the 13th Amendment. Another largely moribund legal fiction proclaimed husband and wife to be one, a fiction that effectively restrained the independent status of women, especially with respect to property matters, for generations.

Lon Fuller's treatise (1967) on legal fictions described several functions of legal fictions, noting their pervasive use in the law, often as a way to reconcile a specific legal result with some premise or postulate. He describes the ways in which fictions serve the process of legal evolution by introducing new law in the guise of the old, so that change will be less threatening to the stability of the law, and thus more readily accepted. Legal concepts such as delivery and possession of property, fraud, and trusts have undergone extensive expansion in meaning through the use of fictions embracing the notions of constructive possession, constructive fraud, or constructive trusts, and so on. One commentator noted, as far back as 1917, "The fiction is frequently resorted to in the attempt to conceal the fact that the law is undergoing alteration at the hands of the judges" (Smith, 1917, p. 150). Thus, in this sense, legal fictions are a kind of linguistic cover. In a more positive light, Julius Stone (1968) in his treatise on the function of law, describes legal fictions as the "swaddling clothes" of legal change (p. 459).

Fictions have other purposes, too. They are sometimes used for convenience. Many have been invented in order to expound legal doctrine already in existence, rather than to change it. In this sense, they have been likened to a "convenient shorthand" (Fuller, 1967, p. 54). For example, the fiction of "corporate personality" serves as an abbreviation for a cluster of legal rights and obligations that would be terribly bothersome to spell out repeatedly in discourse (Fuller, 1967, p. 55).

Why do we need the legal fiction of incompetency? The answer may be fairly straightforward: because we need a trigger to tell us when a state legitimately may take action to limit an individual's rights to make decisions about his or her own person or property. The underpinning of this legal fiction is the doctrine of *parens patriae*—the obligation of the sovereign to care for the vulnerable and less fortunate (Brakel, 1985).

Even though the roots of *parens patriae* go back centuries in our legal system, there is nothing about the doctrine that pinpoints exactly when its principles should "kick in" and permit state intervention into an individual's affairs.

That is why definitions of incapacity become important. They are the triggers defined by society. Recognizing incapacity as a legal fiction is important precisely because a fiction is determined by prevailing values, knowledge, and even the economic and political spirit of the time. In other words, the criteria or elements needed to establish legal incapacity are products of society's prevailing beliefs concerning individual autonomy and social order, tempered by the restraint of legal precedent. Just as societal values and needs have evolved over time, so will the legal criteria for capacity and incapacity. Yet, at any point in historical time, we tend to reify capacity and make it a static "thing" to be discovered. As Margulies (1994) perceptively notes: "Capacity is a shifting network of values and circumstances."

EVOLUTION OF A FICTION

As a starting point to understanding the evolution of the fiction of incapacity, it is important to realize that we have never had a national consensus on a standard for declaring an individual to be incapacitated (Anderer, 1990). Nevertheless, common themes run through the variability, and these themes shed useful light on present assumptions in our legal system concerning autonomy, aging, and disability.

Let us begin with a paradox in the law's approach to incapacity. On the one hand, our legal system has always recognized situation-specific standards of competency that depend on the specific event or transaction in question—such as capacity to make a will, marry, enter into a contract, vote, drive a car, stand trial in a criminal prosecution, and so on (Parry, 1985b). A finding of incapacity in any of these matters could nullify or prevent a particular legal act. On the other hand, at least until very recently, determinations of competency in the context of guardianship proceedings were quite the opposite. They were routinely very global, generalized determinations of one's ability to manage property and personal affairs. Moreover, a finding of incompetency in this latter area traditionally justified quite intrusive curtailments of personal autonomy, and resulted in a virtually complete loss of one's civil rights (Frolik, 1981; Horstman, 1975).

One explanation of this paradox is the nature of the judicial process itself. Specific standards of incompetency for discrete transactions arose through the process of case adjudication. Judges adjudicate specific disputes brought before them about specific transactions. So it is fairly predictable that situation-specific standards of incompetency would emerge. Guardianship, on the other hand, historically sought not to adjudicate specific transactions but rather the status of the person. Moreover, over time the standards for this adjudication of status became shaped primarily by legislators, and not by court-made principles.

Guardianship goes back at least as far as the 14th century English law, *De Praerogativa Regis* (1324),[1] which articulated the concept of special protection for those lacking the ability to care for themselves. It permitted the king to manage the lands and profits of estates of two classes of mentally disabled persons: "idiots" (those born without reason) and "lunatics" (those who later in life lost capacity) (Brakel, 1985, p. 10). The concept behind the English law actually shows up earlier in Roman law, at least as early as the time of Cicero (Brakel, 1985).

As the original model for present day guardianship statutes, the English law was not, as we might hope, driven primarily by humanitarian concerns. It was driven by concern about the management of property, not about care of persons with disabilities. The law was only relevant to the propertied class, where chaos in management might contribute to disorder in the realm. When the alleged incompetent did not possess substantial property, guardianship proceedings were rare.

Following this pattern, several of the American colonies passed legislation designed to protect the estates of "insane persons" (Brakel, 1985; Deutsch, 1949). Gradually, this basic schema of legally sanctioned paternalism received a clear statutory foundation in all states in the form of guardianship laws. These laws, however, shared the social bias of the original concept in that they were largely concerned about and focused on the management of property and not the care of the elderly (Alexander & Lewin, 1972; Schmidt, Miller, Bell, & New, 1981). Protection and management of the ward's personal affairs was essentially unregulated and came much later in the law's development.

Status-Based Incompetency

More importantly, these laws established an amorphous status test for incompetency. Courts and juries could bestow the labels "idiot," "insane person," "lunatic," "*non compos mentis*," and the like with enormous discretion. A requirement that the person be unable to care for himself or herself was included in or added to many of these statutes, but the requirement was largely tautological with the label. The finding of incompetency reduced the putative ward to the legal status of an infant.

Some of the archaic language has actually remained entrenched as late as the 1990s. For example, until 1991, the Rhode Island statute permitted the appointment of a guardian of the person or estate

> of any idiot, lunatic, or person of unsound mind, of any habitual drunkard, or of any person who from excessive drinking, gaming, idleness or debauchery of any kind, or from want of discretion in managing his estate, so spends, wastes, or lessens his estate or is likely so to do, that he may bring himself or his family to want or suffering, or may render himself or family chargeable upon the town for support. (Rhode Island General Laws, 1969)[2]

Similarly, until 1987 Alabama permitted the appointment of a guardian for persons of "unsound mind," defined to include "idiots, lunatics or the insane."[3] As legal fictions, these labels might aptly be characterized as "linguistic covers" to justify the state's preservation of stable property interests within its borders and to prevent the person from becoming a burden on the state (Fuller).

One interesting status category is the puritanical designation of "spendthrift," a not uncommon reason for guardianship until the 1970s or so. Massachusetts still has a spendthrift guardianship provision much like Rhode Island's:

> A person who, by excessive drinking, gaming, idleness, or debauchery of any kind, so spends, wastes or lessens his estate as to expose himself or his family to want or suffering, or the department of public welfare, to charge or expense for his support or for the support of his family, may be adjudged a spendthrift.[4]

While the term spendthrift is not equivalent to mental incapacity, it nevertheless illustrates a status approach to disability, based unashamedly on the outcomes of one's behavior. In fact, unlike the fiction of incompetency, spendthrift provisions at least have the attribute of being more direct about the economic values and purposes furthered by guardianship law.

In time, the status approach was refined in most states in two important respects. First, the laws gradually incorporated a more medicalized approach to adjudicating one's status; and second, most states required a finding that the disabling condition caused some dysfunctional behavior (Parry, 1985a).

Disabling Condition Tests

The medicalized approach required the finding of one or more types of disorders or disabling conditions as a prerequisite for determining incapacity. This new fiction reflected, in part, the ascendancy of modern medicine's authority in health and mental health care in our culture during the middle part of the 20th century. In guardianship proceedings, it enabled diagnostic labels to flourish and weigh heavily in determinations of capacity. By the 1960s, the distinction between medical disability and legal disability became increasingly blurred (Horstman, 1975). At the same time, the distinction between involuntary commitment and guardianship likewise blurred under the medical model. Civil commitment proceedings sought increasingly not only to protect the public from harm (a function of the state's police power), but also to protect the individual from self-inflicted harm and to impose therapeutic objectives upon the individual (a function of the state's *parens patriae* power) (Horstman, 1975; Kittrie, 1971; Parry, 1985a).

With respect to the disabling condition labels used, a 1990 monograph by the American Bar Association (ABA) found that 34 states include "mental illness" among the specified disabilities, 15 include "mental retardation" or "developmental disability," 31 refer to chronic use of drugs or chronic intoxication, 33 include "physical illness" or "physical disability," 15 include "advanced age," and 34 states use audaciously general terms such as "mental deficiency," "mental disability," "mental condition," "mental infirmity," "weakness of mind," or "in need of mental treatment" (Anderer, 1990). This list is not exhaustive; the array of potential disabilities is quite broad.

The finding of one of these putative disabilities presumably offers a sense of objectivity to the adjudication process, although critics of the mental illness paradigm of behavior would find little comfort in this laundry list of disabling conditions (Kittrie, 1971; Szasz, 1984). The disabling-condition requirement ostensibly serves to limit the state's power under an objective, scientific standard. However, any real limitation is belied by the fact that, according to the same ABA report, 27 states concluded their list of disabilities by adding "or other cause" (Anderer, 1990). Thus, the range of disabling conditions may be as broad as the judge's imagination.

Functional Behavior (Outcome) Tests Linked to Disability

Along with the disabling conditions criteria came the addition of a second prong to the test for incapacity—a causally connected dysfunctional behavior test. In order to find incapacity, most states required that individuals be functionally impaired with respect to their ability to manage their property or their person as a result of the disabling condition. This element of capacity theoretically distinguishes clinical incapacity from legal incapacity. In other words, the existence of a behavioral impairment introduces an element of "social necessity" which, unlike the diagnostic task, is within the court's purview and expertise to assess. If the state does not intervene, so the presumption goes, some significant harm will occur to the individual in issue.

While necessity may be a proper conceptual trigger of the *parens patriae* power, the functional behavior tests used to measure it have been notoriously nebulous. Indeed, the functional tests found in state law epitomize statutory draftsmanship at its vaguest and most subjective. Common phraseology includes the criteria "incapable of taking care of himself,"[5] "unable . . . properly to manage and take care of himself or his property,"[6] "unable adequately to conduct his personal or business affairs,"[7] "incapable of taking proper care of himself or his property or fails to provide for his family . . . ,"[8] or "substantially incapable of managing his property or caring for himself."[9]

It is fairly obvious that these kinds of tests openly invite judgments of incapacity based upon the judge's opinion of the reasonableness of one's behavior—essentially, a subjective outcome test. You act crazy, therefore, you must be crazy. Of course, one of the disability labels also had to fit. In concept, it was the disability label that distinguished a "sick" individual, in need of the state's paternalistic intervention, from a competent person who chooses to act eccentric, foolish, crazy, or even self-destructive. In practice, however, the protection is largely illusory.

A provincial but illuminating 1962 probate court opinion from Ohio demonstrates the potential for arbitrariness and capriciousness inherent in the broadly framed two-pronged test. The case, *In re Tyrrell*, presented probate judge Williams with a dispute concerning 85-year-old Mr. Walter Tyrrell, allegedly a victim of a designing person, Mrs. Wise.

The judge's opinion states the presenting problem:

> The evidence discloses that since October 1961 [Mr. Tyrrell] has given Mrs. Wise in excess of two thousand dollars. These have been checks ranging in amounts from ten to fifty dollars.
>
> It is undisputed that Mr. Tyrrell has been an individual who had the good fortune of making considerable money in his earlier days and he also was a gentleman with expensive tastes . . . The ward now has as his life's savings some ten thousand dollars worth of bank stock. (p. 253)

Judge Williams summarizes the in-depth process used to obtain clinical evidence:

> In chambers, immediately preceding the hearing, the [petitioner] requested that two medical doctors . . . be permitted to examine Mr. Tyrrell. This request was granted. For approximately fifteen minutes they had the opportunity to examine the alleged ward in the jury room.
>
> The testimony of the doctors for the proponents was to the effect that a guardian was needed because the alleged ward was subject to undue influence . . . . The one medical examiner asked Mr. Tyrrell why he had given money to Mrs. Wise and he said that he had given it to her because he felt that she needed it. (p. 253)

Judge Williams describes the two-pronged test to be applied:

> [T]he Court, before appointing a guardian for an alleged incompetent, should be fully and completely satisfied that the claimed infirmity or infirmities . . . are of such a nature and character as to prevent such person from fully and completely protecting herself and property interests from those about her who would be inclined to and would take advantage of such person in the way of securing her property or means without giving proper service or value therefor. . . .In applying this principle as enunciated, the Court must first find that a mental infirmity exists, then secondly, find that said infirmity prevents him from dealing at arm's length. (p. 253)

Finally, the judge weighs the evidence against the standard. On the positive side, Judge Williams noted initially that Mr. Tyrrell "sat at the opponent's table and followed the testimony of the witnesses quite carefully," and that he "still had a remarkable memory for past events." Furthermore:

> It is undisputed that Mr. Tyrrell has been an individual who had the good fortune of making considerable money in his earlier days and he also was a gentleman with expensive tastes. The witnesses had knowledge of the expensive parties which he had given for the benefit of his friends. Approximately twenty years ago, when his earning days were over, he retrenched and began to live within his income.
>
> The opponents [of the guardianship petition] claim that Mr. Tyrrell is the same person today that he was earlier in his life; that he is still a spender and one who is extravagant and that he is still showering gifts. (p. 253)

However, the judge was ultimately swayed by absurdly scant evidence of incapacity. He provides the following analysis:

> With respect to the present status of the individual, the Court observed the following: that his smile at times is not normal; his eyes do not focus properly at all times; his gait and reflexes are not normal; and that he is not laying his cane aside, but is dropping it.
>
> These are indications of the lessening of the gentleman's mental capacities. Just what has caused this is not known to the Court. In any event, there has been a deterioration which would be called mental illness.
>
> The second question which must be answered is, can he deal at arm's length? There are instances which have been cited which indicate that he can. However this gentleman has parted with some two thousand dollars during the last six months and there is no indication that he received proper service or value therefor. In review of this, the Court must find, and does so find, that he is subject to undue influence . . . The necessary elements to establish a guardianship having been substantiated, it is the finding of the Court that a guardian of the person and estate be appointed. (p. 253)

Judge Williams' analysis certainly falls below the level of thoroughness and objectivity that we would ideally expect in guardianship decisions. Yet his mistake may have been in demonstrating explicitly a type of ageist and arbitrary analysis that more often occurs subtly under the broad two-pronged tests for competency.

Meeting Essential Needs and Endangerment Elements

Many states responded to the obvious subjectivity of the broad two-pronged test by attempting to further refine the dysfunctional behavior prong. These states took the broad language of "incapable of taking care" of oneself and sharpened it to focus on the ability to take care of the "essential requirements for the person's physical health or safety" (e.g., Alaska,[10] Arkansas,[11] Florida,[12] Kansas,[13] Oregon[14]). The "essential requirements" language has several variations, too. Some states provide a list of essential requirements, such as: "inability to meet personal needs for medical care, nutrition, clothing, shelter, or safety" (Minnesota,[15] New Hampshire,[16] Utah[17]). Connecticut expands this list further by referring to an "inability to provide medical care for physical and mental health needs, nutritious meals, clothing, safe and adequately heated and ventilated shelter, personal hygiene and protection from physical abuse or harm. . . ."[18] Query whether that language really sharpens anything.

Connecticut and a few other states add to the essential requirements test a requisite finding that the inability endangers the person in some way. Thus, Connecticut requires a resulting "endangerment to such person's health."[19] Missouri requires a finding that "serious physical injury, illness, or disease is likely to occur."[20] And New Hampshire requires a finding that the person "is likely to suffer substantial harm. . . ."[21] These endangerment and essential needs provisions raise the threshold for finding that the person is incapable of caring for himself, but they do not eliminate the possibility of unrestrained speculation by judges.

Given the shortcomings of both prongs of the above test—the disability prong and the behavior prong—it was inevitable that, sooner or later, at least some states would throw out either or both elements of these tests or substitute something else. Not surprisingly, both courses have been taken. The following changes represented attempts, not always successful, to refine the trigger we call incapacity so as to be more sensitive to levels of impairment and to situational differences in impairment.

Functional Behavior Test Alone

Rejecting the reliance on diagnoses and labeling, California and a very few other states turned to a purely behavioral impairment test. California law states in part:

> A conservator of the person may be appointed for a person who is unable properly to provide for his or her personal needs for physical health, food, clothing, or shelter.[22]

Washington State requires for appointment of a guardian of the person

> a significant risk of personal harm based upon a demonstrated inability to adequately provide for nutrition, health, housing, or physical needs.[23]

In neither state must a disabling condition be established. Query whether this approach provides an improvement over the use of a diagnosable disorder requirement. Application of the California standard relies heavily on construction and application of the term "unable." Yet, the standard in itself gives no guidance to distinguish whether the inability is, for example, a mental inability or merely a physical impairment that afflicts an otherwise mentally functional person. Nor does it provide guidance to distinguish the person who chooses (on some level) an aberrant lifestyle from the person who is not able to understand alternatives or to make a choice.

"Demonstrated inability" in the Washington statute perhaps strengthens the evidentiary standard but does not really shed additional light on the nature of what must be proved, although Washington adds an additional explanation in the same statute articulating what the statute does *not* mean: "Age, eccentricity, poverty, or medical diagnosis alone shall not be sufficient to justify a finding of incapacity."[24]

Cognitive Functioning

In contrast to the California strategy, other states chose to replace either the disability condition test, or the behavioral test, or both, with a test that focuses more precisely on deficiencies in cognitive functioning. In essence, this represents an effort to define what California and other states mean by "inability." This approach is embodied in the guardianship provisions of the Uniform Probate Code (UPC), first promulgated in 1969, and then expanded and separately published in 1982 as the Uniform Guardianship and Protective Proceeding Act (UGPPA).[25] The UPC retained the disabling condition prong of the test, but replaces the behavioral prong with a test of cognitive ability. The UGPPA defines incapacitated person as:

> any person who is impaired by reason of mental illness, mental deficiency, physical illness or disability, chronic use of drugs, chronic intoxication, or other cause (except minority) to the extent of lacking sufficient understanding or capacity to make or communicate responsible decisions. (UGPPA §5-103(7))

Of course, the phrase "responsible decisions" still keeps the door wide open to significant value judgments based on the court's opinion of what is a responsible outcome of a decision. In addition, this test does not limit in any way the types of decision to which the incapacity must relate. That is, the test on its face does not distinguish decisions of greater or lesser consequence.

According to the uniform law commissioners, the UPC is in effect in 14 states (Uniform Laws Annotated, 1993), although the number is somewhat debatable, since many states depart substantially from the Uniform Act's language. At least 10 other jurisdictions that have not adopted the UPC nevertheless incorporate some form of the cognitive functioning test in their guardianship statutes (English, 1993). Some states have modified or eliminated the "responsible decisions" language in the standard and instead include a recitation of the types of decisions relevant to the determination. These states echo the "essential needs" and endangerment limitations referred to earlier. For example, Arkansas uses the language " . . . to make or communicate decisions to meet the essential requirements for his health or safety or to manage his estate."[26]

Health Care Decisions Statutes

Numerous states have separate health decisions or advance directive statutes that incorporate some form of cognitive functioning test (Choice in Dying, 1993). For example, the District of Columbia's Health-Care Decisions Act (1988)[27] defines "incapacitated individual" as "an adult individual who lacks sufficient mental capacity to appreciate the nature and implications of a health-care decision, make a choice regarding the alternatives presented or communicate that choice in an unambiguous manner'' (§21-2202). A variation of this is incorporated into the new Uniform Health-Care Decisions Act,[28] approved in August 1993, by the National Conference of Commissioners on Uniform State Laws:

> '' 'Capacity' means an individual's ability to understand the significant benefits, risks, and alternatives to proposed health care, and to make and communicate a health-care decision'' (§1(3)).

These enactments reflect a now widely accepted view that capacity in the health care context is a matter of the person's ability to make reasoned decisions. Thus, it is more specifically referred to as ''decisional'' capacity. Also implicit in the standard is a better appreciation of the decision-specific notion of capacity. That is, the level of capacity needed to make a particular decision depends on the complexity and consequence of that decision.

The health care decisions statutes differ from the guardianship context in two significant ways. First, they deal with incapacity to perform a specific task (i.e., make a health care decision). Because of this specificity, it is generally conceded that a finding of general incapacity in a guardianship proceeding should not give rise to a presumption of incapacity to make a health care decision, nor should inability to make a health care decision be dispositive of the issue of capacity in a guardianship proceeding (Applebaum, Lidz, & Meisel, 1987; Meisel, 1989).

A second difference is that most of the health care decisions statutes defer entirely to clinical determinations of capacity. The determinations are made outside the courtroom by health care providers. Many prescribe detailed procedural formalities for certification and documentation of incapacity by one or more physicians. For example, the New York Health Care Proxy Act of 1990[29] requires the following:

> A determination that a principal lacks capacity to make health care decisions shall be made by the attending physician to a reasonable degree of medical certainty. The determination shall be made in writing and shall contain such attending physician's opinion regarding the cause and nature of the principal's incapacity as well as its extent and probable duration. The determination shall be included in the patient's medical record. For a decision to withdraw or withhold life-sustaining

treatment, the attending physician who makes the determination that a principal lacks capacity to make health care decisions must consult with another physician to confirm such determination. Such consultation shall also be included within the patient's medical record (§2983).

The New York provision prescribes additional procedural safeguards for patients whose incapacity results from mental illness or developmental disability. The certification of incapacity then triggers the operation of an advance directive or the recognition of a surrogate decision maker.

Physician certification, at best, ensures objective medical decision making. At worst, it is just a formality for the record. In either case, it provides no answer to the underlying question of how to assess the cognitive functioning of the individual. While the clinical literature provides a burgeoning variety of assessment standards and protocol, no one way to assess cognitive functioning has garnered consensus (Kapp, 1990).

The Mix-and-Match Approach

Returning now to the guardianship context, the cognitive legal standard has been literally mixed and matched with other conventional elements in a variety of ways.

- Some states have connected the cognitive functioning test to the behavioral test of meeting essential requirements of health and safety (e.g., Alaska,[30] Kansas,[31] Minnesota,[32] Missouri,[33] Oregon[34]).
- Some have linked the disabling condition element to the cognitive functioning test. For example, the Arizona law states:

"Incapacitated person" means any person who is impaired by reason of mental illness, mental deficiency, mental disorder, physical illness or disability or other cause to the extent that he lacks sufficient understanding or capacity to make or communicate responsible decision concerning this person.[35]

- Some have linked three elements: disabling condition, cognitive functioning, and dysfunctional behavior impairment (e.g., Arkansas,[36] Oklahoma,[37] Maryland,[38] Utah[39]).

- At least one state, North Dakota, has chosen to combine a little bit of everything in the shopping cart into one grand (and complicated) standard for incapacity:

Disabling con- *dition test*	"Incapacitated person" means any adult person who is impaired by reason of mental illness, mental deficiency, physical illness or disability, or chemical dependency
Cognitive test	to the extent that the person lacks capacity to make or communicate responsible decisions
Essential *needs test*	concerning that person's matters of residence, education, medical treatment, legal affairs, vocation, finance, or other matters,
Endangerment *test*	or which incapacity endangers the person's health or safety.[40]

The North Dakota example, unfortunately, may illustrate the worst tendency of the legal system to solve problems of vagueness by adding more verbiage. It may bolster an appearance of objectivity, but it does not necessarily reflect the way decisions about capacity are really made.

NEW FICTIONS OR NO FICTIONS?

The accumulation of definitional components eventually forces us to reassess our fictions and perhaps chart a direction that will improve the fictions, redefine them, or move beyond definitional fictions altogether. Fuller (1967, p. 14) suggests that: "A fiction dies when a compensatory change takes place in the meaning of the words or phrases involved, which operates to bridge the gap that previously existed between the fiction and reality." We have had an historical gap in the law between the fiction called incompetency and the reality of needing a justifiable trigger for state intrusion in the personal autonomy of its citizens. What compensatory changes have taken or are taking place in our statutory elements of incapacity?

First, it may be argued persuasively that the disabling condition element has become superfluous as a definitional standard in the law of guardianship. Historically, the labels have provided little more than an aura of objectivity without substance. In its place, the clinically based cognitive functioning tests provide a sufficiently objective and justifiable core element, though not the only element, of any legal test of capacity. While tests of cognitive functioning are varied and often rightfully subject to criticism, they nevertheless offer a presently useful tool for distinguishing an inability to function from ways of functioning that merely deviate from social norms.

However, by debunking disabling condition requirements in definitions of incapacity, I do not mean to argue that diagnosis should be entirely discarded from consideration. Rather, diagnosis remains important, but for other reasons. From the clinician's standpoint, diagnosis remains essential as the first step in the process of cure or clinical management. It assigns patients to a clinical category about which there is knowledge of prognosis (Roca, 1994). This knowledge is most relevant to decisions about whether and to what extent guardianship may be an appropriate intervention. For example, let us imagine two individuals, one diagnosed with Alzheimer's disease and the other with major depression. In neither case does the diagnosis itself tell us to what extent their ability to understand, make, or communicate decisions is impaired. That question is the focus of the cognitive functioning test. However, assuming that one finds a significant level of cognitive impairment in both individuals, the diagnosis of Alzheimer's disease implies that the level of functioning will almost certainly grow worse. In contrast, the condition of major depression is likely to be treatable and will improve. In the latter case, guardianship may therefore be less necessary or should be significantly limited in scope or duration.

Another conclusion that emerges from the cumulative experience with capacity standards is that, while a cognitive functioning test may be a necessary component, it is not sufficient in itself to establish incapacity in the guardianship context. Some form of consequential behavior element remains essential to tests of capacity. This is so because courts necessarily look beyond the cognitive functioning level of the individual and ask the question, "So what?" In other words, if the individual is cognitively impaired but is not in any danger of serious injury or loss, then so what? There would be no need or justification for guardianship in that instance. For example, consider the difference in consequence between two individuals who, let us assume, clearly meet tests of cognitive incapacity. However, one of these individuals has established surrogate decision makers for all his or her affairs through the use of powers of attorney and related legal instruments. The other person has done no advance planning. Assuming no confounding factors, a guardianship simply cannot be justified in the first case, but may be essential to the well-being of the individual in the latter.

So how do we distinguish among these kinds of cases? Using dysfunctional behavior tests such as "incapable of taking proper care of himself or his property" to answer the "So what?" question does not work. They are overly subjective and vague, and do not account for the individual's total circumstances. In the example above, such a test would seem to justify a guardianship for both persons described, since neither, individually, can handle his or her affairs.

A test that looks at consequential behavior needs to be constrained without adding new pretenses. One element of constraint is dictated by the dimension of the *parens patriae* principle that is often overlooked— that of "necessity." The king is responsible to take care of those who are vulnerable, but only when it is necessary. Necessity depends not just on the nature of one's disability, but on the environment and circumstances in which one lives. The element of necessity of court involvement has not expressly appeared in any of the tests we have discussed so far, except insofar as the essential needs and endangerment component discussed earlier partially addresses the issue.

Essential needs and endangerment tests, however, do not go far enough, for they still focus primarily on the putative ward's abilities alone. Again, if applied to our two hypothetical individuals, they may still fail to distinguish between the two. Necessity, in this example, remains the real issue in defining the trigger for state intervention.

The District of Columbia Guardianship, Protective Proceedings, and Durable Power of Attorney Act of 1986 incorporates necessity into an essential component of incapacity in the following way:

Cognitive test	"Incapacitated individual" means an adult whose ability to receive and evaluate information effectively or to communicate decisions is impaired
Behavioral test	to such an extent that he or she lacks capacity to manage all or some of his or her financial resources or to meet all or some essential requirements for his or her physical health, safety, habilitation, or therapeutic needs

Necessity   without court ordered assistance or the appoint-
test   ment of a guardian or conservator. (D.C. Code
                   Ann. §21-2011(11))[41]

Two objections to the element of necessity are likely here. One is that necessity has nothing to do with any clinical notions of capacity. This is true. It is a corollary or variant of the principle of "least restrictive alternative," a principle born of the civil commitment reform movement of the 1960s and 1970s, but now a widely acknowledged principle in guardianship reform (Comment, 1980; Gottlich & Wood, 1989). However, the principle of least restrictive alternative may not be applied until after the adjudication of incapacity, when decisions must be made about the type and degree of authority of the guardian (e.g., Colorado[42]). I suggest that, as in the District of Columbia statute, it is important to incorporate necessity into the very definition of legal incapacity. Some states have accomplished this by mandating that a finding of legal incapacity can be made only when the court finds that guardianship is the least restrictive alternative (Minnesota,[43] New Hampshire[44]). Such a "front end" requirement helps defictionalize the capacity trigger for court intervention. It also makes explicit the fact that there is a substantive and practical difference between *de facto* or clinical incapacity and legal incapacity. The latter must be based on necessity.

A second likely criticism is that a necessity test is no less elusive of definition than other tests we have discussed. This criticism would be entirely valid, but for an important difference. The conventional tests of capacity have tended to focus primarily on the characteristics of the individual and not on the context in which they operate. They still normally result in a "yes" or "no" finding, despite attempts to expand limited guardianships. Necessity properly implies, or should imply, a weighing of multiple variables, and a weighing of the possible harms and benefits of court intervention versus other options. Courts must take into account the individual's context—his or her living situation, family, caregivers, the types of decisions that have to be made, alternative legal arrangements that are in place, and so on.

Altman, Parmalee, & Smyer (1992) suggest a similar approach to questions of informed consent, arguing that the legal elements of informed consent should be viewed as a process embodying a complex interplay among personal, environmental, and social factors. This approach to assessment eschews cookbook psychology and offers no easy shortcuts. However, it focuses honestly on the right questions, and it is the type of decision making the court is most suited to make, so long as court resources for investigation and the procedural framework are conducive to a full hearing of the harms and benefits and alternatives.

The recently enacted New York guardianship reform law incorporates the concept of necessity in its criteria for appointment of a guardian, but in a slightly different way. It is not within the definition of incapacity. The provision requires a finding of both incapacity and necessity:

> The court may appoint a guardian for a person if the court determines:
> 1. that the appointment is necessary to provide for the personal needs of that person, including food, clothing, shelter, health care, or safety and/or to manage the property and financial affairs of that person; and
> 2. that the person agrees to the appointment, or that the person is incapacitated as defined in subdivision (b) of this section.[45]

This same subsection of the statute goes on to incorporate several evidentiary and procedural mandates and limitations on the court's decree of guardianship:

> In deciding whether the appointment is necessary, the court shall consider the report of the court evaluator, as required in paragraph five of subdivision (c) of section 81.09 of this article, and the sufficiency and reliability of available resources, as defined in subdivision (a) of section 81.03 of this article, to provide for personal needs or property management without the appointment of a guardian. Any guardian appointed under this article shall be granted only those powers which are necessary to provide for personal needs and/or property management of the incapacitated person in such manner as appropriate to the individual and which shall constitute the least restrictive form of intervention, as defined in subdivision (d) of section 81.03 of this article.[46]

The New York language helps to emphasize the principal consequence of defictionalizing conventional definitions of legal incapacity. As we peel away the fiction of incapacity as some "thing" and attempt to ask the right questions, we are faced with balancing a complex array of variables affecting an individual's functioning and welfare. In this posture, the importance of procedural protections looms ever greater. Procedural protections work to ensure that putative wards are fully informed, properly evaluated, zealously defended, that the issues are fully developed and heard, and that an intervention is finely tuned to the needs and preferences of the individual. Moreover, they may serve to wean judges away from too heavy a reliance on isolated clinical conclusions. The literature indicates that judges' determinations of capacity have been, and continue to be, heavily influenced by clinical opinions concerning capacity (Bulcroft, Kielkopf, & Tripp, 1991; Iris, 1988; Mahler & Perry, 1988).

Determinations of incapacity in the guardianship context will almost always require the exercise of considerable judgment. Given that reality, the thoroughness of the process of deliberation is as important, if not more important, than the substantive standard applied. An examination of recommended procedural and evidentiary protections is beyond the objectives of this chapter. However, much of the guardianship statutory reform occurring today focuses on these procedural protections for potential wards. These procedural protections include:

- improved notice to the alleged incompetent
- a meaningful right to counsel
- presence of the alleged incompetent at the hearing
- conduct of hearings in strict accordance with due process principles
- the use of multidisciplinary assessment resources, trained court visitors, investigators, and guardians-ad-litem to ensure full and fair development of the evidence and an adequate evidentiary record
- specific guidelines for drafting and limiting court orders for guardianship
- Effective training and monitoring of guardians (American Bar Association, 1989, Hurme; 1991)

Failures of these procedural protections are widespread and plague our systems of guardianship. Even where procedural protections are included in state law, they may be diluted in their implementation because of a lack of resources, lack of interest, or because of an abundance of ageism in the form of "We know what's best for Mrs. Doe without subjecting her to the torture of an adversarial proceeding."

A final story illustrates the problem better than any theoretical explanation. Vida Colson, an 88-year-old resident of Maine, became the subject of a guardianship dispute in 1993. A temporary guardian was appointed for her on March 19, 1993, and a permanent guardian two months later on May 26, 1993. Her case was appealed to the Maine Supreme Judicial Court (*In re Colson*, 1993) but was later withdrawn. Maine's guardianship law is based upon the Uniform Probate Code. Thus, it defines "incapacitated person" as

> any person who is impaired by reason of mental illness, mental deficiency, physical illness or disability, chronic use of drugs, chronic intoxication, or other cause except minority to the extent that he lacks sufficient understanding or capacity to make or communicate responsible decisions concerning his person.[47]

The Maine statute, like that of many other states, provides for the right of the alleged incompetent to attend the hearing, for the appointment of a court visitor, a guardian *ad litem*, and/or an attorney, and for evaluation by a physician or psychologist who is expected to provide a diagnosis, a description of the person's actual mental and functional limitations and prognosis.[48] The petitioning party, in this case Mrs. Colson's son, is required to file a guardianship plan with the court, specifying how the ward's needs will be met. Finally, the court is required to grant guardianship orders "only to the extent necessitated by the incapacitated persons's actual mental and adaptive limitations. . . ."[49]

According to the statement of evidence filed by Mrs. Colson's attorney (Appellant's Statement, 1993), Mrs. Colson was not present at her temporary guardianship hearing on March 19, 1993. Her son testified without being put under oath that "an emergency existed regarding his mother's real estate in that there was a possible chance that his mother may be convinced to convey her house to satisfy her husband's debts" (p. 2). Her husband was in a hospital at the time. The son "based his conclusion on a past experience of his brother's former wife" (p. 2). The only other information the son provided to the court was that "his mother was in need of care and a place to live, that her eyesight was a problem, that she needs better nutrition, that she eats at odd hours and that she needs her home cleaned. He further stated that maybe his mother could remain in her own home" (p. 2). The judge appointed the son full temporary guardian and special conservator.

Pending the hearing for a permanent guardian, the judge appointed a visitor, who was a secretary by occupation. The record is silent as to her qualifications to act as a visitor. The visitor met Mrs. Colson at her home once with the son present. As to Mrs. Colson's home, the visitor's report states that the exterior presents a "tidy" appearance but the inside has "a powerful odor of uncared-for animals." Paper napkins were dropped on the floor where animals had apparently had "accidents." Moreover, the kitchen was cluttered and had "unwiped spills." However, the visitor saw only the kitchen, and therefore, "could not judge the rest of the house" (p. 5).

The visitor noted that Mrs. Colson could find her way around her own home by steadying herself on walls and furnishings but would probably have difficulty in unfamiliar surroundings and obviously had trouble seeing detail (p. 5). She also reported that she informed Mrs. Colson of the hearing and tried to explain what a guardian and conservator meant, but that she did not think that Mrs. Colson understood the implications fully. Significantly, she also noted that Mrs. Colson did not want to relinquish her independence and have her son act as her guardian, and that she just wanted her complete freedom. As to Mrs. Colson's desire to attend the court hearing, the visitor reported that Mrs. Colson "probably does" but that she did not say so "outright" (p. 6). Three daughters of Mrs. Colson who did not live in the same geographic area were not contacted by the visitor (p. 5). Nor was the chore worker contacted. The visitor's report was never given to or served upon Mrs. Colson (p. 6).

On or before the hearing for permanent guardianship on May 26, Mrs. Colson's son admitted her to a nursing home. At the hearing, the judge heard from only the son and the son's attorney. Mrs. Coleman was neither present, nor represented by anyone (p. 7). In the record was the son's petition, the visitor's report, and a doctor's letter. Apparently, no guardianship plan was submitted until after the hearing, despite being required as a precondition. The doctor's letter, in its entirety, stated the following:

> I have observed Mrs. Colson over the past 10 years. It has been quite dramatic over the last 12 to 18 months that she has had a marked cognitive decline. Specifically she is not at all as sharp as she had been. Home Health has reported that her home situation is deteriorating, i.e.: her home is no longer as spotless as it was, disorganized and disheveled. She has had close family support but her caring for herself alone or present family setting is certainly problematic. Her functional limitations as per her decreasing mental faculties are certainly there. Diagno-

sis: Decreasing cognitive function and flawed judgement (sic). Prognosis: Mrs. Colson also has had a marked weight loss. This is being investigated. This would certainly color the situation from being less than desirable to quite grave. (p. 4)

As a result of this hearing, the court appointed the son full guardian and conservator.

Mrs. Colson's case may not be the norm for most guardianship cases. Many, if not most, guardianship cases present clear-cut scenarios of incapacity by the time they reach the court. However, neither is Mrs. Coleman's case an anomaly. In every state, there are other Mrs. Colsons who may be determined prematurely to be incapacitated, not because statutory definitions and standards are terribly defective, but because the due process protections are not in place or not used. She needed representation; she needed a thorough evaluation; she needed alternative resources explored that would enable her to stay where wanted; and she needed a court system that would follow its own legislative mandate to intervene only to the extent necessitated by the person's actual limitations. In the end, Mrs. Colson may or may not need a guardian. We simply do not know for sure based upon what is shown by the record, because the necessary work of assessment and deliberation failed dismally.

Such procedural protections have been a high priority of the American Bar Association's (1989) Commission on Legal Problems of the Elderly and others who have been advocating guardianship law reform for some time. While states have been very active in the late 1980s and early 1990s in guardianship reform—improving both the substantive standards and procedures—states have not yet been willing or able to dedicate the resources needed to carry out the spirit of these guardianship reform laws. Indeed, in the final analysis, the problem is largely one of money and resources.

CONCLUSIONS

The case of Mrs. Colson illustrates a simple truth in the search for realistic legal definitions of incapacity or incompetence: When all the fictions are put aside, the more important protection for questionably competent individuals is procedure, not substance. Finely articulated substantive standards are important, and this chapter has suggested ways to improve and "defictionalize" those standards. Specifically, three elements have been articulated: a cognitive test, a consequential behavioral test focusing on essential needs, and a necessity-for-court-involvement test involving a weighing of the individual's personal, environmental, and social context. The District of Columbia and New York statutes provide examples of these criteria.

Substantive standards, though, represent only part of the picture. They are doomed to accomplish little in terms of protecting individual autonomy unless procedural rights are realistically recognized and enforced. The key to evaluating the substantive factors is thorough assessment and thorough deliberation with the emphasis in the judicial arena on procedural protection. The American Bar Association guidelines (1989) provide a useful framework for procedural reform. Unfortunately, these procedural protections require more time, more resources, and more complexity—elements that neither legislators nor public administrators easily embrace. Yet, our success at defictionalizing the notion of "capacity" will depend primarily, not so much on changes to statutory definitions, but on our retooling of the process for determining capacity and the need for guardianship. In the real world, autonomy is messy.

NOTES

1. De Praerogativa Regis, 17 Edw. 2, cs. 9, 10.
2. R. I. Gen. Laws §33-15-8 (1969).
3. Ala. Code §26-2-1 (1975), repealed by 1987 Act 87-590m, §2-333(a).
4. Mass. Gen. Laws Ann., ch. 201, §8 (West 1993).
5. Mass. Gen. Laws Ann. ch. 201, §6 (West 1989).
6. Neb. Rev. Stat. §30-2601 1988.
7. N.Y. Mental Hyg. Law §78.01 (1989), repealed in 1992.
8. Ohio Rev. Code Ann. §2111.01(D) (Anderson 1989).
9. Wis. Stat. Ann. §880.01 (West 1988).
10. Alaska Stat. §13.26.005(4) (1988).
11. Ark. Code Ann. §28-65-101 (Michie 1987).
12. Fla. Stat. Ann. §774.102(10) (West 1989).
13. Kan. Stat. Ann. §59-3002 (1988).

14. Or. Rev. Stat. §126.003 (1988).
15. Minn. Stat. Ann. §525.54 (1989).
16. N.H. Rev. Stat. Ann. §464-A:2 (1988).
17. Utah Code Ann. §75-5-201 (1988).
18. Conn. Gen. Stat. §45-70a (1989).
19. Ibid.
20. Mo. Ann. Stat. §475.010 (1989).
21. N.H., op. cit.
22. Cal Prob. Code §1801 (West 1989).
23. Wash Rev. Code Ann. §11.88.010(1)(a) (West 1989).
24. Ibid, §11.88.010(1)(b).
25. Uniform Guardianship and Protective Proceeding Act (1982).
26. Ark., op. cit.
27. District of Columbia Health-Care Decisions Act, D.C. Code Ann. §21-2202 (1988).
28. Uniform Health-Care Decisions Act (1993).
29. New York Health Care Proxy Act, N.Y. Pub. Health Law §2980-2994 (McKinney 1990)
30. Alaska, op. cit.
31. Kansas, op. cit.
32. Minn., op. cit.
33. Mo., op. cit.
34. Oregon, op. cit.
35. Ariz. Rev. Stat. Ann. §14-5101 (1988).
36. Ark., op. cit.
37. Okla. Stat. Ann. tit. 30, §1-111 (1991).
38. Md. Est. & Trusts Code Ann. §13-705 (1991).
39. Utah, op. cit.
40. N.D. Cent. Code, §30.1-26-01(2) (1992).
41. District of Columbia Guardianship, Protective, Proceedings, and Durable Power of Attorney Act of 1986, D.C. Code Ann. §§21-2001 to-2085.
42. Colo. Rev. Stat. §15-14-304(4) (1988).
43. Minn. Stat. Ann. §525.551(5) (1989).
44. N.H. Rev. Stat. Ann. §464-A:9(III) (1988).
45. N.Y. Mental Hyg. Law, §81.02(a) (1993).
46. Ibid.
47. Me. Rev. Stat. Ann. tit. 18-A, §5-101(1) (1993).

48. Ibid., §5-303.
49. Ibid., §5-304(a).

REFERENCES

Alexander, G., & Lewin, T. (1972). *The aged and the need for surrogate management.* Syracuse, NY: Syracuse University Press.

Altman, W. M., Parmalee, P. A., & Smyer, M. A. (1992). Autonomy, competence, and informed consent in long term care: legal and psychological perspectives. *Villanova Law Review, 37,* 1671–1704.

American Bar Association. (1989). *Guardianship: Agenda for reform.* Washington, DC: American Bar Association Commission on the Mentally Disabled and Commission on Legal Problems of the Elderly.

Anderer, S. (1990). *Determining competency in guardianship proceedings.* Washington, DC: American Bar Association.

Appellant's Statement of Evidence or Proceeding, *In re Colson,* Law Docket No. LAW-WAL-93-349 (Me. July 19, 1993).

Applebaum, P. S., Lidz, C. W., & Meisel, A. (1987). *Informed consent: Legal theory and clinical practice.* New York: Oxford University Press.

Bulcroft, K., Kielkopf, M. R., & Tripp, K. (1991). Elderly wards and their legal guardians: Analysis of county probate records in Ohio and Washingon. *The Gerontologist, 31*(2), 156–164.

Brakel, S. J. (1985). Historical trends. In S. J. Brakel, J. Parry, & B. A. Weiner (Eds.), *The mentally disabled and the law,* (3rd Ed.) (pp. 9–20). Chicago: American Bar Foundation.

Choice in Dying. (1993). *Refusal of treatment legislation: A state by state compilation of enacted and model statutes.* New York: Author.

Comment. (1980). Guardianship of adults with mental retardation: Towards a presumption of competence. *Akron Law Review, 14,* 321.

Deutsch, A. (1949). *The mentally ill in America: A history of their case and treatment from colonial times* (2nd ed.). New York: Columbia University Press.

English, D. M. (1993). The Uniform Guardianship and protective proceedings act—How uniform is it? *National Academy of Elder Law Attorneys (NAELA) Quarterly, 6*(2) 1–15 and *6*(3) 21–29 [Published in two parts].

Frolik, L. (1981). Plenary guardianship: An analysis, a critique and a proposal for reform. *Arizona Law Review, 23*(2), 599–660.

Fuller, L. L. (1967). Legal fictions. Palo Alto, CA: Stanford University Press.

Gottlich, V., & Wood, E. (1989). Statewide review of guardianships: The California and Maryland approaches. *Clearinghouse Review, 23*(4), 426–432.

Grisso, T. (1986). *Evaluating competencies: Forensic assessments and instruments*. New York: Plenum.

Horstman, P. M. (1975). Protective services for the elderly: The limits of parens patriae. *Missouri Law Review, 40,* 215–236.

Hurme, S. B. (1991). *Steps to enhance guardianship monitoring*. Washington, DC: American Bar Association.

In re Colson, Law Docket No. LAW-WAL-93-349 (Me. 1993).

In re Tyrell, 92 Ohio L. Abs. 253 (P. Ct. Preble Co. 1962).

Iris, M. (1988). Guardianship of the elderly: a multi-perspective view of the decisionmaking process. *The Gerontologist, 28* (Suppl.), 39–45.

Kapp, M. (1990). Evaluating decisionmaking capacity in the elderly: A review of the literature. *Journal of Elder Abuse & Neglect, 2*(3/4), 15–24.

Kittrie, N. (1971). *The right to be different: Deviance and enforced therapy*. Baltimore: Johns Hopkins Press.

Mahler, J., & Perry, S. (1988). Assessing competency in the physically ill: Guidelines for psychiatric consultants. *Hospital and Community Psyciatry, 39,* 856–886.

Margulies, P. (1994). Access, connection, and voice: A contextual approach to representing senior citizens of questionable capacity. 62(5) *Fordham University Law Review* 1073-1099.

Meisel, A. (1989). *The right to die*. New York: Wiley.

Nolan, B. (1984). Functional evaluation of the elderly in guardianship proceedings. *Law, Medicine & Health Care, 12,* 210–218.

Parry, J. (1985a). Incompetency, guardianship, and restoration. In S. J. Brakel, J. Parry, & B. A. Weiner (Eds.), *The Mentally Disabled and the Law* (3rd ed.) (pp. 369–433). Chicago: American Bar Foundation.

Parry, J. (1985b). Decision-making rights over persons and property. In S. J. Brakel, J. Parry, & B. A. Weiner (Eds.), *The Mentally Disabled and the Law* (3rd ed.) (pp. 435–506). Chicago: American Bar Foundation.

Roca, R. P. (1994). Determining decisional capacity: A medical perspective. 62(5) *Fordham University Law Review* 1177-1196.

Schmidt, W. C., Miller, K. S., Bell, W. G., & New, B. E. (1981). *Public guardianship and the elderly*. Cambridge, MA: Ballinger.

Smith, J. (1917). Surviving fictions. *Yale Law Journal, 27,* 147–166, 317–330.

Stone, J. (1968). *The Province and function of law. Law as logic, justice and social control: A study in jurisprudence*. Buffalo, NY: Hein.

Szasz, T. S. (1984). *The therapeutic state: Psychiatry in the mirror of current events*. Buffalo, NY: Prometheus.

Uniform Guardianship and Protective Preceedings Act (1993). References and Annotations: Table of Jurisdictions Wherein Act Has Been Adopted.

Uniform Probate Code (1969).

Commentary: A Cognitive Psychologist's Perspective on the Assessment of Cognitive Competency

Timothy A. Salthouse

In chapter 1 of this volume, Sabatino notes that the primary legal concern with respect to competency is the individual's ability to manage property and/or to care for himself or herself. It is apparently for this reason that legal conceptions of competency are typically based on the ability to make responsible decisions and to understand the risks and/or benefits of available alternatives. Sabatino also points out that a key question that emerges from this perspective on competency is how an individual's capability for rational or responsible decision making can be assessed.

This commentary will focus on this latter question because my field of specialization is cognitive psychology, and decision making is an important topic within that field. Specifically, this commentary discusses various types of research related to decision making that are relevant to the assessment of cognitive competency.

OPTIMAL DECISION MAKING

Much of the cognitive research on decision making has been concerned with the question of how close an individual's decision making is to being optimal. Within this framework, decision making has been characterized in terms of the identification of relevant attributes, weighing of the attributes, accumulation of values for the attributes, aggregation of information (i.e., the sum across attributes of the products of weights and values), evaluation of the aggregated information for each alternative, and application of a decision rule such as maximizing expected value or minimizing maximum loss.

Although there has been considerable research concerned with the extent to which these various components are performed in an ideal or optimal fashion, very little research has taken this approach in examining decision making in the elderly. Furthermore, it seems unlikely that this perspective on decision making would be relevant for assessments of competency because the criterion for evaluating optimality of decision making is almost certainly much higher than that appropriate for determining whether an individual is capable of making an informed or responsible decision. For example, even expert decision makers are frequently found to be less than optimal in their decisions (e.g., Camerer & Johnson, 1991), and hence might be classified as incapacitated if a criterion of optimality in decision making were to be adopted.

COMPONENTS OF DECISION MAKING

In the absence of much direct research on decision making in the elderly, a reasonable strategy is to attempt to identify the prerequisites of effective or rational decision making, and then to examine the functioning of elderly adults on measures of the presumed component abilities. That is, rather than simply claiming that nothing can be concluded about decision making in the elderly, plausible inferences could be drawn on the basis of research on abilities hypothesized to be required for effective decision making. Two very broad abilities that appear relevant for decision making are comprehension (the ability to understand and assimilate relevant information) and reasoning (the ability to evaluate and integrate information) (e.g., Kapp, 1990).

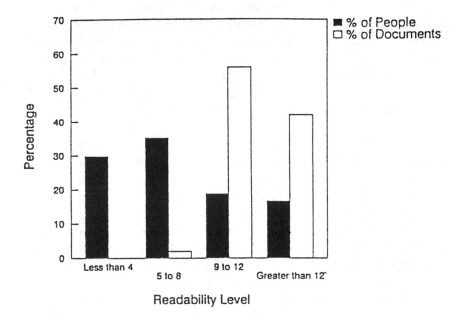

Figure 1.1. Percentage of people and percentage of documents at each level of readability in the Walmsley and Allington (1982) study.

Reasoning is an important aspect of decision making because most decisions involve the selection of an alternative on the basis of different pieces of information that need to be integrated and evaluated. Unfortunately, relatively little research has focused on information evaluation and integration abilities in the elderly (but see Salthouse, 1992, for a review of related research).

Another important ability in decision making, for which a moderate amount of research with elderly adults does exist, is comprehension. Comprehension is a key component of decision making because an informed decision requires that the decision maker understand relevant aspects of the situation, including the risks and benefits of any available alternatives. If comprehension of the information is poor, then the decisions may not be rational, in the sense that they are based on incomplete or inaccurate information.

One indication of a possible problem in comprehension among elderly adults is available in a comparison of the reading level at which documents are written, on one hand, and the reading levels of senior citizens for whom those documents are relevant, on the other hand. Walmsley and Allington (1982) examined the readability of documents (e.g., applications, notifications of acceptance or rejection, claims) pertaining to services provided by Blue Cross, Medicare, Food Stamps, and Social Security. The reading levels of a sample of older adults in a senior citizen center were also measured. The major results of their study are illustrated in Figure 1.1. Many of the elderly adults in this sample were probably not capable of comprehending the documents because their level of reading ability was lower than the level at which the documents were written. That is, almost 65% of this sample had a reading ability of eighth grade or less, but 98% of the documents required readability levels of ninth grade or higher. The sample in the Walmsley and Allington (1982) study may have had relatively low levels of education, but the results are nevertheless meaningful because many elderly adults in the population also have low levels of education.

More direct evidence of comprehension difficulties among older adults derives from recent studies examining the comprehension of prescription information (Morrell, Park, & Poon, 1989, 1990). In these studies, adults of different ages were presented with prescription information, including the dosage and frequency of administration for various medications, and were asked to prepare a schedule indicating when each medication was to be taken and how much of it was to be taken. Even with the prescriptions in front of them, adults in their 60s and 70s made between 16% and 21% errors in specifying either the times at which medications were to be taken, or the amount to be taken. The authors concluded that " . . . compliance with a medical regimen cannot occur if patients do not understand what to do when they read the instructions on the label" (1989, p. 353). For similar reasons, decisions probably would not be considered informed and rational if decision makers did not understand much of the information relevant to their decision.

The most meaningful research for assessing comprehension during decision making may be that concerned with comprehension of information presented in informed consent forms, because these forms are explicitly designed to communicate the risks and benefits associated with an imminent medical procedure. In fact, Stanley, Guido, Stanley, and Shortell (1984) have stated: "Competency to consent has been defined most often as the capacity to comprehend relevant information, the abil-

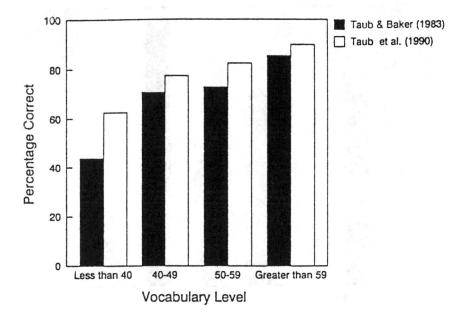

Figure 1.2. Average values of comprehension of informed consent forms by research participants at four different vocabulary levels in studies by Taub and colleagues.

ity to weigh the benefits and risks of the proposed procedure, and the capability to reach a reasonable decision" (p. 1302 1303). A similar view was expressed by Taub, Baker, and Sturr (1986): "The main assumption behind current informed consent regulations is the belief that, when presented with sufficient relevant information, potential volunteers will be able to make a rational decision about participation in research studies" (p. 604).

Stanley and her collaborators conducted a study in which adults of different ages were compared with respect to the accuracy with which they answered questions about the material contained in informed consent forms. Adults 62 years and older were found to make more errors than younger adults in reporting the purpose, procedure, benefits, and risks of the described study—in other words, they were less accurate in understanding all of the specific elements of the informed consent form. These authors concluded that " . . . as a group, geriatric patients may

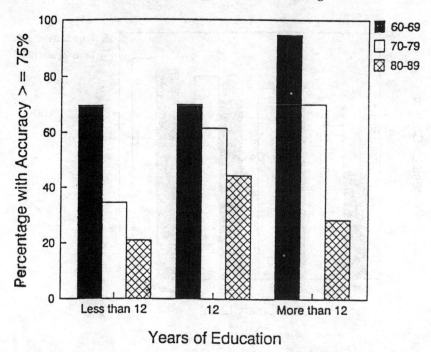

Figure 1.3. Percentages of respondents by age and amount of education with comprehension accuracy of informed consent forms greater than or equal to 75%. Data from Taub et al. (1987).

have some impairment in their competency to give informed consent for research'' (Stanley et al., p. 1305).

It is important to note, however, that even the oldest participants in the Stanley et al. (1984) study were sensitive to the relative risks of the procedures in that they were less likely to agree to participate in projects with high levels of risk. In this respect, therefore, their decisions can be considered rational, even if they were not based on complete understanding of information.

A systematic program of research investigating the comprehension of informed consent forms by elderly adults has been conducted by Taub and his colleagues (e.g., Taub & Baker, 1983; Taub, Baker, Kline, & Sturr, 1987; Taub, Baker, & Sturr, 1986; Taub & Sturr, 1990). A similar procedure was followed in most of the Taub studies, all of which involved adults ranging from about 60 to 90 years of age. First, the individual was presented with the informed consent form to read, and then,

TABLE 1.1   Items on the Mini-Mental Status Examination

1. What is the: Year? Season? Date? Day? Month?
2. Where are we: State? County? Town or City? Hospital? Floor?
3. Repeat these three words: Apple, Penny, Table.
4. Subtract 7 from 100 five times.
5. Recall the three words heard earlier.
6. Name these objects (pencil, watch).
7. Repeat "No ifs, ands, or buts."
8. "Take the paper in your right hand, fold the paper in half, put the paper on the floor."
9. Read and obey the following command: "CLOSE YOUR EYES."
10. Write a sentence of your choice.
11. Copy the following design (overlapping pentagons).

From Folstein, Folstein, and McHugh (1975).

while the form was still visible, he or she was asked questions about the consent form. For example, one question asked about the freedom to withdraw from participation, and another asked about the types of tests or procedures to be administered. Because the consent form could be consulted when answering the questions, it can be assumed that comprehension rather than memory was being assessed.

Figure 1.2 illustrates the average accuracy in answering the comprehension questions for older adults at each of several vocabulary levels in two separate studies. Notice that the level of comprehension is particularly poor for those individuals with low scores on the vocabulary test.

In another study the results were reported in terms of the percentage of respondents who achieved at least 75% accuracy in the comprehension test. These results are portrayed in Figure 1.3 as a function of both educational level and age. Once again, it appears that the level of comprehension was quite low for many older adults, especially those with low levels of education and advanced ages.

Results of the type just summarized do not indicate whether the consent-to-participate decisions were rational on the basis of the information actually available to the individual. However, the findings do suggest that much of the information was functionally unavailable to the decision maker because it was not comprehended. In that sense, therefore, the decisions cannot be considered informed. According to the guidelines of the Uniform Health-Care Decisions Act cited by Sabatino (this volume), then, many of these elderly adults would probably be considered incapacitated because they apparently do not fully understand the benefits, risks, and alternatives relevant to their decision.

MENTAL SCREENING TESTS

Perhaps the most common method of assessing cognitive competency, and indirectly the capacity to make responsible decisions, is with brief tests designed to assist in the detection of dementia or other impairments of mental functioning. The most widely used test of this type is the Mini-Mental State Examination (Folstein, Folstein, & McHugh, 1975; Tombaugh & McIntyre, 1992). The 11 items in this test are listed in Table 1.1.

Notice that the items assess awareness of time and place or orientation, comprehension and production of language, short-term memory, and the ability to attend and concentrate. At least a minimum level of each of these abilities is presumably required in order to make rational and informed decisions. That is, decisions are unlikely to be rational if the individual is disoriented with respect to date or location, if he or she has difficulty in comprehension or communication, and if the ability to attend to, or remember, information over short intervals is greatly impaired.

It should be emphasized that screening tests such as the Mini-Mental exam are useful primarily for identifying the minimum levels of functioning needed for reasonable decision making. In other words, individuals with scores below 24 on this test, which is a frequently used criterion for identifying cognitive impairment, would probably be incapable of making rational decisions, and individuals with scores below 18, which is considered an indication of severe cognitive impairment, would almost certainly not be able to make informed and rational decisions, or even to care for themselves. However, a higher score on this test is only a necessary, rather than a sufficient, condition to ensure that the individual is capable of effective and responsible decision making. For this reason, therefore, mental screening tests should be viewed as providing only lower-bound estimates of when an individual might be capable of making rational decisions.

Another limitation of tests of global cognitive functioning is that the capacity to make rational decisions may vary according to the type of decision being made (e.g., Kapp, 1990; Sabatino, this volume). To the extent that this is the case, situation- specific evaluations of actual decision making would be much more appropriate for the evaluation of decision-making capacity than assessments of overall mental status.

CONCLUSIONS

Let me briefly summarize the three perspectives on decision making that I have discussed. I began by mentioning the optimal decision-making approach in which the goal is to specify how the human decision maker deviates from optimality in his or her decisions. Both because there has been little research of this type on elderly adults, and because a criterion of optimality seems too high to evaluate an individual's capacity for rational decision making, this perspective received little discussion.

The second perspective focused on comprehension as one of the fundamental constituent abilities required for effective decision making. Research with several different types of materials, including informed consent forms designed to communicate the risks and benefits of a procedure one is contemplating, indicated that many older adults fail to comprehend much of the information that is relevant to the decision. In fact, the levels of comprehension in elderly adults with low levels of education are so poor that one can question whether decisions reached by many of these individuals could truly be considered informed.

The third perspective discussed was that of overall mental competency as assessed by short tests intended to help identify individuals with moderate to severe cognitive impairments. The main concern with the use of mental screening tests for the assessment of decision making capability is that they are too gross; that is, the cognitive impairments must be fairly substantial to result in low scores on these tests. It is therefore possible that higher order aspects of cognitive functioning, such as decision making, could be impaired even when performance on tests such as the Mini-Mental State Examination is in the normal range.

What can be concluded about the assessment of an individual's capability for rational decision making? One major conclusion is that the criterion used to determine whether decision making is rational and responsible is extremely important. A very small number of adults of any age would be considered effective decision makers if a criterion of optimality were to be used, whereas only a few individuals with moderate to advanced dementia would not be considered effective decision makers if the mental screening test criterion were to be used.

A second conclusion is that assessment of decision-making capacity should not only be context-sensitive or situation-specific, but should also incorporate evaluations of the individual's comprehension and reasoning relevant to the decision. For example, an examiner could ask a series of questions to ensure that relevant information was adequately comprehended, and could request an explanation of why one alternative was selected and another was rejected to evaluate the processes used to reach the decision. Of course the particular kinds of questions to be asked and the criteria to be used in determining whether the responses were satisfactory would need to be specified, but an approach of this type appears to have the potential to provide a flexible yet sensitive means of evaluating an individual's ability to make reasonable and informed decisions. The field of cognitive psychology can make a contribution to the assessment of cognitive competency, therefore, by specifying questions that can be used to assess specific instances of decision-making competence and by providing methods of evaluating the answers.

REFERENCES

Camerer, C. F. & Johnson, E. J. (1991). The process-performance paradox in expert judgment: How can experts know so much and predict so badly? In K. A. Ericson & J. Smith (Eds.), *Toward a general theory of expertise: Prospects and limits* (pp. 195–217). New York: Cambridge University Press.

Folstein, M. F., Folstein, S. E., & McHugh, P. R. (1975). Mini-Mental State: A practical method for grading the cognitive state of patients for the clinician. *Journal of Psychiatric Research, 12*, 189–198.

Kapp, M. B. (1990). Evaluating decision making capacity in the elderly: A review of recent literature. *Journal of Elder Abuse and Neglect, 2*, 15–29.

Morrell, R. W., Park, D. C., & Poon, L. W. (1989). Quality of instructions on prescription drug labels: Effects on memory and comprehension in young and old adults. *The Gerontologist, 29*, 345–354.

Morrell, R. W., Park, D. C., & Poon, L. W. (1990). Effects of labeling techniques on memory and comprehension of prescription information in young and old adults. *Journal of Gerontology: Psychological Sciences, 45*, P166–P172.

Salthouse, T. A. (1992). Reasoning and spatial abilities. In F. I. M. Craik & T. A. Salthouse (Eds.), *Handbook of aging and cognition.* Hillsdale, NJ: Erlbaum.

Stanley, B., Guido, J., Stanley, M., & Shortell, D. (1984). The elderly patient and informed consent. *Journal of the American Medical Association, 252*, 1302–1306.

Taub, H. A., & Baker, M. T. (1983). The effect of repeated testing upon comprehension of informed consent materials by elderly volunteers. *Experimental Aging Research, 9*, 135–138.

Taub, H. A., Baker, M. T., & Sturr, J. F. (1986). Informed consent for research: Effects of readability, patient age, and education. *Journal of the American Geriatrics Society, 34*, 601–606.

Taub, H. A., Baker, M. T., Kline, G. E., & Sturr, J. F. (1987). Comprehension of informed consent information by young-old through old-old volunteers. *Experimental Aging Research, 13*, 173–178.

Taub, H. A., & Sturr, J. F. (1990). Evaluating informed consent for research: A methodological study with older adults. *Educational Gerontology, 16*, 273–281.

Tombaugh, T. N., & McIntyre, N. J. (1992). The Mini-Mental State Examination: A comprehensive review. *Journal of the American Geriatrics Society, 40*, 922–935.

Walmsley, S., & Allington, R. (1982). Reading abilities of elderly patients in relation to the difficulty of essential documents. *The Gerontologist, 22*, 36–38.

Commentary: Statutory Definitions of Incapacity: The Need for a Medical Basis

Lawrence A. Frolik

C harles Sabatino's chapter, "Competency: Reviewing Our Legal Fictions," is an elegant review and exposition of the concept of legal incapacity. Is there yet more to be said on the subject? I think so, for I believe that the core of the incapacity conundrum is the impossible task of identifying or defining free will. Incapacity is a legal status that occurs when the actor lacks the ability to act autonomously, that is, lacks the ability to exercise free will. If we lack the mental ability to absorb information, understand its implications, correctly perceive our environment, understand the relationship between our desires and our actions, or are unable to behave as we would like to, we lack the ability to exercise free will.

It is ultimately futile to attempt to define the identifiers of the loss of free will (which is what we attempt to do by the legal definition of incapacity). Incapacity is a normative, not an objective, standard, because a finding of incapacity is a statement about the nature of free will, not a measurement of reality. In the vain attempt to define the undefinable, we repeatedly "reform" statutory definitions of incapacity. That does not mean that one definition is as good as the next. As Sabatino has correctly pointed out, some definitions create greater problems than others. Still, we are not going to achieve a perfect definition this side of paradise. The most recent statutory definitions may be an improvement, but like their predecessors they are a not a panacea, because no definition of incapacity can avoid the Scylla and Charybdis of overinclusion or underinclusion. Our language and understanding of mental capacity simply are not precise enough to permit us to create a definition absolutely on target, particularly since the "target" may not exist.

That is, incapacity exists only after we define it. The determination of capacity is necessarily a heuristic undertaking, not a description of reality. Without attempting to plumb the depths of language and reality, I am prepared to contrast the definition of incapacity with the definition, for example, of a bear. We know there is a large furry animal that we call a bear. Because it has a corporeal existence, we can define it by listing its attributes. But incapacity has no such reification. Surely it exists, as does its opposite, capacity, but where one ends and the other begins is an impossible line to draw.[1] This should not disturb us unduly, since it is the problem with so much of the law. We draw lines and draft statutes though unsure of their accuracy with the hope that case-by-case application will bring things closer to the mark.

When it comes to defining incapacity, we are reduced to Justice Stewart's "I know it when I see it" test.[2] We expect the courts to recognize incapacity when they see it, even if we cannot write a statutory definition that operates in a mechanistic manner. A statutory definition of incapacity can only provide guidelines that sketch out the relevant criteria for measuring capacity. The definition is deliberately left vague, because legislatures expect courts to create the necessary specificity in the context of particular facts. They cannot possibly draw a "bright line" that permits a court to measure the loss of capacity in the way that an accountant can total the income of a client. Instead, legislatures expect courts to apply generalized understanding to recognize when an individual has suffered loss of capacity and needs assistance.

The question, then, of what is a "good" statutory definition of incapacity is not whether it is precise (an impossible standard), not whether it is "correct" (there being no such objective standard), not whether it is over-or underinclusive, and not even whether it minimizes the number of guardianships. Rather, a "good" statutory definition is one that causes the courts[3] to give due consideration to the importance of free will (autonomy) when considering whether to invoke the power of the state to protect someone. Conversely, a "bad" statute is one that assumes the primacy of protection while diverting attention from the competing value of autonomy. For example, a statute that equates mental retardation with incapacity fails because it presumes that all mentally retarded individuals at all times need the protection offered by guardianship. The court is not asked to consider whether the particular individual has autonomous needs that would be thwarted by guardianship. Instead, the court is asked only to determine the individual's mental status, and having, determined that, to mechanistically create a guardianship.

Our desire to minimize the use of guardianships, however, should not blind us to the reality that guardianships serve a valuable function. Some individuals, at some times, suffer from a loss of capacity sufficient to require a substitute decision maker. There are two possible solutions: the public one in the form of guardianship, and the private one in the form of durable powers of attorney, living trusts, and advance health care directives. Given the merits of the private approach, the resort to guardianship can only be seen as a failure by the individual to plan properly. Individuals with correctly drawn durable powers of attorney (often in conjunction with a living trust), accompanied by adequate health care directives, should never need a guardianship. The availability of private arrangements for substitute decision making means that guardianship almost always represents a failure to plan effectively.

Who is most likely to fail to plan for substitute decision making in the event of incapacity? Not the rich, for they almost always write wills, and it is when a will is written that the lawyer will suggest durable powers of attorney and health care directives. The middle class is less diligent in writing wills, but they too usually take the necessary steps to appoint surrogate decision makers. The poor, however, rarely write wills and, given their economic pressures, are less likely to plan for possible incapacity. So it is the poor who are more most likely to find themselves as respondents in guardianship hearings, and it is they who may neither appreciate their legal rights nor have the money to hire a competent lawyer. Thus, the most essential protection for alleged incapacitated persons is not found in the statutory procedures, but in the quality of the judges who decide who is incapacitated.

Fortunately, most guardianship hearings concern rather clear-cut cases of incapacity. The issue, if any, is not whether the respondent is incapacitated, but how extensive the guardian's power should be.[4] The definition of incapacity is not significant if the respondent is in a coma or suffering from advanced stage dementia. Some guardianship hearings, however, concern individuals on the margin who exhibit unusual behavior. For these individuals, the decision as to whether they are incapacitated is not at all clear, though too often courts conclude that a guardian is required. In part, decisions are based upon natural judicial caution and a preference for protecting individuals even at the cost of their autonomy. From the judge's point of view, the "harm" of an unnecessary guardian is not nearly so great as the harm that could befall an incapacitated person left without the protection of a guardian. However, even the most pro-guardianship judge may be deterred from a finding of incapacity if the facts obviously do not meet the statutory criteria. In any case, no statute is self-enforcing, and judges, therefore, have a margin of discretion no matter how incapacity is defined. It can be assumed, then, that some judges (perhaps most) err on the side of guardianship and, hence, many individuals who do not deserve or need them have guardians appointed.

Why are not more of these inappropriate guardianships challenged? Why are some persons unnecessarily labeled incapacitated? The answer is probably a combination of three factors: class bias, age bias, and the personality of the incapacitated person. Class bias refers to the likelihood that the poor are disproportionately subject to guardianship, both because of a lack of planning (private solutions) and from a lack of resources to resist unwanted guardians. Consequently, they are likely overrepresented in the group of individuals for whom guardians should not have been appointed.

The poor elderly are also victimized by age bias, or the presumption that older adults are likely to have suffered a loss of mental capacity. It is true that the elderly undergo physical decline, often suffer from diminished hearing and vision, and may experience a loss of short-term memory. As a result, many elderly persons find it hard to keep up with life, and so retreat into a more passive stance. Against a backdrop of prevalent chronic disease among the elderly, it is no surprise that many Americans believe that senility (I deliberately use the lay term) is a natural handmaiden of old age. Judges also are all too willing to assume that an older respondent has lost capacity. Faced with a younger person in otherwise similar circumstances, the judge might be much more reluctant to appoint a guardian.

Finally, the personality of the respondent undoubtedly has a significant impact upon whether a guardian is appointed. Individuals who are assertive and demand control of their lives are more likely to be found to have capacity than are passive, meek individuals who defer to authority.[5] Also, individuals who made "poor" decisions in the past are more suspect, both because of the pattern of their behavior and because questionable decisions, such as refusing to seek health care in a timely manner, may leave the person more vulnerable to life's vicissitudes and apparently in need of the protection that guardianship promises.

A critical test of a good statutory definition of guardianship is whether it counters these biases that influence courts toward excessive findings of guardianship. Some of the older definitions of incompetency actually contributed to the problem, rather than helping. Definitions that refer to the individual's status, for example, assume that all members of the category are incapacitated, or at least create a presumption of incapacity. For that reason alone, we should reject any definition of incapacity that relies upon the individual's status of being elderly. Fortunately, as Sabatino points out, the status definitions of incapacity are quickly giving way to more enlightened definitions, such as the "functional behavior test."

Sabatino cites the California statute as a "pure behavioral impairment test." While he notes that it does not "distinguish the person who chooses (on some level) an aberrant lifestyle from the person who is not able to understand alternatives or to make a choice" (p. 12), his criticism does not go far enough. The functional behavior test fails the essential standard of a good statutory definition of incapacity because it reinforces judicial prejudices about the elderly. Because the functional test does not require a finding of a disabling condition, everything rests upon observation and analysis of the respondent's behavior. Lacking, as we do, any effective test for capacity other than gross measurements of significant cognitive loss due to dementia, courts must rely upon the behavior of the respondent.[6] Since many judges are predisposed to equate being old with a loss of mental capacity, they can all too easily be persuaded that aberrant behavior merely confirms the suspected loss of capacity. Because the court does not have to explain why the respondent behaves the way he or she does, it is too easy for the court to conclude that behavior causing an individual to fail "to provide for his or her personal needs"[7] demonstrates a lack of capacity and not merely a personal predilection for unusual behavior.

Fortunately, better statutory examples exist that do not create a presumption that odd behavior alone is sufficient to warrant the appointment of a guardian. The Uniform Probate Code captures the essential need both to identify the apparent loss of capacity[8] (meaning the individual cannot exercise free will), and to account for the cause or source of the incapacity.[9] Sabatino calls the latter the disability prong. I prefer to refer to it as the medical model because it assumes that incapacity has an identifiable organic basis, and, as with the traditional medical model, equates the loss of capacity with deviance from the norm. Under the medical model, incapacity is an outcome or symptom of a diagnostic disorder. If no disorder exists, the individual cannot be statutorily identified as incapacitated no matter how bizarre, destructive, or foolish the behavior.

Under the medical model, only aberrant behavior that is rooted in an identifiable disorder justifies the appointment of a guardian. Some argue that the need to identify a medical cause for incapacity places too much power in the hands of the physician; essentially what the physician says determines the outcome of the guardianship hearing. This need not be the case. As with any evidence, the probative value of the physician's testimony is determined by the factfinder. It should merely be another piece of evidence that, together with testimony by law observers of the respondent's behavior, cognitive tests, and the testimony of the respondent, combine to form the "truth" of the matter.

Ultimately, we must rely upon the judge to accurately weigh the evidence, which, in turn, depends largely upon the judge's view of the relative merits of autonomy and protection. A judge infused with ageist attitudes, who believes strongly in protection, will find many respondents in need of a guardian, no matter how the statute is written. A judge with a better understanding of the elderly, however, one who appreciates the importance of autonomy, both in life and in the law, can be affected by a good statutory definition. For such a judge, the medical model provides support for protecting individuals from guardianship even though they may act oddly or unreasonably.

Since we have an adequate model of an effective statute[10] in the Uniform Probate Code and the variations on it, what we need are not more model statutes, but better application of those that we have. If we want to have fewer guardians appointed and greater use of limited guardians, the answer lies not in the statute but in the courts. In the end, the use or misuse of guardians is in the hands of the judges who rule on guardianship petitions. Rather than focusing on theoretical concepts of capacity, reformers should turn their attention to sensitizing the judiciary to the value of autonomy and the right to act "unreasonably." Only when judges believe that the elderly have a right to be different will we see a change in guardianship in practice, and not merely in the language of the statutes.

NOTES

1. Consider the problem of trying to determine when black turns to white. The answer is that there is a lot of gray, and it is impossible to state where black leaves off or white begins.
2. Justice Stewart was attempting to define hard-core pornography when he admitted, " . . . perhaps I could never succeed in intelligibly doing so. But I know it when I see it, and the motion picture involved in this case is not that." Jacobellis v. Ohio, 378 U.S. 184, 197 (1964).
3. The term "courts" refers to the fact finder who is most often a judge, but jury determinations of incapacity are permitted in most states and occasionally are used.
4. Too often, the issue is whether the guardianship should be limited at all. Full guardianships remain the rule when they should be the exception.
5. Of course, the elderly (particularly older women) are more likely to defer to authority.
6. Even if reliable and precise cognitive tests did exist, it is hard to believe that they could outweigh the "better" evidence of how the individual acted. For example, if the tests indicated a lack of capacity, but the individual behaved quite normally and effectively, I doubt that any court would find guardianship appropriate. Conversely if the tests indicated that the person had good cognitive skills, but nevertheless acted bizarrely, the court might still find good cause for guardianship if only to protect the individual.
7. Cal. Probate Code §1801 (West 1989).
8. " . . . lacking the capacity to make or communicate responsible decisions." (Uniform Probate Code §5-103(7)
9. " . . . any person who is impaired by reason . . . " Ibid.

10. The Uniform Probate Code definition of an incapacitated person can be improved by modernization of the language. It should not, for example, use the term "mental deficiency" (mental disability is the preferred term), nor should it equate chronic use of drugs or chronic intoxication with incapacity. Ibid.

CHAPTER 2

Frailty, Risk, and Choice: Cultural Discourses and the Question of Responsibility

Sharon R. Kaufman
Gay Becker

This chapter provides an anthropological discussion of frailty, risk, and choice. A central principal of anthropology is that culture informs and structures the way people perceive reality. Culture provides an individual with a framework for making sense of and interpreting his or her own life and its larger contexts. The role of the anthropologist in this particular forum will be to explore a few of the concepts that underlie medical and legal decision making in relation to the elderly, to show how those concepts are embedded in culture, and to draw attention to some of the cultural sources of the perplexing ethical dilemmas about aging.

We attempt to open up the notions of frailty and risk beyond the definitions constructed for them by the field of gerontology, so that what has been tacit and assumed is made visible, and so that what has been taken for granted as basic fact is exposed as cultural construct. For the concepts of frailty, risk, autonomy, and independence, to name a few, are cultural concepts, and not, as years of scientific epistemology would have us believe, value-free notions created by a value-free science (Durbin, 1980; Luborsky & Sankar, 1993). The chapter has two goals: first, to explore briefly the problematic nature of a few of these constructs; and second, to reinforce the view shared by other gerontologists that cultural constructs affect the formulation of our research questions, the activities of service providers, and public policy (Estes, 1979, 1993; Gubrium, 1992; Luborsky & Sankar, 1993). Our interpretations of frailty, risk, autonomy, and dependence are grounded in qualitative research methodologies and are intellectually compatible with what is now being called the critical gerontology perspective. That perspective, developed in recent years by social scientists, philosophers, and other humanistic scholars in the aging field (Cole, Achenbaum, Jakobi, & Kastenbaum, 1993; Moody, 1989), offers a critique of positivist scientific ideology, identifies social and political processes that influence research agendas and policy, and overall, "is concerned with identifying possibilities for emancipatory social change, including positive ideals for the last stage of life" (Moody, 1993, p. xv).

CULTURAL AND GERONTOLOGICAL CONSTRUCTION OF FRAILTY, RISK, AND NEED

Analytic constructs used in gerontology particularly and the social sciences in general are not value-free variables, but are informed by historical and political concerns. The constructs bring shared assumptions about what is right and how things work into the research, explanatory, and policy processes (Luborsky & Sankar, 1993). Most importantly, the way in which a "problem" is perceived and defined will inform the nature and range of "solutions" to it. Frailty, risk, and need are three such constructs. Each is briefly discussed below.

The conceptualization of the elderly as being "at risk" for institutionalization, for falls, for loss of autonomy, for growing dependence, and other outcomes is a recent phenomena. In their detailed historical explorations of the meanings of aging in American society, for example, neither Haber (1983) nor Cole (1992) uncover notions of old people viewed by their families specifically or by society in general, as being "at risk." The construct may not have been conceived, in relation to old people, before the modern era.[1] Recent attention to risk and the elderly may result from the fact that risk is on the rise as a cultural category (Beck, 1992; Becker & Nachtigall, 1994; Douglas & Wildavsky, 1982; Rapp, 1994). It has become a concept which we, the members of late 20th century industrial society, invoke as an important framework for understanding the perils of the postmodern world. It has been said that we live in a "risk society" (Beck, 1992), a world made dangerous by technologies used for the production of war and peaceful progress and by environmental toxins and pollution. Much of our understanding of what constitutes danger, some of our criteria for decision making, and some of our public policies turn on questions of risk assessment, avoidance, and acceptance that we face in our everyday lives.

Public consciousness of risk and its reverberations in all areas of life has perhaps never been higher. Risk awareness is embedded in science and medicine—the two institutions that have come to dominate our ways of understanding the lives and problems of old people in this country (Estes & Binney, 1989). Indeed, Cole (1992, p. xxii) suggests that science and medicine have replaced religion and possibly the family and community as the dominant meaning systems for conceiving the capabilities, limitations, and function of the old. In the realm of contemporary geriatric medicine particularly, much of our activity concerns the biomedically framed "need" to assess, manage, and minimize the risks that both health professionals and the broader public feel older people are exposed to, or that their functionally limited bodies, selves, and lives apparently embody. An old person is linked with the notion of risk when family members, or social service agency personnel, or health care professionals perceive a change in the person's condition, whether it be due to diminishing functional ability, the onset of illness, or "just a feeling that something has gone wrong." At such a time, the health care system is understood to be the arena in which risk can be adequately defined, controlled, and hopefully, diminished.

Biomedical views of risk inform ways in which frailty is constructed. The two concepts are not independent of one another in the context of gerontology. "Frailty" is one of those terms—along with "independence," "life satisfaction," and "continuity"—that trouble gerontologists with multiple and slippery meanings. The *American Heritage Dictionary* defines frailty as "1. physically weak or delicate," and "2. not strong or substantial" (1992, p. 720). Gerontologists define physical frailty as "severely impaired strength, mobility, balance, and endurance" (Hadley, Ory, Suzman, & Weindruch, 1993, p. vii). It has been defined biologically as the state of reduced physiologic reserve associated with increased susceptibility to disability (Buchner & Wagner, 1992). It has been defined medically as limitations in personal mobility; the presence of two or more conditions covering respiratory, circulatory, musculoskeletal, and nervous disorders; or the presence of any single condition that a person characterizes as "serious or restricting" (Reschovsky & Newman, 1990). In their study of frailty and the perception of choice among a sample of old people who live alone, Rubinstein, Kilbride, and Nagy employ an open, qualitative definition: "having one or more health or functioning decrements that seriously affect the person's ability to carry out the expected and usual activities of daily living [ADL]" (1992, p. 4). In that interpretation, frailty suggests that functional losses may interfere with the ability to maintain autonomy in everyday life.

Knight and Walker (1985) note the lack of precision in definitions of frailty and the fact that concepts of independence, dependence, and "at risk for institutionalization" are always intertwined. Their research indicates that frailty can be measured by a variety of criteria, such as medical disorders producing functional disability, memory deficits, other mental disorders, behavior dangerous to self or others, behavior deemed socially inappropriate, and support system breakdown. Other studies of frailty do not necessarily employ those or similar criteria in their analyses. In a study to identify persons at risk for institutionalization, Shapiro and Tate (1985, 1988) considered 28 potential risk factors, and found that having any one of them (e.g., age over 85, living alone, living in retirement housing, ADL problem, mental impairment) was not enough to create such a risk. Discrete, scientifically neutral definitions for constructs such as frailty point to empirical and methodological problems in their objectification. More importantly, such definitions restrict researchers or service providers to concern with measurement and replicability and to the problem of how the elderly fit the definition or fit the range of services available. Objective and measurable definitions also narrow discussion to the elderly's need for services or to assessment of their losses.

The notion that the elderly have special, discrete needs which separate them from the rest of the population is a gerontological construct that both produces and reflects our conceptions of frailty and risk. In the context of gerontology, "needs of old people" can and should be assessed and rated by rational, scientific means so that the old person may be linked with appropriate services.

In a critical examination of the model of need assessment in gerontology, Dill (1993) shows "how organizational imperatives shape the definition of client need" while at the same time obscuring their own role in the production of that need (p. 459). She suggests that in the bureaucratic service organization system, the needy individual is viewed as a passive organism to which care is administered; he or she "is not an agent in the production of the process by which care is delivered" (p. 457). This is an important point. Service organizations claim to honor autonomy in verbal encounters among providers and clients. Yet their work stems from the premise that the individual does not have the ability to act with "agency," with independence of judgment (Clark, 1987, p. 71), and that the institution's own agenda is the real, objective priority.

Need in the context of service organizations is defined by three criteria: (a) as a property of the individual client or patient, rather than as a creation of an institution, (b) in instrumental terms by the evaluation of tests, questionnaires, or other standardized measures, and (c) in reference to outcomes such as home care, a safe environment, and a more healthy lifestyle, that are bureaucratically and professionally defined (Dill, 1993, p. 457). These criteria become taken for granted as the only or the best means to define need. They leave no room for the voices of individual old people to be heard, either in the development of care plans or programs appropriate to their sense of self, or in the shaping and implementation of relevant policy.

ANTHROPOLOGICAL RESEARCH ON FRAILTY

Our research illustrates how these concepts are understood and enacted in the lives of some old people and in the work of some service providers. In the study of growing dependence among a sample of 100 community-living elderly over the age of 80, we wanted to investigate what frailty and risk look like in advanced age. How are those concepts defined, framed, and understood? What mechanisms are employed by older persons, family members, and health care providers to cope with frailty and solve the problems it creates? To explore these questions, we sought out individuals who were perceived by family members, friends, or health professionals to be at risk, that is, whose health had recently changed for the worse and engendered a perceived need for greater medical care, social support, and/or supervision so that they could remain in the community.

Becker observed and interviewed individuals without cognitive impairment who were in a transition, frequently following an acute hospitalization, to a level of greater physical dependence (Becker, 1993a). Kaufman observed a multidisciplinary geriatric assessment team (including physician, nurse, social worker, psychologist, and podiatrist) in their work with individuals over the age of 80 whose mental as well as physical status had recently declined (Kaufman, 1993). This chapter reports on findings from Kaufman's investigation.

For an 8-month period in 1992 and 1993, Kaufman attended assessment team conferences where individual cases were discussed and family conferences, in which diagnoses, prognoses, and choices, recommendations, and solutions to problems were presented to clients and their family members. Two patterns emerged among the 43 cases she observed regarding why the assessment was sought. About half of the clients were brought to the service, usually by family members, because they had experienced a rapid decline in functional status—either mental, physical, or both—following an acute-care hospitalization, fall, or other acute medical incident in the preceding 6 months. The family wanted to know what was wrong and how the older person could be returned to the status quo. The other half were brought to the multidisciplinary team because a family member or other person was experiencing new difficulty in caring for or managing the life of a debilitated person, or simply could no longer cope with the growing strain and responsibility of caring for another person's body, home, finances, and safety. Functional status was not consistent across the 43 cases. Some of the elderly people were driving cars, managing expenses, and controlling their daily schedules at the time they were brought to the assessment service. Others were significantly demented and/or wheelchair bound and homebound when their families sought the team's advice.

Two cases drawn from observations of team meetings and family conferences are presented below. Our goal is to open up the discussion of frailty and risk to their sociocultural dimensions and explore how they are culturally produced through the interaction of older individuals, their caregivers, and their health providers. Frailty is conceived here both as (a) a quality attributed to certain individuals and (b) a dynamic adaptational process on the part of elderly persons, families, and health care personnel. As both quality and process, frailty is open to multiple interpretations. It comes into focus at the moment when any combination of an old person's symptoms and behaviors is construed to tip the balance towards identification of a problem of more dependence than independence with regard to functional ability and social role performance. Frailty thus conceived forces the individuals who encounter it to reconsider and renegotiate the meanings of autonomy and freedom, risk and responsibility, choice and surveillance, and interdependence in their own lives. The close observation of day-to-day frailty shows us that while surveillance of health conditions and risk behaviors may provide a solution to concerns about safety, it is no solution to the highly idiosyncratic desire for emotional well-being in late life.

Our interest lies in existential and experiential expressions of and responses to frailty, rather than objective definitions. We are concerned with what happens when the old and vulnerable *person* becomes a *patient*. While there is growing literature on the need for physicians and other health professionals to treat patients as persons, to approach them in their biopsychosocial wholeness and thus to blur the boundaries between person and patient (Cassell, 1991; Engel, 1977; Kleinman, 1988), here the focus is the construction of frailty through the ascription of the patient role.

THE PROCESS OF FRAILTY

Frailty is proposed when someone conceives there to be a "lived problem" with an old person. Either the old person has a medical condition that has not been diagnosed or resolved, or has a condition that seems to be growing worse or spreading to other bodily systems or areas of the person's life, or a concerned family member can no longer cope with caring for the old person and thus begins to think of symptoms or behaviors as a problem. Unless the caregiver or older person are highly educated or are health professionals themselves, the lived problem, as subjectively experienced, is not usually understood in terms of discrete categories of biomedical knowledge. Thus the family member comes to the health provider with the complaint that the parent "seems to be more forgetful and isn't sleeping lately," or "has lost a lot of weight and stopped taking walks,'' or "can't concentrate on his card game anymore.''

The old person becomes a patient at the time of contact with the health care system. In that transformation, the lived problem is fractured into component parts which are viewed through a biomedical and social service lens. Thus *frailty becomes more fully articulated* within the discourse of risk, safety, and care. A list of discrete diagnoses is made and treatments are created. In some cases, a negotiation process takes place among health provider(s), caregiver, and patient over whether to or how to implement treatment plans. The treatments are conceived as potential or partial solutions both to bodily ailments caused by medical conditions and to the more messy and unbounded dilemmas of social existence caused by inappropriate, irrational, or unsafe behaviors. The solutions, created within the limits of existing medical and social service structures in a particular community, become both the scientific and the moral "facts" of the case. The solutions are frequently claimed as ways to preserve, as completely as possible, the autonomy of the patient in spite of his or her functional limitations. Self-determination is conceived then as valuable, but appropriate only when it is enacted within the structure and rationale of social service and health care intervention. The cases presented below illustrate this process of frailty construction.

The process of constructing frailty is not interpreted as a clear-cut dichotomy between health care provider ideology about risk reduction on the one hand, and patient and family beliefs about autonomy and self-determination on the other. It usually is not that simple. Rather, practitioners, patients, and families share, though to different degrees and in different ways, the strong American values of optimism, determination, and the belief that medicine can cure, can fix things, or at least can provide help in some diffuse way, always. They also share an important Western cultural assumption: that the individual can acquire the ability, through perseverance, to reverse disease outcomes, and in fact, to overcome aging and nature itself (Gordon, 1988).

STORIES OF FRAILTY

Two cases address a number of questions pertinent to this exploration of frailty and risk: What behaviors or symptoms are perceived to place elderly persons at risk? Who considers them at risk, and how do they try to intervene? What problems, in fact, are they trying to solve? The following examples illustrate common problems of people in late life that bewilder, trouble, and sadden families and that are seen regularly by health care providers. Anyone who has observed or worked with old people in the context of health care delivery will recognize these stories.

Case #1

Mrs. A, an 80-year-old woman, was brought to the assessment service by her friend and neighbor of 15 years, M, who was concerned about her increasing inability to remember appointments, pay bills, prepare food for herself, and maintain her personal hygiene. The friend had noticed that Mrs. A's memory was deteriorating and she was worried about Mrs. A's ability to continue living alone safely. Several weeks before the assessment, the friend had discovered Mrs. A on the floor of her apartment, where she had fallen 2 days before, unable to arise unassisted. Mrs. A reported other falls in the past year as well to the assessment team.

According to the friend, Mrs. A's electricity and telephone service had been discontinued in the past year because she had not paid her bills. Mrs. A had also inadvertently run up a $900 bill at the corner grocery store, which was still unpaid. Because she had severe arthritis in her knees and trouble walking, Mrs. A only left her apartment, a task that required climbing 20 steps, once every 2 weeks to get groceries. The friend noticed that Mrs. A was eating mainly snacks and canned food and realized that Mrs. A needed some household assistance. M began visiting her more often and helping her with grocery shopping, cleaning, and paying bills. She also prepared a meal each time she visited.

Mrs. A had a brother, niece and daughter who visited her infrequently. According to M, they did not know the extent of Mrs. A's disabilities, and so were unaware of her problems in daily living. Mrs. A's social life revolved around an organization that provided, in her words, "foster home care to animals." At the time of the assessment, she was caring for nine cats, three birds, and one dog. Aside from M, members of the animal organization were her only regular, though infrequent, social contact. According to M, Mrs. A's apartment was appallingly dirty, she was incontinent, especially at night, and she needed assistance for her animals. She also informed the team that Mrs. A was feisty, resilient, and resented any interference with her life or her affairs.

Two years prior to this assessment, a community agency case manager had attempted to provide a variety of services to Mrs. A, including house cleaning, meal delivery, participation in an adult day health center, and a money management program. Mrs. A rejected all the services offered because she was afraid that anyone who entered her life would have some authority over it and would take her animals away.

Mrs. A was not able to give a detailed medical or social history to the team physician during the assessment because of her memory deficits and she relied on M to answer questions for her. She had not seen a physician for 4 years, claiming that she did not really need to and that she would have great difficulty getting to a doctor's office in any case.

Following the examinations by physician, psychologist, podiatrist and nurse and the meeting with the social worker, the assessment team concluded that Mrs. A was obese, incontinent, visually impaired, had degenerative joint disease, a history of hypertension, anemia, significant gait and balance instability, and severe memory and concentration problems that pointed to progressive dementia. The team nurse, who visited Mrs. A at home to assess her physical and mental capabilities in her own environment, wrote in her report:

> Inside the house there are two bird cages with birds in the front living room. The cages are dirty and the water for the birds has a strong stench. The dining area and kitchen are inhabited by at least nine cats. The room off the dining area is full of old clothes, mail, books, and appliances. Mrs. A is a pleasant woman who is dressed appropriately. When asked if she could locate several phone numbers, including her daughter's phone number and address, she was unable to do so. She has fair grooming and hygiene, although there is an odor of urine on her clothes and about the house. . . .She is borderline functional in her ability to care for herself. The house shows a great need of assistance.

The team wrote in their report that Mrs. A's physical and cognitive condition had deteriorated to the point where she needed "daily intervention" "in an attempt to support her living independently." They agreed that she would be safe in her apartment, temporarily, only if the following conditions were met: (a) her apartment be professionally cleaned, (b) she accept a Medicaid-paid aide to provide personal assistance, hygiene, food preparation, and cleaning on a daily basis, 5 hours a day, 5 to 7 days per week, (c) she have prepared meals delivered to her, (d) she have a money manager, (e) she reduce the number of pets, (f) she attend an adult day health center twice a week to have her physical health monitored, have a meal, and receive physical therapy because her walking was so unstable.

These criteria for her health, well-being, and safety were discussed during the follow-up conference with Mrs. A and her friend. M was informed by the team that even with all such services in place, Mrs. A's mental condition would worsen and that she would be able to remain in her own apartment for another year at most. Mrs. A was congenial during the conference but left without giving her consent for or acceptance of any of the services suggested. She never agreed to participate in any of the treatments suggested. Yet both the team social worker and the agency case manager who had attempted to provide services years before reported they would try to arrange for those services so she would be as safe and healthy as possible at home.

Case #2

The daughter of an 84-year-old woman, Mrs. B, requested an evaluation of her mother's condition in the hope that she could leave the skilled nursing wing of a residential care facility where she had resided for 4 months and return to her independent apartment in the same facility. Mrs. B had been placed in the hospital-like skilled nursing wing by facility personnel following several months of frequent fainting episodes and difficulty in maintaining her balance while walking. Her physical problem had been accompanied by a state of mental confusion and disorientation. The staff at the facility felt that Mrs. B's overall medical condition needed to be watched closely and that she was not safe in an apartment of her own.

Prior to her placement in skilled nursing, Mrs. B had had a series of health assistants living with her in a compromise attempt by facility personnel to monitor her condition daily while she remained in her own home. Mrs. B hated their presence and discharged each one, stating that they restricted her right to make choices for herself. She said, "I can accept the feebleness of my body but cannot deal with restrictions over my ability to make my own decisions."

The assessment evaluation was sought because although Mrs. B's mental and physical condition had seemed to stabilize, that is, she no longer fainted or fell and was not confused, there were conflicting opinions regarding whether Mrs. B continued to be at risk for further falls or other problems. At the time of her evaluation, Mrs. B could not walk unaided. She was diagnosed by the team as having severe memory deficits, difficulty with visual and motor skills, depression, gait and balance instability, chronic alcohol use, allergic dermatitis, normal pressure hydrocephalus, and spinal stenosis. The staff at the facility felt she had not made enough "progress" to return to her apartment. The daughter was unsure about her mother's health, yet wanted to be an advocate for her mother who was angry and frustrated about her loss of freedom and privacy. Mrs. B claimed the skilled nursing wing rules and regulations were too restrictive for her, were making her depressed, and were ruining her life.

Following the assessment, Mrs. B was informed by the team's physician and social worker that "she was in a sticky situation: between independent and assisted living." She was told that if she wanted to return to her own apartment, she "must bend a little with the health aides and not fire them." She was advised that she could return to her apartment only if she had a health aide present 8 hours per day, a call button installed, saw a neurologist about her gait, and appointed someone to take care of her finances. Psychotherapy for her depression was recommended as was the purchase of a medic-alert identification bracelet. The team social worker wrote in Mrs. B's chart, "She is adamant about returning to her apartment but is not realistic about the support services necessary to minimize her risk and maintain her independence."

FINDING SOLUTIONS FOR LIVED EXPERIENCE

The process by which frailty is culturally constructed in the health care context takes a certain form: It is a transformation from lived problem to diagnosis, then to treatment plan, then to rules about what ought to be done, and finally to negotiated compliance. At least three features of frailty's cultural construction emerge from these cases. First, we learn how subjective experience is interpreted in a medical/social service idiom. Though old persons come willingly enough to such services (Epstein et al., 1987), they do not come with the expectation that behaviors, habits, and patterns of a lifetime will be scrutinized along with the symptoms they choose to identify and present as troublesome.

Lived experience is transformed during the medical encounter into a problem list that encompasses personal and social behaviors as well as physiological disorders. It is important to note that the problem list is created through the interaction of older person, family or friend, and health care personnel. No one party is solely responsible for the transformation. Thus Mrs. A, who never sought medical services but was brought to the team by her concerned friend, was diagnosed by the friend and the team as having a dirty house, unpaid bills, too many pets, and not enough cooked food in addition to having medical diseases. Mrs. B's problem was identified by her daughter and herself as wanting to return to her own apartment.

Multidisciplinary health care teams can assess a range of difficulties beyond the biomedical, and in fact can assess the "whole" person, a skill considered essential for good geriatric care (Kane, 1988). But the geriatric imperative of holism has its ironic side: Not only is the problem list frequently more pervasive than patients or families could conceive alone, the proposed solutions are in some cases more invasive than they imagined, requiring active, unsolicited behavior modification. For some persons, such as Mrs. A, treatment plans suggesting behavioral change are not viewed as solutions because patients do not interpret their illnesses, activities, or behaviors as problems in the first place. Instead, treatment plans are viewed as unwanted meddling in their personal affairs. Mrs. A only sees such life management as a threat to her ability to shelter animals. Mrs. B sees the point of proposed treatments, but balks at infringement on her privacy and personal routine. Ironically, failure to comply with health care team proposals does indeed put some persons at risk for institutionalization, the greatest threat to autonomy in American culture.

All participants in this encounter—old persons, family, and health care providers—face an extremely difficult question: How can the health care system "fix" problems that reflect the lived experience of a lifetime? One cultural assumption shared by all participants is that the health care system can, and indeed should, contribute to the resolution of such problems. For frailty, as for other conditions categorized as health problems, is informed by the belief in the power of American medicine to restore, manage, and order (Kaufman, 1988a; Miller, Glasser, & Rubin, 1992). Yet proposals to resolve the problems frailty produces through major or multiple behavioral changes in late life may contribute to a sense of impending identity loss for many old people. We have found that old people, even those with some form of mental impairment, weigh the intrusion on their sense of self against the potential reduction of problems defined by others during the medical encounter (Becker, 1993b; Kaufman, 1988b). That process, in and of itself, can be wrenching for old people and their families. As a result, older persons may feel trapped by solutions proposed to them. And health care providers, who invest much energy and many hours in devising the most appropriate way to keep people out of institutions and in their own homes, may be frustrated when clients reject their proposals.

Second, we see that health care providers, and sometimes family as well, invoke the language of surveillance or safety and risk reduction as the key to maintaining personal autonomy and independence. They try to resolve the lived problem by adapting existing modes of intervention and services to the idiosyncratic forms of autonomy embodied by very old persons. Through the strategy of risk reduction, health care providers and caregivers attempt to resolve the conflict between safety and risk, freedom and supervision by incorporating one into the other. Thus, Mrs. A will have to reduce the number of pets she cares for, receive a meal service, attend an adult day health center, and have her body and environment cleaned by a housekeeper/personal assistant so that she can remain "independent" in her own home. Mrs. B needs to be watched 8 hours a day in order to reside in her apartment alone.

Third, in both of these cases we see how "rules" become "facts" (Arney & Bergen, 1984, p. 5): The lived experience of the old person *becomes* the problem list; risk reduction *is* the key to autonomy. Case management and assessment, with their institutionally created rules and regulations have rationalized and narrowly constructed the meaning of both need and care. The structure of health care delivery and social services, as well as the knowledge its providers share and the ideologies they invoke, create the facts, the only informational context the patients and families have as a basis for making decisions and coping with frailty. The health care context provides the method for addressing frailty. And the legal system reinforces those methods. At the present time, no other institutions in American culture provide alternatives.

THE CULTURAL CONTEXT

The constructs of frailty, risk, and need are articulated within a broader American cultural context. There are two conflicting conceptual frameworks currently applied in American health care delivery, especially (but not exclusively) to older persons. The first framework, most commonly termed *medicalization* by social scientists and other observers of health care, refers to a process in which personal and social problems and behaviors come to be viewed as diseases or medical problems that the medical and allied health professions have a mandate to "treat." Scholars have described how medicine has permeated many behavioral aspects of life, as social deviance or behavioral eccentricities are transformed into medical concerns, or as ordinary life processes (especially birth and death) are reinterpreted as events requiring medical intervention (Arluke & Peterson, 1981; Conrad & Schneider, 1980; Zola, 1972).

In popular thought, medicine is perceived to have spread into many areas of life which were not considered medical or potentially treatable even a generation ago. Problems which in the past were considered social, moral, or personal concerns, or were not publicly identified at all, are now considered medical problems. These include, for example, infertility, teenage pregnancy, and menopause; obesity and anorexia; and alcohol and drug abuse. The irony surrounding the broadening of medicine's influence on these conditions is evident in our confusion toward them. We desire and demand medical treatment (and hopefully cures) for them, and we simultaneously worry about the problems of encroachment, management, and surveillance such treatments create.

The elderly are particularly vulnerable to medical management, since old age is equated with illness in the public view (Estes, 1979; Sankar, 1984): Old people and their families, in increasing numbers, perceive the health care system to be the locus of expertise and resolution as they attempt to solve and cope with the problems created by debility in late life. The personal, social, legal, and political consequences for older persons—and indeed, for society—of exposing more and more areas of life to the clinical "gaze"[2] and to medical intervention are only beginning to be explored (Estes & Binney, 1989; Miller et al., 1992).

The second conceptual framework, called here the autonomy paradigm, represents the widespread application of philosophical principles of ethics to clinical decision making (Beauchamp & Childress, 1989; Pellegrino & Thomasma, 1981; Veatch, 1981). Bioethics as a field of practice places supreme value on the patient's or client's autonomy, self-determination, and right to choose as primary considerations in any medical treatment (Fox, 1990; Rothman, 1990). A variety of scholars have drawn attention to the predominance of individualism in Western, especially American, bioethical theory and practice (Clark, 1991; Marshall, 1992; Thomasma, 1984). They note how individualism has framed and dominated debate about resolving moral dilemmas in medicine and has, until very recently, excluded or muted consideration of other values such as community, interdependence, and mutual obligation in medical decision making.

The bioethics enterprise and its literature has created the most visible framework in contemporary society for defining and understanding dilemmas in medicine. Autonomy, patient rights, death with dignity, control in decision making, and justice, for example, have become familiar words in the public lexicon. Through their repeated use in professional journals and the lay press, these terms have become freestanding, symbolic representations of the valued ends in health care delivery. Although many admit that discussion of any of these terms becomes fraught with ambiguity as soon as they are placed in the context of a real person's situation, the terms have nevertheless become reified, as though they were (or ought to be) tangible, observable outcomes of medical activity and the doctor–patient encounter.

Over the past two decades, the field of bioethics has focused much of its problem-solving attention on the use of life sustaining technology, most specifically, when and why to withhold or withdraw such technology. Fueled by the publicity of the Karen Quinlan (1976) and Nancy Cruzan (1990) cases, bioethicists have brought questions and dilemmas of the patient's and family's role in decisions about quality of life and termination of life to the attention of the wider public. Those debates, taken together with the recent federally mandated Patient Self-Determination Act (1991), have honed the awareness of many people to issues of individual rights, responsibility, and choice in the context of medical care. And the legal mandates produced by highly publicized cases such as *Cruzan* have become part of the cultural context in which physicians, patients, and families act with one another to arrive at important decisions.

The cultural discourses on medicalization and autonomy coexist as powerful but contradictory ways of understanding the old body and old mind and relationships among the person/patient, family, health care system, and society. Those discourses frame conflicting methods of approaching and understanding aging and the dependencies it produces. On the one hand, aging is assumed by both Western popular culture and a great deal of the gerontological literature (Tornstam, 1992) to be demarcated largely and most importantly by physiological change for the worse.[3] Biomedical science is revered, and people want the medical profession to intervene in their distress with the goal of thwarting, monitoring, or managing decline. On the other hand, the cultural ideals of personal autonomy and freedom from institutional constraint and domination compete for expression in medical decision making. People clamor for options, choice, and the right to refuse in their desire to be informed consumers of health care or to be left alone. They—we—want both to passively sit back and let the doctor fix the problem and at the same time to retain full control over our lives.

POLICY IMPLICATIONS, GOALS, AND RESPONSIBILITY

As the two cases studies illustrate, the coexistence of these contradictory frameworks promotes frequently insoluble tension for frail elderly individuals and their families when they encounter the health care and related social service systems. In addition, such encompassing contradiction presents a baffling situation to American society regarding the creation and implementation of appropriate health care policy for the old who are vulnerable. The very old become the field on which the discourse on autonomy and freedom of choice competes with the discourse on intervention, safety, and risk. Dialogues surrounding diagnosis, treatment, management, and care of old or impaired persons invoke the language of these two discourses as persons-turned-patients, families, and health professionals all struggle to solve the problems created by increasing debility. Real and satisfactory solutions to problems of frailty are elusive because the competing discourses are so deeply embedded in the thinking of all the participants in the health care encounter.

It is amply evident that health care policy which does not reflect the actual and complex situations of the elderly simply cannot work. Existing policy has its philosophical foundation in the abstract yet simple cultural ideal of autonomy, understood as unequivocal self-reliance, coupled with the gerontological notion of need described above. Together, these perspectives have prevented us from developing adequate and relevant models of care and choice for a growing elderly population. Our policy seems to be stuck somewhere between the competing discourses: desiring to maximize the self-determination of the elderly while at the same time creating managed care systems which may, in fact, create dependency (Estes, 1993) through the cultural production of risk and frailty and the gerontological construction of need. In reformulating policy, we need to consider the bind in which the contradictory paradigms have placed us. There exists a seemingly permanent tension between safety and supervision on the one hand, and risk and independence on the other. These values compete in the delivery of health care and in our conceptions of who the elderly are and how they should be treated.

Some more expansive ways of thinking about autonomy have been proposed in recent years by a variety of scholars (Agich, 1990; Clark, 1987; Collopy, 1988). Their conceptions of creating and enhancing empowerment, even for severely impaired elders, provide alternatives to our currently conflicting approaches to aging. In those views, independence is not pitted against dependence. Rather, interdependence becomes the most important value. Clark (1987) suggests:

> Rather than being totally autonomous, the elderly must depend on the support of service providers (such as physicians) to provide information about the likely consequences of choosing among various health-related alternatives. Similarly, the community must provide minimal levels of socioeconomic support if real choice and genuine alternatives are to exist. This suggests that a kind of interdependent mutualism—cooperative empowerment—must exist, in which service providers and society support, yet not control, the freedom of individuals to reflect on their own ultimate values and to choose among alternative life options. (p. 73)

We may begin to think of the very old and their families as cultural pioneers, enabling us to consider the idea that both the medicalization and autonomy paradigms are inadequate conceptualizations for the realities of frailty in our aging society. What is called for is a reconceptualization of frailty, risk, and need, and the acknowledgment that interdependence and flexibility in addressing the tasks of day-to-day existence are more important than fitting the elderly to existing models of service delivery or resolving the problem by enhancing safety and reducing risk.

Exploring the tensions between and among these conflicting discourses forces us to consider the following questions: What are the appropriate goals of medicine and the allied social services for the elderly? How much responsibility should health care providers take in assuring safety? Who, ultimately, is responsible for risk reduction and for fostering true interdependence: the doctor? the patient? the family? the law?

These questions are ultimately ethical in nature. They force us to consider which set of values we want to dominate our thinking and our decision making—risk reduction by intervention, or live and let live? They invite us to ponder which set of values is more relevant to quality-of-life considerations. For if quality of life is what we all strive for, which values enable it to be realized in the lived experience of the older person? And in whom should we invest the authority to make it so? Professionals in the field of aging have been grappling with these questions for some time, but the questions also go beyond gerontology. Their answers will affect practices in medicine, law, and public policy.

This chapter offers a constructivist approach to gerontology and to some of the problems of aging in America. Perhaps by shifting and expanding the focus of the gerontological inquiry, we can find our way to a new range of conceivable solutions to the problems of aging that trouble our society.

NOTES

1. Elias Cohen suggests that more extensive historical research might reveal the old were, in fact, considered to be "at risk" in earlier times (personal communication).
2. A term employed by Foucault (1975) and explored in great detail by Arney and Bergen (1984). It refers to the development of an informed, purposeful look at the patient and disease. As notions of disease have expanded in recent history, so too has the clinical gaze expanded to encompass "man within a hierarchy of systems" (Arney & Bergen, 1984, pp. 78–79).
3. This is how aging is largely perceived in the United States and other Western industrialized countries. But neither aging nor frailty are biological givens or objective facts meant to be revealed by health care professionals. Rather, they are socially constructed categories of meaning. For example, Lock (1984) notes that in Japan, where old people go to physicians quite often, the clinical gaze is focused only on the biological body. The social distress of old people is

rendered invisible and is ignored. Cohen (1992) suggests that old age and debility in India are not viewed as states of being that require attention, medical or otherwise, because they are not interpreted as a social threat (p. 144). Thus old age is not medicalized at all and the category of geriatrics is not meaningful or relevant.

ACKNOWLEDGEMENT

The authors' research has been supported through a National Institute on Aging Research Award, # AG09176, "From Independence to Dependence among the Oldest Old," (1991–1994). Gay Becker, Ph.D., Principal Investigator and Sharon R. Kaufman, Ph.D., Co-Principal Investigator.

REFERENCES

Agich, G. J. (1990). Reassessing autonomy in long-term care. *Hastings Center Report*, November/December, pp. 12–17.

American Heritage Dictionary (3rd ed.). (1992) New York: Houghton Mifflin.

Arluke, A., & Peterson, J. (1981). Accidental medicalization of old age and its social control implications. In C. Fry (Ed.), *Dimensions: Aging, culture and health* (pp. 271–284). New York: Praeger.

Arney, W. R., & Bergen, B. J. (1984). *Medicine and the management of living.* Chicago: University of Chicago Press.

Beauchamp, T. L., & Childress, J. F. (1989). *Principles of biomedical ethics.* (3rd ed). New York: Oxford University Press.

Beck, U. (1992). *Risk Society.* Beverly Hills: Sage.

Becker, G. (1993a). The oldest old: Autonomy in the face of frailty. *Journal of Aging Studies, 8*, 59–76.

Becker, G. (1993b). Continuity after a stroke: Implications of life course disruption in old age. *Gerontologist, 33*, 148–158.

Becker, G., & Nachtigall, R. (1994). "Born to be a mother:" The cultural construction of risk in infertility treatment in the U.S. *Social Science and Medicine, 39*, 507–518.

Buchner, D. M., & Wagner, E. H. (1992). Preventing frail health. *Clinics in Geriatric Medicine, 8*, 1–17.

Cassell, E. J. (1991). *The nature of suffering.* New York: Oxford University Press.

Clark, P. G. (1987). Individual autonomy, cooperative empowerment, and planning for long-term care decision making. *Journal of Aging Studies, 1*, 65–76.

Clark, P. G. (1991). Ethical dimensions of quality of life in aging. *The Gerontologist, 31*, 631–639.

Cohen, L. (1992). No aging in India: The uses of gerontology. *Culture, Medicine and Psychiatry, 16*, 123–161.

Cole, T. R. (1992). *The journey of life*. New York: Cambridge University Press.

Cole, T. R., Achenbaum, W. A., Jakobi, P. L., & Kastenbaum, R. (Eds.). (1993). *Voices and vision of aging: Toward a critical gerontology*. New York: Springer Publishing Co.

Collopy, B. J. (1988). Autonomy in long term care: Some crucial distinctions. *The Gerontologist, 28*, 10–17.

Conrad, P., & Schneider, J. W. (1980). *Deviance and medicalization: From badness to sickness*. St. Louis: Mosby.

Cruzan v. Director, Missouri Department of Health, 497 U.S. 261, 110 S. Ct. 2841 (1990).

Dill, A. (1993). Defining needs, defining systems: A critical analysis. *The Gerontologist, 33*, 453–460.

Douglas, M., & Wildavsky, A. (1982). *Risk and culture*. Berkeley: University of California Press.

Durbin, P. T. (Ed.). (1980). *A guide to the culture of science, technology and medicine*. New York: Free Press.

Engel, G. (1977). The need for a new medical model: A challenge for biomedicine. *Science, 196*, 129–136.

Epstein, A. M., Hall, J. A., Besdine, R., Cumella Jr., E., Feldstein, M., McNeil, B. J., & Rowe, J. W. (1987). The emergence of geriatric assessment units. *Annals of Internal Medicine, 106*, 299–303.

Estes, C. L. (1979). *The aging enterprise*. San Francisco: Jossey-Bass.

Estes, C. L. (1993). The Aging Enterprise Revisited. (The 1992 Kent Lecture.) *The Gerontologist, 33*, 292–298.

Estes, C. L., & Binney, E. A. (1989). The biomedicalization of aging: Dangers and dilemmas. *The Gerontologist, 29*, 587–596.

Foucault, M. (1975). *The birth of the clinic*. New York: Vintage.

Fox, R. C. (1990). The evolution of American bioethics: A sociological perspective. In G. Weisz (Ed.), *Social science perspectives on medical ethics* (pp. 201–220). Philadelphia: University of Pennsylvania Press.

Gordon, D. (1988). Tenacious assumptions in western medicine. In M. Lock & D. Gordon (Eds.). *Biomedicine examined* (pp. 19–56). Dordrecht: Kluwer.

Gubrium, J. F. (1992). Qualitative research comes of age in gerontology [editorial]. *The Gerontologist, 32*, 581–582.

Haber, C. (1983). *Beyond sixty-five*. New York: Cambridge University Press.

Hadley, E. C., Ory, M. G., Suzman, R., & Weindruch, R. (Eds.). (1993). Physical frailty [special issue]. *Journals of Gerontology, 48.*

In re Quinlan, 70 N.J. 10, 355A. 2d647, cert. denied sub nom. Garger v. New Jersey, 249, v.s. 922, 50L. Ed. 289, 97S. Ct. 319 (1976).

Kane, R. A. (1988). Beyond caring: The challenge to geriatrics. *Journal of the American Geriatrics Society, 36,* 467–472.

Kaufman, S. R. (1988a). Toward a phenomenology of boundaries in medicine: Chronic illness experience in the case of stroke. *Medical Anthropology Quarterly, 2,* 338–354.

Kaufman, S. R. (1988b). Stroke rehabilitation and the negotiation of identity. In S. Reinharz & G. Rowles (Eds.), *Qualitative gerontology* (pp. 82–103). New York: Springer Publishing Company.

Kaufman, S. R. (1993). The social construction of frailty: An anthropological perspective. *Journal of Aging Studies, 8,* 45–58.

Kleinman, A. (1988). *The illness narratives.* New York: Basic Books.

Knight, B., & Walker, D. L. (1985). Toward a definition of alternatives to institutionalization for the frail elderly. *The Gerontologist, 25,* 358–363.

Lock, M. (1984). Licorice in Leviathan: The medicalization of care for the Japanese elderly. *Culture, Medicine and Psychiatry, 8,* 121–139.

Luborsky, M., & Sankar, A. (1993). Extending the critical gerontology perspective: Cultural dimensions. Introduction. *The Gerontologist, 33,* 440–444.

Marshall, P. A. (1992). Anthropology and bioethics. *Medical Anthropology Quarterly, 6,* 49–73.

Miller, B., Glasser, M., & Rubin, S. (1992). A paradox of medicalization: Physicians, families and Alzheimer's disease. *Journal of Aging Studies, 6,* 135–148.

Moody, H. R. (1989). Toward a critical gerontology: The contribution of the humanities to theories of aging. In J. Birren & V. Bengston (Eds.). *Emergent theories of aging* (pp. 19–40). New York: Springer Publishing Co.

Moody, H. R. (1993). Overview: What is critical gerontology and why is it important? In T. R. Cole, W. A. Achenbaum, P. L. Jakobi, & R. Kastenbaum (Eds.). *Voices and visions of aging* (pp. xv–xli). New York: Springer Publishing Co.

Patient Self-Determination Act, Omnibus Budget Reconciliation Act of 1990, Pub. L. No. 101-508 4206, 4751.

Pellegrino, E. D., & Thomasma, D. C. (1981). *A philosophical basis of medical practice.* New York: Oxford University Press.

Rapp, R. (1994). ''Risky business:'' Genetic counseling in a shifting world. In J. Schneider & R. Rapp (Eds.). *Articulating hidden histories: Anthropology, history, and the influence of Eric R. Wolf.* Berkeley: University of California Press.

Rechovsky, J. D., & Newman, S. J. (1990). Adaptation for independent living by older frail households. *The Gerontologist, 30*, 543–552.

Rothman, D. J. (1990). Human experimentation and the origins of bioethics in the United States. In G. Weisz (Ed.), *Social science perspectives on medical ethics* (pp. 185–200). Philadelphia: University of Pennsylvania Press.

Rubinstein, R. L., Kilbride, J. C., and Nagy, S. (1992). *Elders living alone: Frailty and the perception of choice.* New York: Aldine de Gruyter.

Sankar, A. (1984). "It's Just Old Age." In D. Kertzer & J. Keith (Eds.). *Age and anthropological theory* (pp. 250–280). Ithaca, NY: Cornell University Press.

Shapiro, E., & Tate, R. (1985). Predictors of long-term care facility use among the elderly. *Canadian Journal on Aging, 4*, 11–19.

Shapiro, E., & Tate, R. (1988). Who is really at risk of institutionalization? *The Gerontologist, 28*, 237–245.

Thomasma, D. C. (1984). Freedom, dependency, and the care of the very old. *Journal of the American Geriatrics Society, 32*, 906–914.

Tornstam, L. (1992). The quo vadis of gerontology: On the scientific paradigm of gerontology. *The Gerontologist, 32*, 318–325.

Veatch, R. M. (1981). *A theory of medical ethics.* New York: Basic Books.

Zola, I. K. (1972). Medicine as an institution of social control. *Sociological Review, 20*, 487–504.

Commentary: Managing Incapable People's Financial Affairs in England and Wales

A. B. Macfarlane

In England and Wales, there is a special body responsible for overseeing the administration of the financial affairs of people who are unable to manage their own property and affairs by reason of mental disorder. That body is called the Court of Protection, and it is partly a court and partly an office. The administrative or office functions are carried out by a sister body in the same building, called the Public Trust Office. The judicial decisions are made by my assistants and me. I am a lawyer and the principal judge of the Court of Protection, although there is a right of appeal by anyone aggrieved by a decision to a judge at a higher level and eventually to the House of Lords, which is the highest appeal court in England. As far as I know, no decision has ever gone through that entire process. The whole organization is at present constituted under the Mental Health Act 1983.[1]

The history of the Court of Protection is relevant to this volume, since it indicates how long some of the issues now being discussed in the United States have been considered a problem in England. Jurisdiction over persons "of unsound mind" is believed to have been taken over by King Edward I (who reigned from 1272 to 1307) from the feudal lords and exercised as part of the royal prerogative. The first written reference appears as an attempt to restrict the royal prerogative by the statute called *De Prerogativa Regis*, probably dated 1339. The statute provided that "the King shall have the custody of the lands of natural fools, taking the profits of them . . . "and shall find them their necessaries . . . " and that "the King shall provide when any, that beforetime hath had his wit and memory, happen to fail of his wit . . . that their lands and tenements shall be safely kept . . . and the residue beside their sustentation shall be kept to their use, to be delivered unto them when they come to their right mind. . . ." So it is clear that from a very early date there was felt to be a public interest in looking after the assets of mentally disordered people. It is from the royal prerogative that the office of the Master in Lunacy derived and the Court of Protection is the successor in title to that office.

Several factors regarding the Court of Protection should be stressed. First, it deals directly only with a person's financial affairs, not with welfare or personal care decisions nor with decisions relating to consent to or refusal of medical treatment. Geographically, also, jurisdiction is limited only to England and Wales, and not Scotland, Ireland, or the islands off the British shores. Second, the nature of the legal system differs in different parts of the United Kingdom. England and Wales is a single legal jurisdiction which has a common law system, for example, while Scotland has a civil law (Roman law) system.

Third, the Court of Protection has a total caseload at any one time of about 30,000. These are all people decided by the court to be mentally unable to manage their financial affairs. In addition, the court acts as a registration office for the particular class of documents called "enduring powers of attorney," which are created by a person when capable and which give power to an agent (called an "attorney" but who need not be a lawyer) to act on his/her behalf in financial matters in the future. This enduring power of attorney is required by English law to be registered with the Court of Protection when the attorney believes that the donor (the person creating the document) is or is becoming mentally incapable. The Court's "customers" are called "patients" (or, in the case of enduring powers of attorney, "donors"). Of those who are patients, 69% are aged 70 or over and 12.4% are over 90. Most of this group of elderly patients come within the Court's jurisdiction because of senile dementia of one form or another. These statistics reveal the interesting fact that there is a large number of potential patients whose affairs are never brought to the Court's attention. For instance, the population of the United Kingdom is about 56 million people; the Alzheimer's Disease Society in the United Kingdom estimates that there are 750,000 people in the country suffering from Alzheimer's disease. Some of those, of course, are in Scotland or Northern Ireland, but the bulk are in England and Wales. Some of them may still be capable of managing for themselves, many will not have funds of a size or type which need sophisticated management, and there exists a system in simple cases through which an "appointee" is authorized to act for the purpose only of drawing welfare benefits and spending them for the patient's benefit. But even supposing those categories account for 500,000 Alzheimer's disease sufferers, who is managing the financial affairs of the rest? The court's 30,000 include people of all ages and all types of mental disorder, although 69% (20,700 people) might fall into the Alzheimer's disease group. What is happening to the other 230,000 or so?

Fourth, there is the matter of how the court works in relation to patients. An application is first made by a relative, adviser or friend of a patient asking the court to appoint a receiver, that is to say, a financial manager. An application must be supported by a certificate as to the patient's assets and family circumstances and by a medical certificate from at least one doctor, explaining in detail the nature of the patient's mental disorder, confirming the incapacity to manage affairs and answering certain questions, such as how long the disorder has lasted and what is the patient's life expectancy. The court then takes up a reference from someone who can answer written questions about the proposed receiver's reliability and competence. The court also arranges for the proposed receiver to take out a security bond to guarantee the performance of the receivership duties. The patient is notified of the application personally (not just by letter) and is invited to make any objection, either as to the appointment of a receiver at all or as to the particular receiver proposed. The patient does not, however, see the medical evidence or the evidence as to family and property unless an objection is made. If there is an objection, the dispute is heard by the court in an adversarial, but comparatively informal, way, and all parties, including the patient, may attend and/or be represented by a lawyer. The number of objections and contested hearings is very small, perhaps 35 or 40 a year out of a yearly intake of about 6,200 cases.

As a final piece of background material, certain provisions are made in England for elderly people's needs. Everyone is entitled to a retirement pension. There are other allowances payable to people who need attendance, either during the day or for both day and night, and to people who are unable to walk; the amount of these allowances is not dependent on the patient's other means. There are other benefits payable to people in certain cases, which may or may not be means tested. Free medical treatment is available to everyone, as is free hospital care, but the number of beds is limited and, in the psychiatric sector, is diminishing. Official government policy is to discharge patients from geriatric and psychiatric hospitals into the community, and to maintain in the community those who would at one time have been admitted to hospital. Local governmental bodies (the county councils and district councils, which have considerable powers and duties of their own and by whom, for example, most social workers are employed) have a considerable degree of responsibility for the elderly people in their area and maintain residential homes of their own for infirm people, although not facilities which provide nursing care. Local government authorities have been given the main functions of assessment and provision of care under the community care legislation which took effect in April, 1993. For people in private residential or nursing homes, the local authority has the responsibility of meeting the difference (formerly met by central government) between the fees charged by the home and the social security benefits which the patient receives, once the patient's own resources have fallen to below £ 3,000 ($4,350). Obviously, there can be considerable conflict between the patient's relatives, who try to persuade the hospital (which is free) that it should keep the patient there, and the doctor, who believes there is a suitable place for the patient in a fee-charging home nearby and wants to free the hospital bed for some other person who needs it. The patient may be made to feel like the parcel nobody wants in the game of "pass the parcel."

The Court of Protection must decide questions of capacity of four types: (a) capacity to manage and administer one's property and affairs, (b) capacity to make a will, (c) capacity to create or revoke an enduring power of attorney, and (d) capacity to resume management of one's property and affairs. All these problems are familiar to American workers in this field. In spite of international differences in language and procedure, there is complete universality in the difficulties faced by professionals who work with older persons, and there is a tremendous need for multidisciplinary discussions to enhance knowledge and skills.

One is reminded of the anecdote about the rather slow-witted judge who asked counsel to explain an abstruse point to him. After the explanation, he said to counsel, "I'm afraid, Mr. Brown, I am still no wiser." "No, my lord," replied counsel, "but you are considerably better informed."

There is a great deal of significant information in Dr. Kaufman and Dr. Becker's chapter. It seems as true for British society as for American society that older people have become more likely to be regarded as "at risk" today than they were only a few decades ago. The heightened perception of risk has led to considerably increased medical intervention, particularly since the introduction of the National Heath Service in the late 1940s, and to some extent to intervention into the whole life of the patient, by the mechanism described in the main essay in this chapter.

On the other hand, there is no doubt that in financial matters, the idea of vulnerability to exploitation of one's assets has been a live issue in England since the 14th century. However, this concern has not spilt over into the welfare or personal care aspects of a person's life. Hence, only minimal rules regulate guardianship of adults in England and Wales. There is extensive legal regulation of compulsory and voluntary admission of psychiatric patients to hospital, but very little of elderly people whose only mental disorder is dementia.

In present day England, as in the United States, the two principles of protection and autonomy of patients frequently come into conflict. The devil's advocate should ask how possible or advisable it is to overcome the normal perception of society about risk and frailty. Is autonomy the higher good? There is an argument that would say not. This discussion referred earlier to the number of people who might be expected to need someone to manage their financial affairs, compared with the number of cases where there is actually a legal receiver. This disparity can to some extent be explained if one thinks of those who do not become patients as having bargained or negotiated for the level of autonomy which they are willing to accept. There may be an express or, more likely, a tacit agreement within the family, as a result of which each side makes concessions, and the overall result, although not perfect, is sufficiently acceptable to form a way of living which works. Alternatively, the patient may have bargained with herself when younger to give up some pleasures in order to provide for the expensive contingency of losing mental capacity later in life. Investing heavily while young in life assurance policies, coupled with endowment insurance, is a simple example. Other people may build up their savings by sacrificing holidays or may buy or rent smaller property than they would otherwise like. Later, the savings may be ploughed into the purchase of an annuity to procure guaranteed income. Yet others may use their energies when young to cultivate and get close to family or friends, or to build up contacts in the community in preparation for less independence. The individual may interpret this as a bargain with society at large, and may then arrange her life so that, even if she becomes confused and incapable of making decisions, the arrangements will hold. A condition of the bargain will be a limit to complete self-determination and this will be recognized from the start and adhered to when the time comes. This phenomenon applies especially to elderly women on their own, who in England form the largest number of people in the category of elderly confused people.

We must also return to the question of why, in the Court of Protection, so few objections and disputes arise. Partly, it may be explained by the fact that most applications are made late; often, the medical evidence shows that the onset of the mental disorder occurred up to five years before the application. Some of this delay is understandable when one considers a condition like dementia, which develops at different speeds in different people and which might not be recognized by a lay person until well after its beginnings have been noted by a doctor. However, even allowing for that, some of the explanation must lie in the willingness of patients to acquiesce in having their financial management taken away from them; it is a relief to many people not to have to struggle any longer. They may be confused and unable to cope, but they can still see the bills coming through the letter box and can tell that they are short of cash for food, or that the heating had been turned off, even if they are not entirely sure all the time why this is happening. At that stage, many people are prepared to realize, in a blurred way, that they need to make other arrangements and are prepared to sacrifice autonomy, well knowing that in consulting the doctor or a social worker about the problem, they are surrendering their rights in all sorts of areas for the sake of increased care. (Incidentally, in England doctors would not necessarily invoke a professional team to investigate the situation and suggest holistic solutions. Because doctors' lists are always overfull, there seems more of a tendency to treat the specific complaint and to ignore the home circumstances of the patient who can be brought to the physician.)

There has been considerable debate among British social workers about the ethical implications of fitting patients in residential homes (where they are not held under compulsory detention powers) with electronic tags to alert the staff if they attempt to leave the home. Although a lawyer can argue both sides of this issue, relatives of an elderly, disoriented person likely to wander out of the home into a busy main road would certainly see that possibility as a very real risk to life and many would support the home in any attempt to prevent it, even if it were theoretically the crime of false imprisonment.

The Kaufman and Becker approach to thinking about autonomy as a matter of interdependence has much merit. This may be what is actually happening and why there are so many fewer problems than one would expect. Mrs. A and Mrs. B, although standing for many others, do not represent the majority of elderly incapable people. We should be working toward educating people into realizing that they should learn, early in life, how to negotiate for what they will need from society later on. This negotiation may take the form of creation of a detailed enduring power of attorney (on one level) or of working to ensure that relationships with the younger generation are securely bonded with trust and affection (on a deeper level). Education of this kind would pay dividends to everyone in a world that has increasing numbers of older people.

NOTE

1. 1983, chapter 20.

Commentary: Protection and Empowerment of the Elderly: Whose Needs Does the Law Really Serve?

John J. Regan

Several provocative themes emerge from Dr. Kaufman and Dr. Becker's chapter that are relevant to the way our legal system deals with incapacity:

1. Frailty has been medicalized by our society, thus leading us to seek medical answers to the problems arising from frailty.
2. Frailty and risk are social constructs, characteristics of aged persons framed by those who have a familial or public responsibility to provide care for these persons.
3. A system of service organizations, the "aging enterprise," (Estes 1979, 1992) has developed to meet the "needs" of these persons. The needs are themselves defined by these agencies in the light of the organizational imperatives of these agencies.
4. The medicalized interventions offered by these organizations

sometimes run counter to aged persons' deeply held values of independence and autonomy.

5. What is needed is greater empowerment of aged clients through systems of service delivery that balance care and choice and that emphasize interdependence and flexibility in addressing the tasks of day-to-day existence.

To what extent does the legal system reflect, support, or even create these propositions? Do the legal mechanisms designed to protect the incapacitated and to empower those with capacity sometimes subvert these goals and instead promote the interests of the protectors?

The presence of frailty and risk in an older person often gives rise to an inquiry into the person's competency, or (a better word) capacity, typically through the vehicle of a guardianship proceeding. For many years, these proceedings authorized intervention solely on the basis of a finding that the person was of "advanced age" or had a mental or physical illness or disability which caused the functional deficits exhibited by this older person.[1] Typically, the primary evidence supporting a petition for a guardianship was an affidavit from a physician describing the person's physical and mental condition and classifying the individual as incompetent to manage his or her affairs. Often the petition and evidence were presented without any opportunity for the judge to actually see the incapacitated person or to hear the person's point of view (Legal Counsel for the Elderly, 1987). Clearly the guardianship process had been medicalized (Horstman, 1975).

Recent reforms in the law of guardianship have discarded the so-called medical model of incapacity (American Bar Association, 1986). The process now places greater emphasis on evidence of functional deficiency as the measure of incapacity. It gives the person a better opportunity to participate in the hearings by requiring his or her presence and by guaranteeing the right to appointed counsel. It expands the options available to the judge by requiring a report from a court investigator who assesses the person's needs and recommends a plan of action to meet those needs.

In light of Kaufman and Becker's observations, however, one may question whether these reforms fully address the problems they have identified, or whether the difficulties have simply been moved into the background. For example, are the functional deficiencies that justify a guardianship another way of defining frailty, risk, and need from the perspective of a proposed intervenor? To what extent is a court's finding that a person is functionally disabled prompted by the availability of the proposed guardian, or even a reflection of the self-interest of an intervenor anxious to preserve the person's assets for others or himself (Alexander, 1969)? How much actual attention do judges pay to the possibility that a guardianship will foster more dependence rather than promote the incapacitated person's autonomy? Are court visitors and evaluators trapped in the cycle of defining the person's needs only in the light of those services which are available from the service agencies? Or worse, are these court investigators likely to be attorneys who are only 1990s versions of the former guardians *ad litem*, who offer to the judge a cramped legal vision of what they believe is best for the incapacitated person but who lack expertise in assessing need and devising a service plan?

Another example of a problem where our perception of incapacity may be distorted by the lens through which we view it is elder abuse. The appearance of a few fragmented and unscientific studies of elder abuse in the late 1970s (Block & Sinnott, 1979; Douglass, Hickey, & Noel, 1980) and the publication in 1981 of a report by the U.S. Congress, House Select Committee on Aging supposedly documenting this tragedy provoked a storm of public outrage over this previously unknown phenomenon. State legislatures rushed to enact mandatory reporting laws, create hotlines, and order immediate investigations of all such reports to deal with this horrendous practice, though seldom was any new money appropriated to fund these efforts. Estimates of the incidence of abuse indicated that the nation had up to 2 million cases a year (Tatara, 1990), most of which unfortunately were hidden and unreported. State elder abuse agencies and adult protective services programs proliferated, academic centers to study the problem were established, and a national clearinghouse was created. Never mind that no real data existed to demonstrate the incidence of abuse, or that no true consensus on the legal definition of abuse had emerged.

At the end of 1993, however, new data were published which may challenge the justification for these developments. A study based on actual state reports of abuse found that the number of substantiated reports of abuse in 1991 was only 52,000, which by extrapolation led to an estimate of 735,000 nationwide (Tatara, 1993). Obviously, the earlier estimate of 2 million cases is in jeopardy.

Besides mandating reporting and investigation, the protective services legislation of the 1980s attempted to control forced intervention by requiring consent of the client with capacity for these services and court authorization on behalf of incapacitated clients (Legal Counsel for the Elderly, 1987). The cases of Mrs. A and Mrs. B recounted by Dr. Kaufman and Dr. Becker suggest, however, that the consent/court order legal dichotomy is too simplistic. The shaping of the packages of services offered to these women seems to have lacked a process of negotiation and gradualism to gain their consent and instead had overtones of a take-it-or-leave-it approach. If this impression is accurate, should one conclude that the interventionist ethic, which these laws sought to control, is alive and well beneath the surface, and is it perhaps beyond legal control?

No one denies that cases of domestic violence against the elderly or of their own self-neglect exist. Rather, the real issues are how broadly abuse should be defined, whether it is as widespread as some maintain, and what type of social response to it is appropriate. To what extent is the problem of elder abuse another example of frailty, risk, and need identified by intervenors but shaped by the service imperatives of the social agencies? Is there at work here a "social- industrial complex" which is the counterpart of the medical–industrial complex described by Carroll Estes (Estes, 1979; Estes, 1992)?

Still another area where intervention and autonomy often clash is the nursing home. How often is admission to a nursing home a voluntary act by a resident? The elderly are frequently "placed" in a nursing home by exhausted caretakers, but this decision may be a product of defeat and lack of choice rather than a freely chosen option. If the elderly person appears to lack capacity, the family may sign him into the facility without legal process of any sort. If the person already has a guardian, the guardian's action goes unchallenged. No inquiry into alternatives is required or wanted. Thus, institutionalization of the frail elderly not only verifies the risk of institutionalization previously assessed by the intervenor, but is conducted in a manner which drives home to the elder the point that his or her autonomy has vanished.

Once admitted to the nursing home, the frail elder is still at risk for further intervention. Physical and chemical restraints, especially antipsychotic drugs, are all too common, often used by staff for patient management rather than prescribed by a physician as a last resort for the welfare of the resident (Garrard et al., 1991). Recent studies of the use of these restraints have shown how widespread they are but how inappropriate in many cases (U.S. Congress, Senate Special Committee on Aging, 1989). Is this another example of risk and need of the elderly being defined and managed by caretakers for institutional and organizational purposes?

The same tension can be found in the process of medical decision making. No better example of the philosophy of empowerment for the elderly can be found than the remarkable spread of advance directives. Although only a fraction of the older population has executed a living will or a durable power of attorney for health care, a philosophy of personal responsibility and control over health care decisions has become deeply embedded in the American psyche (Kapp, 1989). Yet barriers to a greater exercise of this responsibility are still erected by the helping professions. The durable power of attorney for health care should be a "people's document," a simple and straightforward delegation of authority over health care decisions during incapacity to one's agent. In practice, however, many states have made it so complex that a person must consult (and pay) a lawyer to have one drafted. Even worse, New York's simplified health care proxy form, designed to avoid the need for a lawyer, has nonetheless been so customized by many attorneys, without any real change in substance, that many people are afraid to execute one without legal advice.

Or consider the reluctance of many physicians to carrying out patients' advance directives (Danis et al., 1991; Wolf et al., 1991). Some would rather not discuss them at all, or believe that such discussion takes too much time and requires special training and competence. Others reject these directives entirely because they think that patients cannot really anticipate their preferences in a future medical situation, or that the forms are too vague to be useful guides to future action, or that the patient simply may have changed his or her mind since the time when the form was executed (Cantor, 1992).

The enactment of laws authorizing advance directives or informing the patient about them on admission to a hospital or nursing home is really only the first step in empowering the patient. Physicians must accept the responsibility for initiating and engaging in discussions with the patient about future health care decisions much earlier in their relationship. The physician should anticipate the possible future frailty of the patient, the risk of unwanted health care decisions, and the importance of having the patient articulate his or her values and preferences before a crisis occurs.

Another reflection of the tension between professional dominance and patient prerogatives lies in the current debate about medical futility and the limits of patient autonomy. No consensus has developed to date concerning the definition or scope of the concept of futility beyond the principle that there are some treatments which confer no benefit on a patient and, therefore, the physician has no duty to provide them. Nor is there agreement as to who should decide that a particular treatment is futile (Cranford & Gostin, 1992; Daar, 1993). The obvious danger here lies in giving individual providers the power to make this determination for specific patients without any guidelines. If they do so, such decisions might reflect the provider's perspectives on the cost-effectiveness of treatment or the social value of a particular patient's life (Applebaum, 1993; Hall, 1993). This is the threat posed by the facts of the *Wanglie* (Capron, 1991) and *In re Baby K* (1993) cases, although the court in both of these cases refused to authorize the withdrawal of treatment. My preference is for a public process within which the medical profession and society at large develop these guidelines, which are really principles for rationing medical care.

Finally, the current debate about whether physicians should be authorized to assist a patient in committing suicide may be an example of misjudged patient capacity and mistaken empowerment. Some background will help explain this position. Last year, after Dr. Timothy Quill published the now famous description of his role in the case of a patient who committed suicide (Quill, 1991), a New York grand jury refused to indict him and the State Office of Professional Medical Conduct did not impose any disciplinary sanctions on him. Instead, the Office asked the New York State Task Force on Life and the Law to study whether New York law should be changed to permit physicians to assist patients who wish to commit suicide. After consulting extensively with physicians and nurses who specialize in care of the terminally ill, the Task Force concluded (New York State Task Force on Life and the Law, 1994) that the state of the art of pain control, as practiced by large numbers of physicians, is primitive and unresponsive to the needs of many suffering patients (Foley, 1991), a judgment recently confirmed in the release of new clinical practice guidelines for the management of pain (Jacox, Carr, & Payne, 1994). The inadequacy of current pain control measures is compounded by the fact that a significant number of these patients also experience clinical depression which is neither diagnosed nor treated by many attending physicians (Breitbart & Holland,

1990). This combination of inadequately managed pain and overlooked depression has contributed to the public perception that there exists a large class of incapacitated patients who are dying in unremitting pain and for whom suicide is the only way to regain some measure of self-determination.

If these observations are valid, it would be a mistake at this time to authorize physician-assisted suicide as a method for empowering these suffering patients. A better approach for the near term is to insist that medicine deal with pain and depression in terminally ill patients in an aggressive and sophisticated manner. Such efforts will not make all pain controllable nor will they prevent some quite rational patients from choosing suicide. But later, after we are satisfied that medicine is doing its best to control pain and to relieve depression, society can then determine whether the remaining group of patients who need a physician's assistance in ending their lives is large enough to justify changing our laws to legitimate such action. In sum, the danger is that the contemporary movement to authorize physician-assisted suicide in the name of enhancing patient autonomy may be another form of intervention defined by well-meaning intervenors without adequate appreciation of and action to remove those factors, pain and depression, which inhibit truly autonomous action by the patient.

NOTE

1. Uniform Probate Code, §5-101.

REFERENCES

Alexander, G. (1969). Surrogate management of the property of the aged. *Syracuse Law Review, 21*, 87-173.

American Bar Association. (1986). *Statement of recommended judicial practices*. Washington DC: American Bar Association.

Applebaum, P. S. (1993). Must we forgo informed consent to control health care costs? A response to Mark A. Hall. *The Milbank Quarterly, 71*, 669-676.

Block, M. R. & Sinnott, J. D. (1979). *The battered elder syndrome: An exploratory study*. College Park, MD: University of Maryland, Center on Aging.

Breitbart, W., & Holland, J. (1990). Psychiatric aspects of cancer pain. In K. Foley (Ed.), *Advances in pain research and therapy* (pp. 73–87). New York: Raven.

Cantor, N. L. (1992). Prospective autonomy: On the limits of shaping one's postcompetence medical fate. *Journal of Contemporary Health Law and Policy, 8,* 13–48.

Capron, A. (Sept/Oct, 1991). In re Helga Wanglie. *Hastings Center Report, 21,* 26–28.

Cranford, R., & Gostin, L. (Eds.). (1992). Medical futility [symposium]. *Law, Medicine and Health Care, 20,* 307–339.

Daar, J. F. (1993). A clash at the bedside: Patient autonomy v. a physician's professional conscience. *Hastings Law Journal, 44,* 1241–1289.

Danis, M., Southerland, L. I., Garrett, J. M., Smith, J. L., Hielema, F., Pickard, C. G., Egner, D. M., & Patrick, D. L. (1991). A prospective study of advance directives for life-sustaining care. *New England Journal of Medicine. 324,* 882–888.

Douglass, R. L., Hickey, T., & Noel, C. (1980). *A study of maltreatment of the elderly and other vulnerable adults.* Ann Arbor: University of Michigan, Institute of Gerontology.

Estes, C. L. (1979). *The aging enterprise.* San Francisco: Jossey-Bass.

Estes, C. L. (1992). The aging enterprise revisited. *The Gerontologist, 33,* 292–298.

Foley, K. M. (1991). The relationship of pain and symptom management to patient requests for physician-assisted suicide. *Journal of Pain and Symptom Management, 6,* 289–297.

Garrard, J., Makris, L., Dunham, T., Heston, L. L., Cooper, S., Ratner, E. R., Zelterman, D., & Kane, R. L. (1991). Evaluation of neuroleptic drug use by nursing home elderly under proposed Medicare and Medicaid regulations. *Journal of the American Medical Association, 265,* 463–467.

Hall, M. A. (1993). Informed consent to rationing decisions. *The Milbank Quarterly, 71,* 645–668.

Horstman, P. (1975). Protective services for the elderly: The limits of parens patriae. *Misouri Law Review, 40,* 215–278.

In re Baby "K", 832 F. Supp. 1022 (E.D. Va. 1993).

Jacox, A., Carr, D., & Payne, R. (1994). New clinical-practice guidelines for the management of pain in patients with cancer. *New England Journal of Medicine, 330,* 651–655.

Kapp, M. B. (July/Aug, 1989). Medical empowerment of the elderly. *Hastings Center Report, 19,* 5–7.

Legal Counsel for the Elderly. (1987). *Decision-making, incapacity and the elderly.* Washington, DC: American Association of Retired Persons.

New York State Task Force on Life and the Law. (1994). *When death is sought: Assisted suicide and euthanasia in the medical context.* New York:

Quill, T. E. (1991). Death and dignity: A case of individualized decision making. *New England Journal of Medicine, 324,* 691–694.

Tatara, T. (1990). *Summaries of national elder abuse data: An exploratory study of state statistics.* Washington, DC: National Aging Resource Center on Elder Abuse.

Tatara, T. (1993). Understanding the nature and scope of domestic elder abuse with the use of state aggregate data: Summaries of the key findings of a national survey of state APS and aging agencies. *Journal of Elder Abuse & Neglect, 5,* 35–57.

U.S. Congress, House Select Committee on Aging. (1981). *Elder abuse (An examination of a hidden problem).* Washington, DC: U.S. Government Printing Office.

U.S. Congress, Senate Special Committee on Aging. (1990). *Untie the elderly: Quality care without restraints.* Washington, DC: U.S. Government Printing Office.

Wolf, S. M., Boyle, P., Callahan, D., Fins, J. J., Jennings, B., Nelson, J. L., Barondess, J. A., Brock, D. W., Dresser, R., Emanual, E., Johnson, S., Lantos, J., Mason, D. R., Mezey, M., Orentlicher, D., & Rouse, F. (1991). Sources of concern about the Patient Self-Determination Act. *New England Journal of Medicine, 325,* 1666–1671.

CHAPTER 3

Assessing Everyday Competence in the Cognitively Challenged Elderly

Sherry L. Willis

W hat the elderly fear most, often even more than dying, is the loss of independence—the inability to care for oneself, to manage one's affairs, and to live independently in the community. The Solomon-like decision that must be made in guardianship or conservatorship cases involves weighing the legal rights and desires of the elderly for autonomy and independence versus beneficence, society's obligation to protect and care for the incompetent or disabled. The purpose of this chapter is to relate the psychological literature on cognitive

Research reported in this paper was supported in part by funding (AG 08082) from the National Institute on Aging to S. L. Willis.

competence to issues regarding legal decisions and judgments concerning the capability of older adults to care for themselves and to manage their affairs (Appelbaum & Grisso, 1988; Kapp, 1992; Parry, 1985). For the past decade or so there has been a new specialty in the study of cognitive aging that has focused on everyday problem solving or practical intelligence (Poon, Rubin & Wilson, 1989; Puckett & Reese, 1993; Sinnott, 1989). This chapter relies heavily on this perspective, including much of my recent research, which has been in this domain (Willis, 1991; Willis & Marsiske, 1990; Willis & Schaie, 1993).

This chapter involves two major sections. The first part will consider characteristics of legal competence from a psychological perspective. Scholars such as Kapp (1992), Grisso (1986, 1994), and Sabatino (this volume) have suggested that there are several characteristics that provide a common structure in defining legal competencies. The second part of the chapter will deal with issues related to forensic assessment instruments and their use in the evaluation of everyday competence in the cognitively challenged older adult.

The emphasis is on the cognitively challenged elderly, not solely the cognitively impaired elderly. The terms *cognitive impairment* or *disability* often suggests a disorder that is pathological in etiology and is considered irreversible. However, there are many elderly who are cognitively challenged by the tasks of daily living due to socioeconomic and/or cultural disadvantages throughout life, although they suffer from no diagnosed disorder. Given recent rapid technological advances and positive cohort trends in education, today's elderly are particularly likely to be challenged as a function of sociocultural change (Pifer & Bronte, 1986). The fastest growing segment of our population are the oldest old—those in their 80s and 90s (Suzman & Riley, 1985; U.S. Congress, Senate Special Committee on Aging, 1987–1988). They are most likely to be vulnerable to the effects of rapid sociocultural change, as well as to normative nonpathological age-related change in intellectual functioning (Schaie, 1983; 1990). If the judgments of legal incompetence are now to focus largely on functional abilities, then broader consideration must be given to elderly who are cognitively challenged for reasons other than mental disorders or pathologies.

DEFINING COMPETENCE

We must first begin with the definition of the term competence as it has been used in the law and in psychological theory and research. Table

TABLE 3.1   Definitions of Competence

LEGAL:

Incapacitated Person: One "who is impaired by reason of mental illness, mental deficiency, physical illness or disability, advanced age, chronic use of drugs, chronic intoxication or other cause (except minority) to the extent of *lacking sufficient understanding or capacity to make or communicate responsible decisions*" (Uniform Probate Code and Uniform Guardianship and Protective Proceedings Act).

"In the past few years, several states have made substantive changes in their guardianship laws..by substituting . . . more objective standards, designed to focus on the individual's *functional ability to manage personal care or finances on a daily basis*—that is the focus more on the person's ability to meet basic needs rather than just his or her 'condition' " (Kapp, 1992; Wang, Burns, & Hommel, 1990).

"A legal finding of incompetence signifies that a person, because of a lack of the capacity to contemplate choices rationally, *cannot care adequately for person or property*" (Kapp, 1992).

PSYCHOLOGICAL:

"Everyday competence represents the adult's *ability or potential to perform adequately those activities considered essential for living on one's own*" (Willis, 1991).

"Cognitive competence . . . can be loosely interpreted as *the utilization of one's abilities-cognitive, interpersonal, and others—in adapting to particular situations*. Cognitive ability and cognitive competence are at least somewhat independent because it may be possible for a person with a low level of cognitive ability to achieve a high degree of competence by maximizing his or her usage of available abilities for functioning in specific situations" (Salthouse, 1990).

"Behavior under control of *cognitive processes* and employed toward the *solution of problems which challenge the wellbeing, needs, plans, and survival of individuals*" (Charlesworth, 1976).

3.1 presents several definitions from both legal and psychological perspectives. Although psychological definitions focus on competence, in contrast to legal definitions that focus on incapacity or impairment, there are several areas of similarities. First, there is an emphasis on cognition and on decision-making capacity, in particular. Second, the focus is on functional tasks, or applied cognition—the ability to make decisions and to carry out activities essential for daily living. Third, the context in which competence is of concern is the naturalistic or everyday environment of the individual, not the scientific laboratory or the courtroom, in most instances.

LEGAL COMPETENCIES: COMMON CHARACTERISTICS

A review of the legal literature suggests that a common structure can be identified in legal competencies as diverse as competency to stand trial, competency as caretaker of a child, and competency to manage one's property. Six common characteristics of legal descriptions of competencies have been identified by Grisso (1986) and others (Altman, Parmelee & Smyer, 1992; Anderer, 1990; Kapp, 1992). These characteristics are:

(a) A recent trend in the literature on legal competencies has been a focus on *functional abilities* (that which a person knows, understands, believes, or can do). The principal objective of forensic assessment, then, is viewed as the evaluation of the older adults functional abilities that are conceptually relevant to the legal competency in question.

(b) Historically, judgments of legal incompetence have included a statement of *cause*—a disorder or disability that was considered to be the basis for the elderly person's functional deficits (Anderer, 1990; Sales, Powell & Van Duizend, 1982). Many legal statutes continue to include causal inferences in their definitions of competence.

(c) What functional abilities are relevant in order for an older adult to function competently at a given point in time is defined by the *general environmental context*. The critical functional abilities for an older adult do not exist in limbo, but are circumscribed by the sociocultural context.

(d) Although the broad sociocultural environment dictates what functional abilities are most important to live independently, the *person–context interaction* determines the level of competence required of an elderly individual. The congruency or incongruency between a person's level of functional ability and the demands of the older adult's environment must be determined (Lawton, 1982).

(e) Legal competencies are *judgmental* in that they require a legal or moral evaluation that there is sufficient incongruence between a person's abilities and contextual demands to warrant a finding of incompetence, and

(f) Finally, judgments of legal competency are *dispositional* in that they may involve depriving the older adult of fundamental rights, such as decision making about the care of oneself and the maintenance of one's property.

Functional Abilities or Capacities

The central question in guardianship and conservatorship cases is whether the individual's level of functional abilities are sufficient for the contextual demands experienced by that elderly individual.

Domains of functional competence.

Most older adults are not totally incompetent. Until quite late in a dementing illness, for example, an older adult may remain competent to perform selected tasks of daily living (Vitaliano, Breen, Albert, Russo, & Prinz, 1984). In most forms of dementia, cognitive deficits are evident before deficits in basic self-care activities. Moreover, there is some evidence that cognitive functioning declines in a progressive manner, with deficits being first exhibited in complex cognitive tasks such as those involving inductive reasoning or decision making in novel, unfamiliar situations (Ashford, Kolm, Colliver, Bekian, & Hsu, 1989).

Recognition of the fact that competence is not an all-or-nothing phenomenon is reflected in the recent trend toward choosing the "least restrictive alternative" in guardianship judgments (Parry, 1985). There is a trend for guardians to be appointed as surrogate decisions makers in only selected domains of activity, such as the management of financial affairs.

Although there is a trend toward legal judgments regarding guardianship being increasingly domain-specific, rather than being global or inclusive in nature, most state statutes remain very broad and general. Legal statutes typically mention only very general capacities, such as the ability to "make or implement decisions" to "provide health care, food, clothing, and shelter" or to "know the nature of business transactions." The two most common very broad domains of functional competence found in legal statues are: 1) Caring for self and 2) Managing one's property. The Uniform Probate Code (UPC, 1989) distinguishes between proceedings regarding care of the person (guardianship) and those related to property (conservatorship). A major challenge in assessing competency and in making judgments is defining the particular functional abilities associated with "caring for self and/or managing one's property" that are relevant in a given case.

The theoretical and empirical work in psychogerontology can contribute significantly to scholars' attempts to categorize functional abilities associated with self-care and property management (Grisso, 1986; Kapp, 1992; Quinn, 1989; Quinn & Tomita, 1986). Two major categories of functional abilities have been espoused in the gerontological literature (Fillenbaum, 1987a,b,c; Kane & Kane, 1981): (a) activities of daily living, commonly known as ADLs, that focus primarily on self-care, including feeding, bathing, toileting, and basic mobility (Katz, Ford, Moskowitz, Jackson, & Jaffee, 1963); and (b) instrumental activities of daily living, commonly known as IADLs (Fillenbaum, 1987a,b). The IADLs are viewed as fairly complex, but essential, abilities required in order to live independently in our society. Seven IADL activity domains (see Table 3.2) are commonly cited: managing medications, shopping for necessities, managing one's finances, using transportation, using the telephone, maintaining one's household (housekeeping), and meal preparation and nutrition (Fillenbaum, 1985; Lawton & Brody, 1969). In terms of the distinction made in the Uniform Probate Code (1989), "caring for self" may include the IADL domains of managing medication, meal preparation and nutrition, using transportation, and using the phone. "Managing property" includes the IADL domains of maintaining one's household, shopping for necessities, and managing one's finances.

Grisso (1986) and others have argued that it is the IADLs that are of primary interest in legal guardianship cases. The elderly person may be able to engage in basic self-care activities and still have serious deficiencies in making decisions regarding independent living and in managing property. In cases where the individual is lacking in these most basic self-care functions (ADLs), the deficiencies are often sufficiently obvious and serious that institutionalization is required.

TABLE 3.2   Instrumental Activities of Daily Living

DOMAIN	EXEMPLAR TASK
Managing medications	Determining how many doses of cough medicine can be taken in a 24-hour period.
	Completing a patient medical history form
Shopping for necessities	Ordering merchandise from a catalog
	Comparison of brands of a product
Managing one's finances	Comparison of Medigap insurance plans
	Completing income tax return form
Using transportation	Computing taxi rates
	Interpreting driver's right-of-way laws
Using the telephone	Determining amount to pay from phone bill
	Determining when telephone discounted time rates apply
Maintaining one's household	Following instructions for operating a household appliance
Meal preparation and nutrition	Evaluating nutritional information on food label

Deficits in capacity and in decision making versus in performance.

Two distinctions are important in defining, assessing, and making judgments regarding competence. The first distinction focuses on the individual's capacity to care for self and to manage property versus what the individual actually does routinely in daily life. The terms *competence*, *ability*, and *capacity* are used frequently in both the legal and psychological literature. These terms have been used to denote constructs in both the psychological and legal literature (Grisso, 1986). Constructs are conditions or states that cannot be observed directly; only their behavioral signs or reflections can be observed. In the psychological literature, the terms ''competency'' and ''ability'' represent the *potential* or *capability* of the individual to perform certain tasks, not necessarily the actual daily behaviors of the individual (Salthouse, 1990; Willis, 1991). Competence represents the ability to carry out, when necessary, a broad array of activities considered essential for independent living, even though in daily life the adult may not perform these activities or only perform a subset of these activities.

Functional assessment has traditionally addressed the question, "*Can* the individual perform an activity?" not "*Does* the individual perform the activity on a regular basis?" This distinction is important because psychological research indicates that different factors may be involved in determining (explaining) whether an individual has the requisite functional competence or ability than in determining whether the individual carries out an activity when it is required or needed. Organic brain syndromes are often cited as a major explanatory variable in determining competence. The individual lacks the cognitive capability. On the other hand, the nondemented individual may be capable of carrying out necessary activities but may not do so due to factors such as self-efficacy beliefs or depression (Fitten & Waite, 1990; Swartz & Stewart, 1991).

The second distinction focuses on whether the elderly have the capability to *make decisions* regarding care of self and property versus whether they can actually perform the necessary activities themselves (Anderer, 1990; Bersoff, 1992; Smyer, 1993). It has been argued that competence rests not on whether the elderly can perform tasks themselves without assistance, but on capability to make decisions regarding care and to direct others in managing their affairs. In the legal literature, the distinction between capacity and actual behavior has focused on the elderly's functional capacity to make decisions, rather than on the *reasonableness* of their decisions. An "unreasonable" decision such as refusing medications may be implemented if the patient has the functional capacity to make the decision (Legal Counsel for the Elderly, National Protective Support Center, 1989; National Conference of the Judiciary on Guardianship Proceeding for the Elderly, 1986).

Components of decision making.

Research on decision making and problem solving in the psychological literature becomes of interest, given the increasingly salient role in legal judgments that is being given to the capacity of the elderly to make decisions. Numerous models of problem solving are present in the literature (Nezu & Nezu, 1989; Sternberg & Kolligian, 1990; Voss & Post, 1988). In previous work (Willis & Schaie, 1993) we have suggested that at least five components are involved in making decisions related to tasks of daily living (Figure 3.1). There is a hierarchical relationship among components in this framework. Basic mental abilities and domain-spe-

A. Relevant Mental Abilities and Skills
B. Domain-specific Knowledge Base
C. Understanding of:
    1. Personal Circumstances
    2. Interpersonal Context
D. Attitudes, Beliefs, Preferences
E. Integration of Dimensions

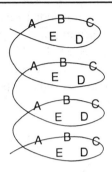

Everyday problem solving is a recursive process. At each cycle in the recursive process, any or all of the dimensions in problem solving may have changed.

Figure 3.1.   Components of everyday decision making and the recursive nature of everyday decision making.

cific knowledge bases are necessary components in decision making, but are not sufficient for generation of adequate problem solutions; there must also be consideration of the elderly's perception of the social and physical environment associated with the problem or task and the individual's beliefs and preferences regarding alternative solutions.

    a. *Mental abilities.* Our prior research has indicated that many of the basic abilities (e.g., verbal, reasoning, memory) studied by psychologists in their laboratories are required in solving tasks associated with daily living. However, tasks of daily living are often very complex and thus involve more than one mental ability (Willis, 1991; Willis, Jay, Diehl, & Marsiske, 1992; Willis & Schaie, 1986). For example, comparing alternative medigap health insurance plans was found to involve both verbal ability and inductive reasoning. While verbal ability is required to read the benefits chart, making comparisons among different insurance plans involves inductive reasoning. The individual must determine the similarities and differences among the insurance plans and determine which set of services fits his/her needs. Different constellations of mental abilities and processes will be required for various practical problems (Willis, 1991; Willis et al., 1992). Spatial orientation and verbal ability will be more important for reading a map, whereas inductive reasoning and verbal ability will be more salient for interpreting a medication label.

b. *Domain-specific knowledge.* Decision making also involves specialized knowledge related to the problem at hand. Whereas the research literature on expertise has shown relationships between a single, specialized knowledge domain and competence in a skill or profession (Ceci & Liker, 1986; Salthouse, 1990), solutions for many everyday types of tasks will require accessing several different knowledge domains (Christie, 1984). In considering medigap insurance plans, for example, the problem solver needs to have at least rudimentary knowledge not only about insurance policies and health care, but also about the Medicare system.

c. *Understanding personal circumstances and the interpersonal context.* Considered next are the more individualized, personal, affective, and social dimensions of everyday decision making in which individuals take into account their own personal circumstances and contexts (Sternberg & Kolligian, 1990). Which insurance plan, for example, represents a viable option for an elderly woman will be partially determined by personal circumstances, namely, her understanding of her financial status, as well as her understanding of her current and future health status. Likewise, the individual's understanding and assessment of his or her interpersonal context must be taken into account. For example, what types of health care services need to be purchased will depend in part on the older adult's assessment of the social support network.

d. *Attitudes, beliefs, and preferences.* Understanding and assessing one's personal circumstances reflects in part certain attitudes, beliefs, and preferences (Baltes & Baltes, 1986; Masterpasqua, 1989; Rodin, Timko, & Harris, 1985). For example, health-related locus-of-control and self-efficacy beliefs (Wallston & Wallston, 1982) will influence decisions regarding health insurance. Locus-of-control beliefs deal with whether an individual perceives control over one's life to lie primarily under one's own control or whether control is external, determined largely by fate or by powerful others (e.g., doctors, lawyers). Likewise, self-efficacy beliefs reflect one's beliefs regarding one's own competence. Current research on age-related changes in self-efficacy indicates an increased dependence on powerful others in old age (Lachman & Leff, 1989; Levinson, 1974; Willis et al., 1992). Some elderly persons may therefore increasingly seek and depend on the advice of significant others (doctors, lawyers, ministers, adult children) in making important decisions in everyday life.

In his book *Geriatrics and the Law*, Marshall Kapp (1992) repeatedly refers to how decisions by the elderly may be influenced by their "awe" or "deferential respect" for their doctor or a lawyer. From a psychological perspective, this "awe" may reflect an age-related increase in beliefs regarding powerful others—the belief that one is less competent to make decisions and therefore should depend on the advice of powerful others (Levinson, 1974; Wallston & Wallston, 1982). Several studies indicate that the belief that one needs to depend on "powerful others in making decisions increases with age" (Lachman & Leff, 1989; Willis et al., 1992). There is considerable debate whether or when increases in dependence on powerful others is efficacious (Lachman, 1986; Lachman & Leff, 1989). Nevertheless, it is important that clinicians and legal professionals involved in assessing competence and in making judgments regarding guardianship be aware of these age-related belief systems.

e. *Integration of decision-making components*. Reaching an effective solution involves integration of the above dimensions. Integration is continually occurring at various phases of the problem-solving process. In medical cases assessing the older patient's ability to give informed consent, an important component is the elderly person's ability to articulate the decision-making process and to state the rationale for the decision (Appelbaum & Grisso, 1988; Kapp, 1990). Integration of the multiple components in the decision process and articulation of the rationale for the decision reached may involve several steps: (a) identification of solution alternatives, (b) ruling out options that will not work given the individual's personal circumstances, and (c) prioritizing the remaining viable options.

Change in everyday problem-solving competence in old age.

Those involved in guardianship cases need an understanding of the normative age-related changes in capacity to make everyday decisions that occur for elderly persons with no known pathologies. Data on normative changes in decision-making competence can serve as a baseline for assessment and for decisions regarding elders who do suffer from dementia

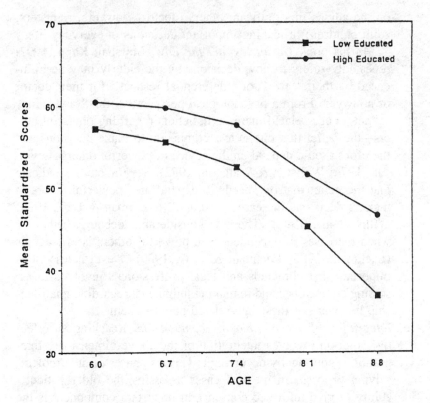

Figure 3.2. Longitudinal change in performance on everyday problems test for Low-Educated (12 or less years of schooling) and High-Educated (over 12 years of schooling) elderly.

and who may be subject to guardianship decisions. We have examined change over a 7-year interval in everyday decision-making performance (Willis & Marsiske, 1990). Figure 3.2 presents longitudinal findings regarding the pattern of change for elders with no known mental disorder; patterns of age-related change are shown for elders with 12 or fewer years of education and for those with more than 12 years. Note that, at each chronological age, less educated elders are functioning at a lower level than those with above average levels of education. While age-related decline in young-old age (60–75 years) is modest, the rate of average decline increases in old-old age (75+ years). Our data suggest that the educationally disadvantaged elderly in very old age (in their 80s or 90s) are increasingly likely to need assistance in everyday decision making, even though they do not suffer from a specific mental disorder.

There are personal characteristics of adults that make them particularly vulnerable to functioning at lower levels of competence as they age. Education is significantly related to level of everyday competence (Willis et al., 1992). Adults with lower levels of education have greater difficulty, on average, in everyday decision making throughout their adult lives. These less educated adults become particularly vulnerable in old age when their level of functioning becomes even further diminished by age-related change in performance. The relevance of education in assessment of everyday decision making is very salient in old age, since today's cohorts of elderly people have a lower mean level of education than the total adult population. The median school years completed for elderly who are 60–74 years is 12 years, while those 75 years and older have completed only 11 years of schooling, on average (U.S. Bureau of the Census, 1989).

The need for follow-up assessment in guardianship cases.

Quinn (1989) observes that most state laws do not provide for effective review of conservatorship or guardianship decisions. One of the unique mandated roles of the court investigator in California is to review existing conservatorships, one year after appointment and every 2 years thereafter. Follow-up assessment of competence in guardianship cases is critical for several reasons. The elderly's competence in everyday decision making is likely to change either due to progression in the disorder that led to guardianship or as a function of advancing age. Follow-up assessment is particularly important given the trend toward limited guardianship in selected domains of daily living (Parry, 1985; Kapp, 1992). In the case of dementia, further decline in competence is to be expected, and hence, more extensive guardianship provisions are likely to be required.

On the other hand, if deficits in functioning are due to short-term disorders (e.g., delirium, depression) or due to lack of experience in a domain (e.g., management of finances) in which training can be provided, then future assessments may lead to removal or reduction of the guardian role. Given the negative stereotypes of aging, the potential for positive change in the elderly can be underestimated.

Research findings supporting the potential for positive change is found both in the epidemiological literature and in cognitive training research. In an epidemiological study involving large representative samples of older adults, Blazer (1978) compared the proportion of community-dwelling versus institutionalized elderly respondents who reported themselves to have remained stable, to have declined or to have improved in everyday competence over the past year. Significant proportions of both community-dwelling elderly (18%) and institutionalized elderly (17%) perceived themselves to have improved in the past year. In our experimental training research, we have found that educational training was effective in remediating decline on a target mental ability in 40% of nondemented elderly (Schaie & Willis, 1986; Willis & Schaie, 1994).

Mental Disorders and Functional Incompetence: The Causal Link

Until recent times, most states' statutes regarding incompetency equated incompetency with a mental disease or disorder (Parry, 1985; Sales et al., 1982; Sabatino, this volume). Mental disorders were described in vague terms (lunacy, idleness, madness, senility) that lack scientific meaning in today's parlance. In some cases, "advanced age" was included in state statutes as an admissible cause of incompetence. An affidavit signed by a physician was sufficient for determination of incompetence. A single sentence was often accepted, such as "I have examined the person and she is incompetent by reason of senility." (Horstman, 1975). More recently, simply the diagnosis of a mental disorder is insufficient support for a judgment of incompetence. The critical criterion is evidence of functional impairment in domains considered essential for care of self and property. For many states, a mental disorder must still be identified, but the emphasis is on demonstration that a disorder offers a causal explanation for the functional deficits observed (Nolan, 1984). The functional deficit must be the product of some underlying disabling condition over which the adult currently has no control. If the functional deficiency can be remediated or modified there may be no need for a guardian or a guardian may need to be appointed for only a limited time span necessary for the remediation. Consider, for example, the need for differential decisions when memory problems are due to Alzheimer's disease, a progressive, irreversible dementia, versus due to reactive depression, a condition that is susceptible to treatment and is typically remediable. At its best, causal inference involves (a) demonstration that functional deficits can be logically related to a specific underlying disorder, and (b) supporting evidence that can rule out other possible explanations.

Functional deficits and measures of mental ability.

Recent legal writings have called into question efforts to draw inferences regarding functional level from data based on neuropsychological exams or intellectual ability measures (Altman & Parmelee, 1992). Grisso (1986, p. 16) states that "the expert's inferences about functional abilities specific to the legal competencies (paying bills, understanding police warnings) when based on these more general observations may be no more than common sense or speculation of which nonexperts are fully capable when they are provided with the same information."

However, my recent research as well as that of others, suggests that the legal scholars are in danger of "throwing the baby out with the bath water" when they take the position that important inferences regarding functional ability cannot be drawn from intellectual ability data (Camp, Doherty, Moody-Thomas & Denney, 1989; Cornelius & Caspi, 1987; Schaie, 1987; Willis et al., 1992). In our own work we have assumed a hierarchical relationship between the basic intellectual abilities that have been traditionally studied by psychologists and the functional tasks associated with daily living that are the concern in judgments of legal competency (Willis & Marsiske, 1990; Willis & Schaie, 1986, 1993). As was illustrated with the decision-making model discussed above (Figure 3.1), we assume that basic mental processes are necessary, but not sufficient, determinants of functional competence. Given that everyday tasks are complex, we assumed that performance on a given task requires a unique constellation of mental abilities.

The question for us has been how well could we predict an older adult's performance on critical everyday tasks if we had information on their performance on a number of mental ability measures. We assessed functional abilities by examining older adults' performance on tasks related to each of the IADL domains discussed previously (see Table 3.2). In our first study, we examined whether intellectual abilities assessed at one point in time could predict older adults' performance on functional abilities 7 years later (Willis et al., 1992). Approximately 67% of the individual differences in functional abilities could be accounted for by performance on intellectual processes 7 years previously (Willis et al.,

1992). We have replicated these findings in subsequent research studies (Diehl, Willis, & Schaie, 1995; Willis & Marsiske, 1990).

Research on the relationship between basic mental processes and functional abilities has several important implications for making judgments regarding legal competence. First, findings from this research provide information on the specific types of mental abilities that underlie functional competence. Second, prior longitudinal research on these mental abilities (Schaie, 1990) provides the best predictions available regarding what to expect in the future—what trajectory of functioning is to be expected given current level of performance. Third, there has been over a decade of research on the modifiability of these basic abilities and on the individual difference variables associated with remediation (Schaie & Willis, 1986; Willis, 1987). Findings from this research provide important information on what types of interventions might be profitable and with what types of individuals.

Education, mental disorders, and competency.

It might be argued that the presence of a mental disorder in combination with functional deficits should satisfy the causal question. However, the functional deficit may have predated the organic condition, highlighting the importance of determining the *premorbid functional competency* of the older adult.

There has been little attention in the legal literature to the moderating effect of individual difference variables on functional competence, even though individual difference variables are well known to have a major influence on cognitive functioning (Schaie, 1989, 1990). As noted above, educational level is significantly related to cognitive functioning throughout the life course. Recently, the influence of education on the diagnosis and progression of dementias, such as Alzheimer's disease have become of increasing concern (Uhlmann & Larson, 1991; Wiederholt et al., 1993). The important issue for those involved in guardianship cases is whether functional deficits are attributable primarily to low educational level, to a mental disorder, or to a combination of these factors.

Figure 3.3 presents the proportion of everyday problems solved correctly on our measure of functional ability for a nondemented group of elderly, stratified by age and educational level. Note that subjects with less than 12 years of education are functioning at a significantly lower level than those with average or higher levels of education. The old-old

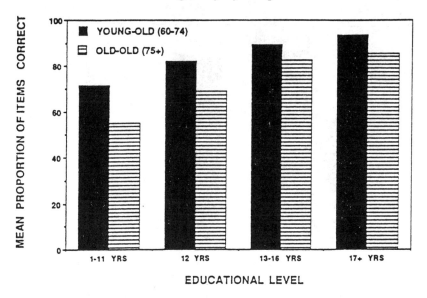

Figure 3.3. Proportion of everyday problems items answered correctly: Non-demented elderly by educational level.

(75+ years) with 1–11 years of education are particularly disadvantaged and may be said to be at cognitive risk, although having no organic impairment.

The graph in Figure 3.4 presents data on the same task for nondemented and community-dwelling Alzheimer's patients. The combination of low level of education plus an organic impairment results in serious deficits in functioning. However, given the previous data (Figure 3.3) on the low level of performance of the nondemented old-old with low levels of education, it is likely that comparably educated Alzheimer's patients were functioning quite marginally even prior to diagnosis of an organic impairment. Given the significant relationship between education and almost all measures of cognitive function, the increased risk of misdiagnosis for a dementia in an older adult with low educational and socioeconomic status should be a major concern in competency judgments (Wilson, Grant, Witsey, & Kerridge, 1973). On the other hand, Alzheimer's patients with high levels of education may be competent to engage in some forms of decision making early in the disease progression.

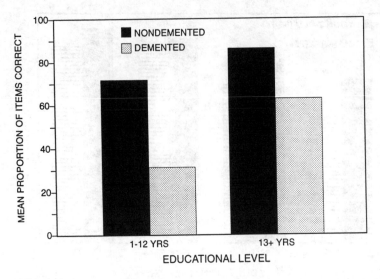

Figure 3.4.   Proportion of everyday problems items answered correctly: Nondemented elderly and Alzheimer's elderly by educational level.

Functional Abilities: The Role of Environmental Context

The elderly do not live in a vacuum and, thus, competence cannot be considered without taking into account the environment in which they function (Lawton, 1982; 1987). Grisso (1986) and others have argued that the environmental context is critical in defining which specific functional abilities are most salient in legal competency judgments. The term environmental context refers to the external situations to which the older adult must respond. Different contexts require different functional abilities. The legal system cannot assess functional abilities without taking into consideration the environmental context in which these abilities are required.

The gerontological literature (Lawton, 1987) has defined the sociocultural context to include both the physical and the social environment in which the individual must function competently in order to maintain independence. The physical environment includes factors such as geographical location, climate, and architectural features of facilities; characteristics of the physical environment influence the types of tasks required to function independently in that context. For example, functional abilities associated with independent living would be expected to vary whether the older adult lived in an urban versus rural environment and/or in inner city or suburbia. This distinction was made very real when we began to utilize the Lawton & Brody (1969) functional assessment measure developed at the Philadelphia Geriatric Center in inner-city Philadelphia. When we asked farm women in rural central Pennsylvania about their ability to use mass transportation, one women gently reminded us that she would have to drive 20 miles to catch a bus, and several hundred miles to use a subway system!

Likewise, the social environment plays a critical role in determining social roles and the functional abilities associated with these roles. For example, several of the IADL domains (e.g., housekeeping, meal preparation, shopping) deal with activities that traditional gender roles might define as "women's work." Although some IADL scales utilize the same items for older men and women (Lawton & Brody, 1969), gender differences in perception of competence are widely reported for the elderly in the epidemiological literature (Fillenbaum, 1985).

The sociocultural context is dynamic and ever changing; hence, the requisite functional abilities would be expected to change with the historical context. For example, use of computers in some form (e.g., ATM machines, microwaves, VCRs, programmable phones) has become quite pervasive. What is of interest is the selective adoption by older adults of computer-driven technologies. For example, most senior citizens own and use microwaves, but fewer than one third use an automatic teller machine.

An important question is what criteria are to be used in determining the functional abilities considered most salient in a given context. The professionals and/or social service providers that work directly with the elderly are on the "front line" and often are involved in making decisions (often by default) regarding competency and functional abilities. For example, it is frequently service providers such as senior citizen directors, rehabilitation specialists, and the managers of senior citizen housing who determine whether an older adult is competent to live independently. Interestingly, there has been relatively little research on whether providers of different types of social services agree on which of the IADLs are most critical for independent living (Loeb, 1983).

As part of our program of research, we asked three different groups of providers working with the elderly (occupational therapists, managers of housing for the elderly, senior citizen center directors) and the elderly themselves to rate 75 tasks related to daily living according to how essential competence on each task would be for independent living (Diehl & Willis, 1991). The tasks represented five IADL domains. There was considerable consensus among the different groups of service providers and the elderly regarding the relative importance of IADL domains. Management of finances and taking of medications were rated as the two most important domains by all three service provider groups and also by older adults. Shopping for necessities was rated as the least essential functional ability for independent living by all groups.

Person–Context Interaction

While the broad sociocultural context is instrumental in defining which specific functional abilities are most salient, assessment of a particular individual's competence must consider the person–context interaction. At issue is the congruence or incongruence between the elder's level of competence on key functional tasks and the complexity of the environmental demands in the immediate context (Kahana, 1982; Lawton, 1982; Lawton & Parmelee, 1990). The question is whether the individual has the level of functional ability to cope effectively in a particular environmental context.

Let us consider whether a recently widowed 80-year-old woman with severe arthritis living in a retirement community has the requisite level of competence to manage her financial affairs. Two different scenarios can illustrate how the interaction of intraindividual ability and contextual demands may lead to different conclusions regarding the level of competence required of the individual. In scenario one, the deceased husband had managed the couple's financial affairs throughout the marriage and the wife had little knowledge of how her considerable inheritance had been invested. The retirement community offered no banking or financial advisory services. The wife did not drive and her only child lived on the other side of the country. In scenario two, the deceased husband had suffered from Alzheimer's disease for a number of years and the wife had managed their financial affairs. Full banking services and financial consultation were provided at the retirement community and her only child lived in a near-by community.

The central question is one of the congruence or lack of congruence between intraindividual capabilities and the resources and demands of the physical and social environment (Drane, 1984). With regard to ability

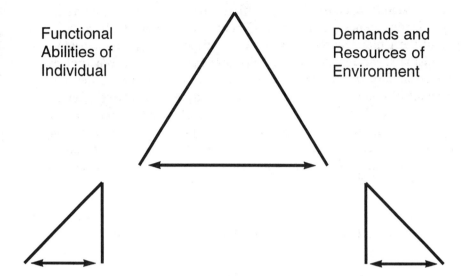

Functional
Abilities of
Individual

Demands and
Resources of
Environment

Figure 3.5.   Incongruence in person–environment interaction: Three types.

to manage one's financial affairs, the size, type, and complexity of the
individual's property and resources will influence the level of competence required. Figure 3.5 presents three different conditions under
which there could be incongruence between intraindividual capabilities
and contextual demands and resources. This is illustrated by three types
of triangles. In the central triangle, the increasing lack of congruence is
attributed to shifts in both intraindividual and contextual components;
intraindividual capabilities decrease and contextual demands increase (or
contextual resources decrease). In the left-hand triangle, the increase in
incongruence is due primarily to a decrease in intraindividual capabilities, such as organic impairment or severe physical health problems;
environmental resources and demands remain constant. In the right hand
triangle, the increasing disparity is attributable primarily to an increase
in contextual demands; for example, in scenario one the woman's functional abilities and health problems remained relatively stable but, due
to the death of a spouse who had managed the financial affairs, the
contextual demands increased significantly.

Judgment and Disposition

The final two characteristics of legal competency determination focus on
the question of whether the incongruency between individual capacity

and environmental demands is of sufficient magnitude to warrant a finding of incompetency. A judgment of incompetence is solely the prerogative of the judicial system. Likewise, the disposition of guardianship is a decision made by the judge. Behavioral scientists and practitioners provide important information and advice to the judge in making these decisions. In addition, the clinician may play a critical role after the judgment and disposition in counseling the older adult and guardian regarding the meaning and implications of the judgment. Counseling may be particularly useful if there was disagreement among parties regarding whether the older adult was incompetent and/or who was to be appointed guardian.

FORENSIC ASSESSMENT INSTRUMENTS

The use of Forensic Assessment Instruments (FAIs) is becoming increasingly common in assessment of older adults involved in guardianship or conservatorship cases. The popularity of FAIs has increased as a result of the recent emphasis on deficits in functional abilities as the primary criteria for judgments of incompetence and the rejection of diagnosis of a mental disorder as a sufficient justification for guardianship rulings. Grisso (1986, p. 34) has described a forensic assessment instrument as "an operational definition of a legally relevant functional ability concept." Therefore, FAIs are intended to provide data that can manage the conceptual gap between legal constructs and psychological constructs.

Currently two major categories of measures to assess functional ability in the elderly are discussed in the literature. The most commonly cited type of measure is a *self-report* instrument. The second category provides an *objective* assessment of functional abilities. In the following sections, we will briefly review the gerontological literature with regard to each category of instrument.

Self-Report Instruments

In a self-report instrument, the older adult is asked to rate his or her level of competence on each of the IADL domains. There is a single question for each domain (e.g., telephone), in which the elder is asked to self-rate functional ability on a 3-to 4-point scale: "Can you use the telephone: (a) without help, (b) with some help, or (c) not at all?'' In cases in which the elderly person is incapable of answering for himself or herself, a family member is usually asked these questions. In studies using comprehensive assessment batteries, such as the Older Americans Resources and Services (OARS) (Fillenbaum, 1978; Fillenbaum & Smyer, 1981) and the Multilevel Assessment Instrument (MAI) (Lawton & Moss, undated), a summary rating across the five domains is then made by the interviewer.

This approach to assessment of functional abilities has been used in large-scale epidemiological surveys of noninstitutionalized elderly. Previous survey research suggests that 80% or more of community-dwelling elderly adults report having no difficulty in performing each of the functional abilities (Fillenbaum, 1985; Galanos, Fillenbaum, Cohen, & Burchett, 1991). There has been limited survey research on ethnic differences in level of competency. In the recent Duke epidemiological study, approximately one third of blacks and one quarter of whites reported needing assistance in one or more of the domains (Galanos et al., 1991).

Figure 3.6 shows the proportion of young-old (60–74 years) and old-old (75+ years) and the proportion of men and women who reported themselves to perform competently in each domain without assistance (Fillenbaum, 1985). The data speak to the need to be attentive to age and gender differences in considering what is normative. Comparisons of young-old and old-old indicate a smaller proportion of old-old capable of functioning independently in each of the domains. The magnitude of age differences vary by domain and are most evident for the three domains of shopping, transportation, and housekeeping; over 40% of the old-old report needing some assistance. Both blacks and whites reported the greatest limitations with regard to the domains of transportation, shopping, and housekeeping, although a higher proportion of blacks reported needing assistance in each domain (Galanos et al., 1991).

Comparisons of men and women indicate no gender difference with respect to telephone usage, taking medications, or financial management (Fillenbaum, 1985). Men report themselves to be somewhat more competent with respect to shopping, housekeeping, and traveling to locations outside walking distance. Why is there this gender difference in favor of men on some tasks (shopping, housekeeping) traditionally ascribed to women? Fillenbaum (1985) has suggested that data on physical competence and mobility do not support the rationale that these gender differ-

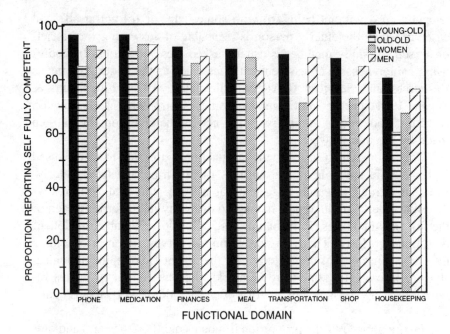

Figure 3.6. Proportion of community-dwelling elderly reporting themselves fully competent in functional domains.

ences can be attributed to differences between men and women in physical mobility. It has been argued that men and women may have different standards for housekeeping, thus resulting in more men than women reporting continuing competence in this domain.

Strengths and limitations of a self-report approach to functional assessment.

There are advantages and limitations to the self-report approach, as with any assessment procedure. At least three advantages can be noted. First, this approach is efficient, since the assessment interview can be administered in a relatively brief time period. The temporal efficiency of this approach has made it very attractive for use in epidemiological surveys in which large numbers of individuals needed to be interviewed in order to achieve representative samples. Second, the procedure does not require a highly skilled professional; technicians have been trained to administer the instrument. Third, acceptable levels of both interrater reliability and intrarater reliability have been reported.

There are also a number of limitations to the self-report approach that should be taken into account when using this method to judge competency. First, older adults tend to overestimate their level of competence when compared to ratings by professionals or to actual performance. Significant differences have been found between ratings based on clinical interviews and self-report data. Fillenbaum (1978, p. 28) writes with regard to the OARS that the questionnaire tends to give too rosy a picture, for clinicians, in personal contact with clients notice difficulties which are not so evident from questionnaire data alone.

Self-reports may reflect either over-or underestimations of functional competence. Healthy, community-dwelling elderly tend to overestimate their actual level of functioning (Ford et al., 1988). However, in impaired populations, the etiology of the disorder affects whether competence is overestimated or underestimated. In a study of geriatric psychiatric patients, Kuriansky, Gurland, Fleiss, & Cowan (1976) found that only 41% of patients evaluated their level of physical ability at the same level as exhibited on a performance test. Patients diagnosed as having an organic disorder were more likely to overestimate competence, whereas those with a functional disorder were more likely to underestimate performance.

In our own work, we have examined the relationship between healthy, community-dwelling older adults' self-ratings of competence and their performance on an objective measure of performance. Figure 3.7 presents a comparison of the proportion of older adults rating themselves as able to perform without assistance in each IADL domain versus the proportion of subjects who answered 75% or more of items correctly on an objective measure of performance. A score of 75% correct was considered to represent a relatively high level of functioning. Note that the discrepancy between perceived level of functioning and objective performance differs by IADL domain. The greatest discrepancies occur for the domains of taking medications, phone usage, and financial management.

A second limitation of the self-report approach is that each competency domain has been assessed by a single item. Reliance on a single item to assess functional ability provides little information on the specific behavioral competencies of an individual (Grisso, 1986; Willis, 1991).

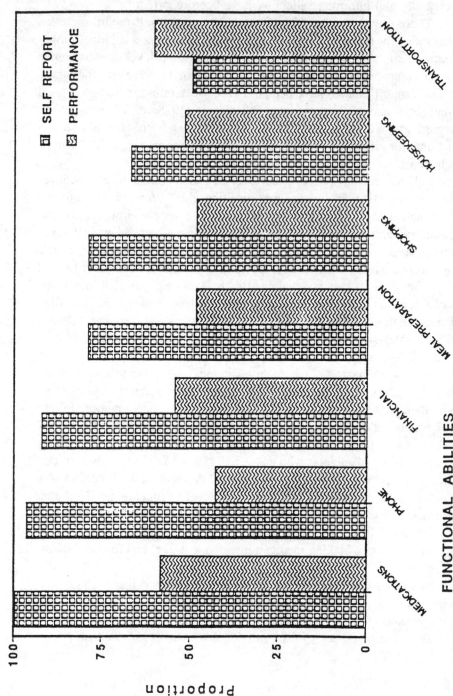

FUNCTIONAL ABILITIES

Figure 3.7.   Comparison of elderly's self-report of functional competence versus performance on everyday problems measure.

There are wide individual differences in interpretations of what it means to "use the phone," "manage one's finances," or "shop for necessities" without assistance. A third limitation of this approach is that it provides little information on the perceived cause of the incapacity. Inability to use the phone may be due to sensory deficits, memory problems, or inexperience with recent information technologies.

Objective Measures of Functional Ability

Objective measures of functional abilities are fewer in number and tend to have been developed fairly recently. Examples of objective measures include the Community Competence Scale (Loeb, 1983), the Everyday Problems Test (Diehl et al., 1995; Marsiske & Willis, 1995; Willis & Marsiske, 1992), and the Direct Assessment of Functional Status Scale (Loewenstein et al., 1989). These measures involve presenting the elderly adult with specific tasks of daily living (e.g., telling time, counting change, addressing an envelope, determining medication information from a prescription drug label, ascertaining the amount to be paid from a phone bill). The adult's response to the tasks is assessed objectively by: (a) having the adult verbally indicate the solution to the task or (b) observing the adult's behavioral response.

Strengths and limitations of objective measures.

The major strength of these measures is that they provide an objective measure of competence with respect to the functional abilities associated with guardianship cases. They focus primarily on the higher order, more complex functions associated with the IADL domains, rather than with the more basic self-care, or ADL, domains. Second, each functional domain is assessed by several items, compared to a single item in self-report measures. For example, in our Everyday Problems Test, tasks assessing the domain of financial management include (a) comparing benefits for several medigap insurance plans, (b) completing a portion of a tax return form, and (c) determining what form of medical assistance one is eligible for from various plans. Assessment of an individual's performance on multiple tasks related to a functional domain is critical in order to assess competence with greater accuracy and reliability. Also, the measures make clear the types of tasks on which competency is being judged, in contrast to the very subjective nature of the self-report questions. Finally, these measures have high face validity, since they focus on tasks encountered by most elderly in their daily lives.

However, a number of limitations of the measures need to be noted. Some of the limitations are due to the recent development of these instruments and the need for time to complete ongoing data collection related to them. There is first the question of whether the problems being assessed represent the most critical or essential tasks required for independent living. What are the essential tasks on which competence is required in order to manage one's finances? One may answer that the tasks will vary with the individual and the environmental demands. However, the authors of the tests have taken the position that there is a subset of critical tasks that can serve as the core for assessing competence in each domain; these tasks can then been supplemented with tasks unique to an individual case. How then should we go about determining this core of critical tasks?

Objective assessment comes at a cost in terms of the time to administer the instruments. Task performance is usually self-paced by the elderly, since the focus is on assessment of behaviors approximating how the elderly perform these tasks in their everyday environment. Thus, administration of the Community Competence Scale requires 60–90 minutes. Administration of the Everyday Problems Test ranges from 25 to 90 minutes, depending on the version of the test administered. The length of test administration is a major factor in assessing cognitively impaired elderly who typically have short attention spans and a low tolerance for ambiguous or stressful conditions, such as might occur in a testing situation. An additional concern is the need to develop norms for these objective measures on larger and more representative samples. Since the objective measures focus primarily on the cognitive demands of everyday tasks, it is critical that norms stratified by age and education be developed.

Issues in Forensic Assessment

As the preceding discussion has illustrated, the development of forensic assessment instruments for use in guardianship cases is in its infancy. In some cases, existing measures, developed for other purposes, such as assessment of eligibility for health and social services, have been adopted

(Fillenbaum, 1985; Kane, 1993). Recently, several new measures specifically targeted toward functional assessment have been presented in the literature; virtually all these measures are quite new and the instruments are in need of further development. There are several issues that need careful consideration as measurement development continues (Willis & Schaie, 1994).

Construct validity: The search for the gold standard.

Perhaps the most salient question with respect to any assessment instrument is, "Does the instrument measure what it is intended to measure?" In guardianship cases, the question is whether the FAI assesses the older person's competence with respect to the functional ability in question (Schaie, 1978). The construct validity of an instrument has traditionally been assessed with respect to a "gold standard." For example, in medicine, a test or battery of tests becomes accepted as the gold standard for the diagnosis of a disease or health condition. The effectiveness of alternative diagnostic procedures are assessed in comparison to the gold standard.

A critical problem in functional assessment is that there is no agreed upon gold standard. Epidemiological studies have largely depended upon the self-report of the adult; limitations of this approach were discussed above. Clinician ratings have often been cited in validity studies, but the criteria employed by the clinician are often vague and vary from clinician to clinician. A leading scholar in geriatric assessment wrote recently that clinical judgment still plays a major role in what is sometimes described as the "*art* of diagnosis" (Kane, 1993, p 27; underline added).

In guardianship cases, the problem appears to be further complicated by two opposing trends:

1. Legal statutes tend to provide only very vague definitions of the construct (i.e., functional competence) upon which a judgment is to be made; but
2. there is a movement toward guardians being appointed in fairly limited domains of decision making (Parry, 1985).

For example, the older adult may be judged competent to make decisions regarding everyday financial decisions, but be considered incompetent to manage financial assets. If guardianship decisions are to be made regarding fairly narrow domains of competence, then assessments need also to be targeted to quite specific domains of behavior.

Global versus function-specific assessment of competence.

In the preceding discussion, we have suggested that functional assessment instruments may need to focus on specific areas of competence, given recent trends in guardianship judgments. However, both existing and newly developed measures of functional competence often rely on a summary or global score. For example, although the OARS examines perceptions of competence in five IADL domains, the most commonly reported finding is a summary score of the total number of activity domains with deficits. Likewise, new functional assessment instruments also often involve summary scores (Loeb, 1983; Loewenstein et al., 1989). Summary scores, from a measurement perspective, are often the most appropriate level to report assessment findings, since specific abilities (e.g., ability to balance a checkbook, comprehension of a medicine label) are commonly assessed with a single item, and competencies cannot be reliably measured with a single item. However, the congruence between the specificity of assessment of competence and the particular domains of activity over which a guardian is appointed needs further careful consideration.

Measurement of environmental demands and resources.

Competence is considered to involve an interaction between the individual's level of functional abilities and the demands and resources in his or her environment. While there has been some progress made in development of measures to assess the functional abilities of the individual, much less attention has been given to assessment of the environment. Although consensus appears to be emerging on some of the critical functional abilities associated with competency, there has been much less conceptual work or research on defining the dimensions of the environment associated with competency (Krauss & Popkin, 1989; Lawton, 1987).

Measures such as the OARS (Fillenbaum, 1978) have enumerated categories of services, including: transportation, social/recreational, employment, educational, mental health, and personal care. There appears to be a primary focus on services provided by formal support mechanisms (agencies, community programs). Less emphasis is given to the informal services that may be provided by friends and relatives, although most caregiving in our society is provided by an informal network (Horowitz, 1985).

An alternative approach to assessment of environmental demands has been proposed by Scheidt and Schaie (1978), who developed a taxonomy of competency-requiring situations encountered by community-dwelling elderly adults. Elderly judges rated 300 everyday situations according to a set of situational attributes derived from the social-psychological literature. Four attribute dimensions were identified that characterized these situations: social-nonsocial; active-passive, common-uncommon, and supportive-depriving. Older adults were then asked to rate their perceived individual level of competence with regard to situations representing these dimensions. The two attribute dimensions that most influenced the elderly in their perception of their own competence in a given situation were: common-uncommon and supportive-depriving. That is, the elderly perceived themselves to be significantly more competent in situations that may be characterized as being common or as being supportive. They perceive themselves to be much less competent in situations characterized as being uncommon or depriving. Gender differences also affect perceptions of situational competence. Women perceived themselves as more competent than men in social, common, and supportive situations. Again, the findings on gender-based differences in situations of perceived competence are quite congruent with those from the traditional sex role literature. A substantial literature indicates greater concern among females for social competence, for acquiring the approval of others, and for avoiding competitive conflict situations.

SUMMARY

In this chapter we have considered the geropsychological literature related to four characteristics of legal competence: focus on functional abilities, causal linkage between incapacity and mental disorder, role of the general environmental context in defining the critical functional domains, and the congruence between the individual's competence and environmental demands. Most older adults are not totally incompetent, and thus guardianship decisions often are concerned with the "least restrictive alternative.'' The task is to determine the specific domains of functional abilities in which the older adult is deficient and for which a guardian needs to be appointed. Since most legal statutes describe only very general capacities, a major challenge for those involved in assessment and judgment of competence is to define the domains of functional abilities associated with living independently in our society. We suggest that prior research on the instrumental activities of daily living (IADLs) may be particularly useful to those concerned with guardianship issues.

Competence represents the older adult's potential or capacity for making decisions necessary for care of oneself and maintenance of one's property. Competence is not necessarily reflected in the older adult's everyday behavior. Competence addresses what the individual is able to do, not what he or she actually does. Likewise, competence focuses heavily on the older adult's mental ability to make critical decisions regarding care of self and management of property; it does not necessarily require that the older adult be physically able to carry out the required tasks of daily living. Given this perspective on functional competence, we discuss the multiple components that may be involved in decision making. Basic mental abilities and domain-specific knowledge bases are necessary components in decision making, but are not sufficient for generation of adequate problem solutions. There must also be consideration of the elderly individual's perception of the social and physical environment and beliefs and preferences regarding alternative problem solutions.

We present data on longitudinal change in problem-solving performance for elderly adults with no known pathologies. Data on normative change in decision-making competence can serve as a baseline for assessment and for decisions regarding elderly persons who suffer from mental disorders. While age-related decline in young-old age is modest, the rate of average decline increases in old-old age. At all chronological ages, elderly people with below average educational level function at a lower level. Our research suggests that the educationally disadvantaged elderly in very old age are increasingly likely to need assistance in everyday decision making, even though they do not suffer from a specific mental disorder.

It may be argued that the presence of a mental disorder in combination with functional deficits should be sufficient grounds for guardianship decisions. However, the functional deficit may have predated the organic condition, highlighting the importance of determining the premorbid functional competence of the older adult. Given the significant relationship between education and functional competence, elderly persons with low socioeconomic status may have functioned marginally even prior to diagnosis of an organic impairment. Increased risk of misdiagnosis for dementia in poorly educated older adults is also a concern in competency judgments.

The elderly do not live in a vacuum, and thus competence cannot be considered without taking into account the environment in which the elderly function. Both the physical and social environment need to be considered in determining which functional abilities are most salient for independent living. An important issue is what criteria to use in determining the functional abilities considered most salient in a given context. Family members, clinicians, social workers, legal professionals, and the elderly themselves may disagree regarding the most salient functional domains for defining competence.

While the broad sociocultural context is instrumental in defining which specific functional abilities are most salient, assessment of a particular individual's competence must consider the congruence or incongruence between the person's capabilities and the demands and resources in the immediate environment. Person–environment incongruence can occur in three ways: decreasing individual competence and increasing environmental demands, stability in individual competence but increasing environmental demands, and decrease in individual competence but stability in environmental demands.

The second part of this chapter deals with the use of forensic assessment instruments (FAIs) to assess older adults' competence to live independently. Two major types of measures are currently in use: self-report instruments and objective measures. Both types of measures have strengths and limitations. Advantages of self-report instruments are that they can be administered in a relatively brief time interval and they can be administered by trained technicians rather than highly skilled professionals. A major limitation of the self-report approach is that older adults tend to overestimate their level of competence when compared to ratings by clinicians or compared to actual performance. A second limitation is that each competency domain is traditionally assessed by a single item and there is little information on the source (physical, mental, social) of the perceived deficit in competence.

Most objective measures of functional ability have been developed fairly recently and thus psychometric information on the instruments is limited. A major strength is that they provide an objective measure of functional ability. They tend to focus on higher order, more complex tasks of daily living. A limitation of these measures is that they require more time to administer than self-report instruments. Due to the recent development of the measures, there is limited normative data, especially with respect to individual difference variables, such as age, educational level, or ethnicity.

Finally, we discuss three issues in the development and use of forensic instruments that need to be addressed. First, there is the issue of the construct validity of the instruments and the lack of a "gold standard" by which to evaluate recently developed measures. Second, most measures involve a summary score that provides information on overall functional competence. However, recent trends are toward appointing guardians for specific functional domains. Forensic assessment instruments need to provide information on competence in the specific domains of interest in guardianship cases. Third, there has been even less effort expended toward development of measures to assess the environmental demands and resources. Assessment of the environmental demands, as well as the capabilities of the individual, is critical if incompetence is seen to result from incongruence between the person and the environment.

Our review of the legal and geropsychological literatures suggests that each field has much to contribute to the other. The shifting age structure of our society makes the need for interdisciplinary exchange all the more urgent. Functional competence in old age is the foremost concern of the elderly themselves and will become an increasing societal concern as the baby boomers reach old age early in the next century. The joint efforts of the legal and psychological communities are needed to meet the challenge.

REFERENCES

Altman, W. M., & Parmelee, P. A. (1992). Discrimination based on age: The special case of the institutionalized aged. In D. K. Kagehiro & W. S. Laufer (Eds.), *Handbook of psychology and law* (pp. 416–417). New York: Springer Publishing Co.

Altman, W. M., Parmelee, P. A., & Smyer, M. A. (1992). Autonomy, competence, and informed consent in long term care: Legal and psychological perspectives. *Villanova Law Review, 37,* 1671–1704.

Anderer, S. J. (1990). Determining competency in guardianship proceedings. *American Bar Association Public Service Monograph Series*, 1. Washington, DC: American Bar Association.

Appelbaum, P. S., & Grisso, T. (1988). Assessing patients' capacities to consent to treatment. *New England Journal of Medicine, 319*, 1635–1638.

Ashford, J. W., Kolm, P., Colliver, J. A., Bekian, C., & Hsu, L. (1989). Alzheimer patient evaluation and the Mini-Mental State: Item characteristic curve analysis. *Journal of Gerontology, 44*, P139–P146.

Blazer, D. (1978). The OARS Durham survey: Description and application. In Duke University Center for the Study of Aging (Eds.), *Multidimensional functional assessment: The OARS methodology* (2nd ed.), Durham, NC: Duke University.

Baltes, M. M., & Baltes, P. B. (1986). *The psychology of control and aging.* Hillsdale, NJ: Erlbaum.

Bersoff, D. N. (1992). Autonomy for vulnerable populations: The Supreme Court's reckless disregard for self-determination and social science. *Villanova Law Review, 37*, 1569–1605.

Camp, C., Doherty, K., Moody-Thomas, S., & Denney, N. (1989). Practical problem solving in adults: A comparison of problem types and scoring methods. In J. Sinnott (Ed.), *Everyday problem solving: Theory and applications* (pp. 211–228). New York: Praeger.

Ceci, S., & Liker, J. (1986). In R. Sternberg & R. Wagner (Eds.), *Practical intelligence* (pp. 236–270). New York: Cambridge University Press.

Charlesworth, W. R. (1976). Intelligence as an adaptation: An ethnological approach. In L. Resnick (Ed.), *The nature of intelligence* (pp. 147–168). Hillsdale, NJ: Erlbaum.

Christie, B. (1984). Guardianship in Alberta, Canada. In Appolloni, T., & Cooke, T. P. (Eds.), *A new look at guardianship*. Baltimore: P. H. Brookes.

Cornelius, S., & Caspi, A. (1987). Everyday problem solving in adulthood and old age. *Psychology and Aging, 2*, 144–153.

Diehl, M., Willis, S. L., & Schaie, K. W. (1995). Everyday problem solving in older adults: Observational assessment and cognitive correlates. *Psychology and Aging, 10*(3), 478–490.

Diehl, M., & Willis, S. L. (1991, November). *Relationship between psychometric measures of intelligence and measures of everyday problem solving in older adults.* Paper presented at the annual meeting of the Gerontological Society of America, San Francisco, CA.

Drane, J. F. (1984). Competency to give informed consent. *Journal of the American Medical Association, 252*, 925–927.

Fillenbaum, G. G. (1978). Reliability and validity of the OARS multidimensional functional assessment questionnaire. In Duke University Center for the

Study of Aging (Eds.), *Multidimensional functional assessment: The OARS methodology* (2nd ed.) (pp. 20–28). Durham, NC: Duke University.

Fillenbaum, G. G. (1985). Screening the elderly: A brief instrumental activities of daily living measure. *Journal of the American Geriatrics Society, 33,* 698–706.

Fillenbaum, G. G. (1987a). Activities of daily living. In G. L. Maddox (Ed.), *The encyclopedia of aging* (pp. 3–4). New York: Springer Publishing Co.

Fillenbaum, G. G. (1987b). Multidimensional functional assessment. In G. L. Maddox (Ed.), *The encyclopedia of aging* (pp. 460–464). New York: Springer Publishing Co.

Fillenbaum, G. G. (1987c). OARS Multidimensional Functional Assessment Questionnaire. In G. L. Maddox (Ed.), *The encyclopedia of aging* (pp. 496–497). New York: Springer Publishing Co.

Fillenbaum, G. G., & Smyer, M. A. (1981). The development, validity and reliability of the OARS Multidimensional Functional Assessment Questionnaire. *Journal of Gerontology, 36,* 428–434.

Fitten, L. J., & Waite, M. S. (1990). Impact of medical hospitalization on treatment decision-making capacity in the elderly. *Archives of Internal Medicine, 150,* 1717,1719–1729.

Ford, A. B., Bolmar, S. J., Salmon, R. B., Medalie, J. H., Roy, A. W., & Galazka, S. S. (1988). Health and function in the old and very old. *Journal of the American Geriatrics Society, 36,* 428–434.

Galanos, A., Fillenbaum, G. G., Cohen, H. J., & Burchett, B. (1991). *Limitations of functional health status in the comprehensive assessment of community-dwelling elderly.* Unpublished manuscript, Duke University, Durham, NC.

Grisso, T. (1986). *Evaluating competencies: Forensic assessments and instruments.* New York: Plenum.

Grisso, T. (1994). Clinical assessment for legal competency of older adults. In M. Storandt & G. R. Vanden Bos (Eds.), *Neuropsychological assessment of dementia and depression in older adults: A clinician's guide* (pp. 119–139). Washington, DC: American Psychological Association.

Horowitz, A. (1985). Family caregiving to the frail elderly. In C. Eisdorfer, M. P. Lawton, & G. L. Maddox (Eds.), *Annual review of gerontology and geriatrics* (Vol. 5). New York: Springer Publishing Co.

Horstman, P. (1975). Protective services for the elderly: The limits of parens patriae. *Missouri Law Review, 40,* 215–278.

Kahana, E. (1982). A congruence model of person-environment interaction. In M. P. Lawton, P. Windley, & T. Byerts (Eds.), *Aging and the environment: Theoretical approaches* (pp. 97–121). New York: Springer.

Kane, R. L. (1993). The implications of assessment. *Journal of Gerontology, 48,* 27–31.

Kane, R. A., & Kane, R. L. (1981). *Assessing the elderly: A practical guide to measurement.* Lexington, MA: Lexington Books.

Kapp, M. B. (1990). Evaluating decision making capacity in the elderly: A review of recent literature. *Journal of Elder Abuse and Neglect, 2,* 15–29.

Kapp, M. B. (1992). *Geriatrics and the law: Patient rights and professional responsibilities* (2nd ed.). New York: Springer Publishing Co.

Katz, S., Ford, A., Moskowitz, R., Jackson, B., & Jaffee, M. (1963). Studies of illness in the aged: The Index of ADL, a standardized measure of biological and psychological function. *Journal of the American Medical Association, 185,* 94–99.

Krauss, I. K., & Popkin, S. J. (1989). Competence issues in older adults. In T. Hunt & C. J. Lindley (Eds.), *Testing older adults: A reference guide for geropsychological assessments.* Austin, TX: Pro-Ed.

Kuriansky, J. B., Gurland, B. J., Fleiss, J. L., & Cowan, D. (1976). The assessment of self-care capacity in geriatric psychiatric patients by objective and subjective methods. *Journal of Clinical Psychology, 32,* 95–102.

Lachman, M. (1986). Locus of control in aging research: A case for multidimensional and domain-specific assessment. *Psychology and Aging,1,* 34–40.

Lachman, M., & Leff, R. (1989). Perceived control and intellectual functioning in the elderly: A 5-year longitudinal study. *Developmental Psychology, 25,* 722–728.

Lawton, M. P. (1982). Competence, environmental press, and adaptation of older people. In M. P. Lawton, P. Windley, & T. Byerts (Eds.), *Aging and the environment: Theoretical approaches* (pp. 33–59). New York: Springer.

Lawton, M. P. (1987). Contextual perspectives: Psychosocial influences. In L. W. Poon (Ed.), *Handbook for clinical memory assessment of older adults.* Washington, DC: American Psychological Association.

Lawton, M. P., & Brody, E. (1969). Assessment of older people: Self maintaining and instrumental activities of daily living. *The Gerontologist, 9,* 179–185.

Lawton, M. P., & Moss, M. (Undated). *Philadelphia Geriatrics Center Multilevel Assessment Instrument: Manual for Full-length MAI.* Philadelphia, PA: Author.

Lawton, M. P., & Parmelee, P. A. (1990). The design of special environments for the aged. In J. E. Birren & K. W. Schaie (Eds.), *Handbook of the psychology of aging* (3rd Ed.). San Diego: Academic.

Legal Counsel for the Elderly, National Protective Support Center. (1989). *Informational Mailing 89-1.* American Association for Retired Persons.

Levinson, H. (1974). Activism and powerful others: Distinctions within the concept of internal-external control. *Journal of Personality Assessment, 38,* 377–383.

Loeb, P. A. (1984). *Validity of the Community Competence Scale with the*

Law and Older Adults' Decision Making

elderly. St. Louis University. (Dissertation Abstracts International, *45*(6), 1919.)

Loewenstein, D. A., Amigo, E., Duara, R., Guterman, A, Hurwitz, D, Berkowitz, N., Wilkie, F. Weinberg, G., Black, B. M., Gittelman, B., & Eisdorfer, C. (1989). A new scale for the assessment of functional status in Alzheimer's disease and related disorders. *Journal of Gerontology, 44,* P114–P121.

Marsiske, M., & Willis, S. L. (1995). Dimensionality of everyday problem solving in older adults. *Psychology and Aging, 10*(2), 269–283.

Masterpasqua, F. (1989). A competence paradigm for psychological practice. *American Psychologist, 44,* 1366–1371.

National Conference of the Judiciary on Guardianship. Proceedings for the Elderly. (1986) Reno, Nevada. *Statement of Recommended Judicial Practices* adopted by the National Conference of the Judiciary on Guardianship, Proceedings for the Elderly, June 15–18, Reno, Nevada. Reno, NV: National Judiciary College.

Nezu, A. M., & Nezu, C. M. (Eds.). (1989). *Clinical decision making in behavior therapy: A problem-solving perspective.* Champaign, IL: Research Press.

Nolan, B. (1984). Functional evaluation of the elderly in guardianship proceedings. *Law, Medicine, & Health Care, 12,* 210–218.

Parry, J. (1985). Incompetency, guardianship, and restoration. In J. Brakel, J. Parry, & B. Weiner (Eds.), *The mentally disabled and the law.* Chicago: American Bar Foundation.

Pifer, A., & Bronte, L. (Eds.). (1986). *Our aging society.* New York: Norton.

Poon, L. W., Rubin, D. C., & Wilson, B. A. (Eds.). (1989). *Everyday cognition in adulthood and late life.* Cambridge: Cambridge University Press.

Puckett, J. M., & Reese, H. W. (Eds.), (1993). *Lifespan developmental psychology: Mechanisms of everyday cognition.* Hillsdale, NJ: Erlbaum.

Quinn, M. J. (1989). Probate conservatorships and guardianships: Assessment and curative aspects. *Journal of Elder Abuse and Neglect, 1,* 91–101.

Quinn, M. J., & Tomita, S. K. (1986). *Elder abuse and neglect: Causes, diagnosis, and intervention strategies.* New York: Springer.

Rodin, J., TImko, C., & Harris, S. (1985). The construct of control: Biological and psychosocial correlates. In M. P. Lawton (Ed.), *Annual review of gerontology and geriatrics* (Vol. 6, pp. 3–55). New York: Springer.

Sales, B., Powell, D., & Van Duizend, R. (1982). *Disabled persons and the law.* New York: Plenum.

Salthouse, T. A. (1990). Cognitive competence and expertise in the aging. In J. E. Birren & K. W. Schaie (Eds.), *Handbook of the psychology of aging.* (3rd ed.). New York: Academic.

Schaie, K. W. (1978). External validity in the assessment of intellectual development in adulthood. *Journal of Gerontology, 33,* 695–701.

Schaie, K. W. (1983). The Seattle Longitudinal Study: A twenty-one year exploration of psychometric intelligence in adulthood. In K. W. Schaie (Ed.), *Longitudinal studies of adult psychological development* (pp. 64–135). New York: Guilford.

Schaie, K. W. (1987). Applications of psychometric intelligence to the prediction of everyday competence in the elderly. In C. Schooler & K. W. Schaie (Eds.), *Cognitive functioning and social structure over the life course* (pp. 50–59). New York: Ablex.

Schaie, K. W. (1989). The hazards of cognitive aging. *Gerontologist, 29,* 484–493.

Schaie, K. W. (1990). Intellectual development in adulthood. In J. E. Birren & K. W. Schaie (Eds.), *Handbook of the psychology of aging.* (3rd ed.). New York: Academic.

Schaie, K. W., & Willis, S. L. (1986). Can decline in adult intellectual functioning be reversed. *Developmental Psychology, 22,* 223–232.

Scheidt, R. J., & Schaie, K. W. (1978). A taxonomy of situations for the elderly populations: Generating situational criteria. *Journal of Gerontology, 33,* 848–857.

Sinnott, J. D. (Ed.). (1989). *Everyday problem solving.* New York: Praeger.

Smyer, M. (1993). Aging and decision-making capacity. *Generations, 17,* 51–56.

Sternberg, R., & Kolligian, J. (Eds.) (1990). *Competence considered.* New Haven, CT: Yale University Press.

Suzman, R., & Riley, M. W. (Eds.). (1985). The oldest old. *Milbank Memorial Fund Quarterly/Health and Society 63*(2), 177–451.

Swartz, C. M., & Stewart, C. (1991). Melancholia and orders to restrict resuscitation. *Hospital and Community Psychiatry, 42,* 189.

Uhlmann, R. F., & Larson, E B. (1991). Effect of education on the Mini-Mental State Examination as a screening test for dementia. *Journal of the American Geriatrics Society, 39,* 876–880.

Uniform Probate Code. (1989). Chicago: National Conference of Commissioners on Uniform State Laws.

U.S. Bureau of the Census. (1989). *National data book and guide to sources: Statistical abstract of U. S. 1989.* Washington, DC: U.S. Government Printing Office.

U.S. Congress, Senate Special Committee on Aging. (1987–88). *Aging America: Trends and projections.* Washington, DC: United States Department of Health and Human Services.

Vitaliano, P. P., Breen, A. R., Albert, M. S., Russo, J., & Prinz, P. N. (1984). Memory, attention and functional status in community-residing Alzheimer type dementia patients and optimally healthy aged individuals. *Journal of Gerontology, 39,* 58–64.

Voss, J. F., & Post, T. A. (1988). On the solving of ill-structured problems. In M. T. H. Chi, R. Glaser, & M. J. Farr (Eds.), *The nature of expertise* (pp. 261–285). Hillsdale, NJ: Erlbaum.

Wallston, K. A., & Wallston, B. S. (1982). Who is responsible for your health: The construct of health locus of control. In G. S. Sanders & J. Suls (Eds.), *Social psychology of health and illness* (pp. 65–95). Hillsdale, NJ: Erlbaum.

Wang, L., Burns, A. M., & Hommel, P. A. (1990). Trends in guardianship reform: Roles and responsibilities of legal advocates. *Clearinghouse Review, 24,* 561–569.

Wiederholt, W. C., Cahn, D., Butters, N. M., Salmon, D. P., Kritz-Silverstein, D., & Barrett-Connor, E. (1993). Effects of age, gender and education on selected neuropsychological tests in an elderly community cohort. *Journal of the American Geriatrics Society, 41,* 639–647.

Willis, S. L. (1987). Cognitive interventions in the elderly. In K. W. Schaie (Ed.), *Annual review of gerontology and geriatrics* (Vol. 7) (pp. 159–188). New York: Springer.

Willis, S. L. (1991). Cognition and everyday competence. In K. W. Schaie & M. P. Lawton (Eds.), *Annual review of gerontology and geriatrics* (Vol. 11) (pp. 80–109). New York: Springer Publishing Co.

Willis, S. L., Jay, G. M., Diehl, M., & Marsiske, M. (1992). Longitudinal change and prediction of everyday task competence in the elderly. *Research on Aging, 14,* 68–91.

Willis, S. L., & Marsiske, M. (1990). A life-span perspective on practical intelligence. In D. Tupper & K. Cicerone (Eds.), *The neuropsychology of everyday life* (pp. 183–198). Boston: Kluwer.

Willis, S. L., & Marsiske, M. (1992). *Manual for the Everyday Problems Test.* University Park, PA:

Willis, S. L., & Schaie, K. W. (1986). Practical intelligence in later adulthood. In R. Sternberg & R. Wagner (Eds.), *Practical intelligence* (pp. 236–270). New York: Cambridge University Press.

Willis, S. L., & Schaie, K. W. (1993). Everyday cognition: Taxonomic and methodological considerations. In J. M. Puckett & H. W. Reese (Eds.), *Lifespan developmental psychology: Mechanisms of everyday cognition.* Hillsdale, NJ: Erlbaum.

Willis, S. L., & Schaie, K. W. (1994). Assessing the elderly. In C. B. Fisher & R. M. Lerner (Eds.), *Applied developmental psychology.* New York: Mc-Graw Hill.

Willis, S. L., & Schaie, K. W. (1994). Cognitive training in the normal elderly. In F. Forette, Y. Christen, & F. Boller (Eds.), *Cerebral plasticity and cognitive stimulation* (pp. 91–113). Paris: Foundation National de Gerontologie.

Wilson, L., Grant, K., Witsey, P., & Kerridge, D. (1973). Mental status of elderly hospital patients related to occupational therapist's assessment of activities of daily living. *Gerontologia Clinica, 15,* 197–222.

Commentary: Everyday Competencies and Guardianship: Refinements and Realities

Mary Joy Quinn

eciding when or if an older adult should have a guardian[1] appointed has bedeviled scholars and practitioners in the legal and clinical professions for decades. Various standards have been proposed, mulled over, refined, been found wanting, and then discarded, sometimes with disillusionment. Those standards have focused variously on old age, the quality of decision making, the role of undue influence, the medical or psychiatric diagnosis, the risk of impoverishment through heedless spending, physical endangerment, and both the **capacity** of an elder to carry out the activities of daily living necessary for health and safety and **actual** daily functional behavior. More recently, there has been a focus on evaluating whether or not a guardianship is the most appropriate legal alternative for an individual elder in a given situation, and if it is, how to tailor the guardianship especially for that elder in the least restrictive way possible (Wood, 1986; Sabatino, this volume).

In her chapter entitled "Assessing the Everyday Competence in the Cognitively Challenged Elderly," Dr. Sherry Willis approaches the above standards from the viewpoint of the research psychologist. Dr. Willis divides her chapter into two main parts. In the first part, she focuses on aspects of legal competence from a psychological perspective. In the second part of the chapter, she examines assessment tools that might be helpful in determining if a guardianship should be established, including the strengths and weaknesses of each tool. For the sake of clarity, this response follows the outline of Dr. Willis' chapter.

Beginning by looking at the definitions of competence, Willis makes concrete points throughout the chapter regarding the links between psychology and the law. She offers insights into the areas where the two fields might "speak" to each other. For instance, those who work mainly in the law will be intrigued to learn that psychology looks at the issue of competence in positive terms and centers on what a person is capable of doing, in contrast to the law, which focuses on what the person in incapable of doing. While this may appear to be a simplistic, even trite, formulation, it has deep implications for the way in which we view and approach those elders we seek to serve. Further, it has implications for the types of assessment tools we will develop and the manner in which we will use them. Because we have so few assessment tools now, or even reliable guidelines to assist in determining if an individual elder is in need of a guardianship, it is difficult to imagine what "positive" tools would look like and how they would be used. However, it is safe to say that most of us personally would like to be approached in a positive manner with an emphasis on what we are able to do.

LEGAL COMPETENCIES: COMMON CHARACTERISTICS

In the first part of her chapter, Willis examines common characteristics of legal competencies from the psychological viewpoint. These characteristics include functional abilities, mental disorders and functional incompetence, the role of environmental context (e.g., climate, geographical location, architectural features of the building, available social services, gender roles) as related to functional abilities, and then, the abilities of the individual elder to function in a particular environment. The two remaining characteristics which are examined are judgment and disposition, which refer to the judicial determinations that are made once evidence is submitted, examined, and weighed.

Functional Abilities or Capacities

Functional ability is one of the more recent standards to be proposed (Nolan, 1984; Nolan, 1990; Quinn, 1989; Quinn, 1990). Indeed, some state laws have completely abandoned all other standards and look only at functional abilities.[2] As Willis notes, "The central question in guardianship and conservatorship cases is whether the individual's functional abilities are sufficient for the contextual demands experienced by an elderly individual" (p. 91, this volume). However, the criteria for guardianship or conservatorship need to be more sophisticated than functional abilities tests alone. As Willis notes, there are elders who have the capacity to make decisions but lack the physical capacity to execute those decisions. However, they may be able to direct others to perform the needed tasks such as housekeeping, preparing food, assisting with bathing, or banking. Still other elders have the capacity to function but fail to do so, possibly as the result of lagging behind technological advances, as noted by Willis, but also perhaps as the result of a lack of interest or cultural conditioning. Wealthy people who fall on hard times in old age, for example, may never have had to keep house or cook and therefore, literally do not know how to do so. Other conditions that come to mind are "learned helplessness," infantalization by a now deceased spouse, acute or prolonged grief reactions, alcoholism in the early and middle stages, and clinical depression or outright mental illness. Likewise, there are people who are able to carry out the activities of daily living but would not do well on tests for decision-making capacity, possibly due to lower education levels, as noted by Willis, but also due to immigrant status, language problems, and culturally biased tests (J. Lim, personal communication, January 24, 1994).

Case study.

In one dramatic case, a son caused a petition for guardianship to be filed for his mother, naming himself as the proposed guardian. His father had recently died and he felt it was his duty as the only son to see to his mother's financial affairs. He was also incensed that his mother had already made future arrangements by executing a durable power of attorney for health care and a trust. A medical declaration was submitted as part of the son's petition. The mother was diagnosed as having dementia despite the fact that the physician could not converse with the woman in her own language! The mother had not informed her son of her planning nor had she included him in any way because she did not want him to have knowledge or control of her medical care or her funds. When the mother learned of her son's petition for guardianship, she retained an attorney who initiated an elegant assessment process which resulted in the withdrawal of the petition. First, the attorney retained the services of a neurologist, an internist, and a psychiatrist. An occupational therapist was retained on the recommendation of the court investigator. Each professional spoke the mother's particular Chinese dialect.

The occupational therapist's evaluation is of particular note. She personally went to the home and watched the woman prepare meals. She also went out into the neighborhood with her and asked the woman to take her around to her commercial support network. She observed the woman making purchases and appropriately dealing with her money (i.e., counting her change). She reviewed health, money management, community resources and use of leisure time. She also reviewed emergency telephone numbers and showed the woman photos of houses, some with dangerous situations, to see if the woman could identify dangerous situations—she could. The occupational therapist ascertained that there were family members other than the son who were available as needed and that the woman had assistance in managing her property. Upon a review of all the meticulous evaluations, the son and his attorney were convinced to withdraw their petition for guardianship.

As can be seen from this case description, the question of the proposed ward's actual behavior with regard to decision making, functional behavior, and freedom from psychological pathology was resolved by clear and convincing evidence, the usual standard of proof for guardianships. This case clearly demonstrates that we often overrely on physicians to tell judges if someone needs a guardianship when we could have been consulting other professionals for appropriate information. Over the years, most medical declarations have proved to be notoriously lax, generalized, and incomplete. Also, we may have been asking physicians to make judgments they were not in a position to make (i.e., need for a guardianship). It would be more appropriate to rely on physicians for the information they have been educated to give (i.e., diagnosis, treatment plans, and prognosis of a given medical condition). Historically, however, physicians' reports have been the only third party information that judges have had to assist them in deciding whether a guardianship should be imposed. The only other input came from the petitioner and the attorney of record, who may or may not be self-serving, but who definitely want the guardianship established.

Least restrictive alternative.

Once the concept of functional abilities or actual functional behavior as the criterion for guardianship is accepted, then comes the recognition that almost all humans have capacities to function in some areas and not others (Quinn, 1990). Therefore, it is desirable that courts remove rights from elders and delegate those rights to others only in those areas where the elder is not functioning. Most states have addressed that issue by including the concept of "limited guardianship" or the "least restrictive alternative" in their laws. For instance, California law mandates that, before a guardianship is established, the court must determine if the elder is living in the least restrictive setting and if there is any sufficient legal alternative to a guardianship.[3]

There are several results when the concept of the least restrictive alternative is fully implemented by a court that has the support of appropriately educated court investigators. Some guardianships are not granted at all, while others are carefully tailored for the individual elder. For instance, a reverse annuity mortgage may be ordered to help keep the elder in her/his own home, a bank account from which to manage daily expenses may be mandated, or the court may order that the elder cannot be moved without its review. In some instances, the proposed guardian is not appointed; the court appoints someone else whom the elder prefers after making the determination that the person is trustworthy, capable, and willing to serve as guardian.

Another result of fully implementing the concept of least restrictive alternative is that there are more petitions which include substantiated allegations of severe neglect or abuse. The most extreme cases are coming to court now, possibly due to heightened educational efforts regarding elder abuse and neglect (Quinn & Tomita, 1986; Wolf & Pillemer, 1989), but also because less restrictive alternatives are more available and being used for less complex situations. Still another unanticipated result from the promulgation of less restrictive alternatives is the apparent increase in abuse of those alternatives, which include powers of attorney and trusts. These alternatives do not carry the protections that guardianships include, such as notice to appropriate parties of the pending action, bonding, formal court procedures, and some measure of monitoring. Courts are beginning to see guardianship petitions filed in order to get the decision making away from an abusive trustee or attorney-in-fact and into the hands of a trustworthy (and court-supervised) guardian. Once a guardianship is established a lawsuit can be filed against the abuser by the guardian. For instance, the lawsuit might attempt to recover real property, or to get payment for medical treatment as the result of the physical abuse, or win an award for damages.

Courts are even seeing some abuses in connection with durable powers of attorney for health care.

Case study.

In one instance, a son who was the attorney-in-fact under his mother's durable power of attorney for health care kept his mother alive with a nasogastric tube even though she had expressly stated that she did not want that intervention. The procedure was performed after she had become severely mentally impaired to the point that medical personnel relied on the son for medical decision making. When the treating physician found out that the woman had actually written a book on the subject of the right to die without medical interference, he contacted the court and a neutral party guardianship was established. The guardian revoked the durable power of attorney for health care and directed that the tube be removed and the woman fed by hand. The son had been keeping his mother alive so that he could collect payments on an unsecured loan he had made with his mother's money and so he could collect her Social Security checks.

This case makes it clear that legal and clinical practitioners must be thoughtful and cautious when recommending legal alternatives. It is always wise to ask, "The least restrictive alternative—for whom?" (J. Ferdon, personal communication, March 3, 1992).

Decision making.

The process of decision making and the issue of decisional incapacity have been studied for years. As Kapp (1990) notes, the search for a

precise, easily measurable and applied legal definition of decisional incapacity has been likened to a "search for the Holy Grail" (Roth, Meisel,
& Lidz, 1977). It is in this arena that research psychology can clearly
make contributions to the legal field. Certainly legal scholars have not
been able to find a cogent consensus on any definition for decision-
making competence. Willis notes that efforts have been made in research
psychology to define decision-making capacity, and she details seven
components related to daily living. This discussion is valuable for stating
in precise terms the exact conflicts front line practitioners face.

One of the biggest dilemmas that practitioners struggle with over
and over is whether someone who is self-neglectful or remains in an
abusive situation has the capacity to choose their condition. It would be
helpful if Willis and other research psychologists would devote more
attention to this area. The clinical need for valid material is readily
apparent to anyone familiar with the field. Valid instruments or guidelines would find immediate clinical application.

Another arena where psychological research could be helpful is with
regard to the concept of "undue influence." Some states refer to this
issue in their laws and therefore practitioners must be aware of it. It has
been defined as the substitution of one person's will for the true desires
of another. It can be accompanied by fraud, duress, threats or different
types of pressure on persons who are particularly susceptible. It is possible to be "competent" and still be subject to undue influence (Grant &
Quinn, in press). Undoubtedly, there are features of undue influence that
are unique to older adults and, in fact, it may be an aberration of the
natural desire many older people have to help the next generation.

Case study.

In one psychological and financial abuse case, a woman in her eighties
allowed herself to be virtually impoverished because she felt she ought
to help her nephew who was also her godson. The initial court investigation found that she had given him over $13,000 in money orders in less
than a year. He would call collect, sometimes from prison, and tell
woeful stories, asking his aunt to send a money order to some person.
He also induced her to write two checks amounting to $9,000 by telling
her he was coming into money and would pay her back when he did.
The woman was alert, oriented, and totally functional in her everyday
activities. She felt enormous relief when another nephew petitioned to

be her guardian of estate. She realized that once she no longer had control of her money, she could not be induced to give it to her godson/nephew.

Other features of cases in which undue influence is suggested include loneliness and early dementia. A common scenario involves the elder who is suspicious by nature and does not trust friends or family members even if they are reliable and honest. Paradoxically these elders often end up placing their wholehearted and unshakable faith in the very person who defrauds them, usually a new acquaintance.

Length of guardianship.

It is possible that functional abilities may vary over time and, contrary to stereotyped views of aging, improve. People who have psychotic breaks recover, alcoholics stop drinking alcohol, and people who have the diagnosis of bipolar disorder find an effective treatment. For those reasons, it may be more appropriate to view an assessment of capacity as "a snapshot in time," that is, a measure of the person's functioning only at the time the guardianship is being considered. Court monitoring, which is routinely taking place in a few states, greatly enhances the courts' abilities to know if a guardianship is still needed or if the terms need to be changed.

Termination of guardianships should be a cause for celebration, and court personnel react that way when termination is ordered. It means that an elder has recovered or that other sufficient means short of court involvement have been found to assist the elder. Willis makes the point that research findings indicate that improvement and positive change have been reported among the elderly. While self-reports may be suspect, particularly among those who suffer from dementias, educational and therapeutic efforts may be able to mediate decline. Certainly, practitioners working in the field would like to see more efforts in these areas. For too long, the only psychotherapeutic intervention available to elders has been medication. Educational efforts such as memory training have not found widespread application, although they appear to be promising.

Mental Disorders and Functional Incompetence: The Causal Link

There is another standard with which to measure an elder's competence. States have enumerated many mental conditions or disorders, including alcoholism and gambling, old age, and "weakness of mind" (Sabatino, this volume) as the "causes" of incompetence. In other words, the emphasis is on the cause of the impaired functioning. This standard is passing out of favor, although in a few state laws old age alone is enough reason for the imposition of guardianship.

However, Willis notes that it may not be prudent for legal scholars and practitioners to completely abandon consideration of the causal link. Diagnosis can be helpful in determining what types of powers a guardian should be given initially, as well as forecasting the length of the guardianship. This presumes that an accurate diagnosis has been made in the first place. Diagnosis, however, is difficult to perform due to the complexity of human beings, the current state of medical knowledge and technological testing, and the continued ageism in general society. Again, court monitoring, which involves personal interviews with the elder, is critical. Human healing and recovery are not always predictable, and termination of guardianships may be possible in the most unlikely situations. Alternatively, in the face of a well-determined diagnosis and prediction of decline and dependence, a court and a guardian will have a clearer path. However, continued effective court monitoring will ensure that the elder's rights are protected in those cases and that the estate is used for the elder's welfare as he or she becomes less capable of personal care or of supervising others in the discharge of activities of daily living (Keith & Wacker, 1992).

Willis notes that there are individual variables in cognitive functioning related to education and that those elders with less education may be functioning at a lower level initially. Poorly educated Alzheimer's patients have been found to function quite marginally even prior to diagnosis of an organic impairment, while those with higher levels of education may be able to function longer into the course of the disease. Other variables which could be explored include family support, self confidence, self approval of how one has lived one's life, previous styles of decision making, socioeconomic background, and so on. Again, guardianships should be carefully and humanely tailored and monitored.

Functional Abilities, Environmental Context, and Person–Context Interaction

The categories of environmental context and person–context interaction relate to the skills and abilities an elder needs to function in a particular environment. A useful study asked elders and three occupational groups of care providers (managers of housing for the elderly, senior citizen center directors, and occupational therapists) to state the most important components of daily living necessary to remain independent (Diehl & Willis, 1991). There was a high degree of agreement; management of finances and taking of medication were rated the two most important aspects of staying independent. This finding has definite clinical implications:

1. Money management education and assistance are important services.
2. There is a need for patient education and monitoring of medication.

Willis proposes two scenarios, each composed of a woman who was newly widowed, living in a retirement community and suffering from arthritis. In one scenario, there was sufficient environmental support (financial and banking services, a son living nearby), and the elder possessed a number of skills that made functioning possible. In the other scenario, the elder was a woman who had always been dependent on her husband and who consequently had developed few skills in taking care of her financial affairs. Additionally, her retirement community offered fewer supportive services. The second woman is more likely to be the subject of a guardianship petition especially if her social support system is meager.

Judgment and Disposition

As Willis notes, the ultimate judgment of incompetence or incapacity is the sole prerogative of the judicial system. If judges had fully developed evaluations in the areas mentioned in the previous sections, true judicial deliberation and weighing of evidence could take place. No reporter or evaluator, including court visitors, guardians *ad litem* or court investigators, can perform this task. The judge who automatically defers to reporters and evaluators and does not independently determine if the standard of clear and convincing evidence has been met is not acting in the best interests of the elder who is before the court. Reporters and evaluators may know only one part of the story; clinical incompetence or incapacity is simply a threshold question for guardianship, not the final determinant. Consider that the great bulk of older people's affairs are handled by them or by others without guardianship and conservatorship. In fact, it has been estimated that only 500,000 to 1,000,000 older people in the United States are under guardianship or conservatorship (Frolik, 1990). Other practical considerations that may determine whether a petition for guardianship will be filed are listed below.

1. There is a sudden and catastrophic physical impairment due to a stroke or accident.
2. There are transactions which require a surrogate decision maker, such as divorce, selling the house or other property, establishing a trust, splitting assets when one spouse is in a convalescent hospital, or settling a personal injury lawsuit or other type of lawsuit.
3. An elder does not grasp the severity of a situation and refuses desperately needed assistance.
4. A family is quarreling over custody or assets of the elder. Sibling rivalry can persist even among those who are in their seventies and eighties.
5. One adult child wants to claim an inheritance prematurely or influence the elder to make a new will.
6. Guardianship is a condition for probation or for receiving funds from a trust or the Social Security Administration or in the settlement of a lawsuit.
7. There has been a gradual decline in the elder's functioning resulting in incapacity. There now is a crisis precipitated by a physician or banker who becomes uncomfortable about medical consent or the handling of financial assets. Alternatively, there is a need for placement and the doctor says a guardianship is needed. Perhaps someone tells the family that the general power of attorney they have been using for years is no longer valid because the elder lost capacity some years previously.
8. There is an inadequate support system or the elder does not trust the support system.
9. The estate is complex and everyone is more comfortable with it being under court supervision.
10. There is abuse of a less restrictive legal option.

Because state laws are so vague and overgeneralized, even with the sweeping reforms since 1987, many older people fall within the legal definitions of incapacity. Practical considerations as outlined in the above-stated list are more apt to provide the trigger for a petition for guardianship petition than the theoretical standards stated earlier in this response chapter. In states where the court employs a neutral party to perform investigations and advise proposed wards or conservatees of their rights, however, and where the investigator is charged with determining if a less restrictive legal alternative will suffice, the rights and wishes of the proposed ward are more likely to be observed. Of course, much depends on the investigator's education, commitment, and perspective. Cost is always a factor, also. Some states, notably California, have financed court investigations by charging a fee to the estates that can afford to pay. In 1994, that fee averaged $430 per investigation in the San Francisco Bay area regardless of the complexity of the case.

FORENSIC ASSESSMENT INSTRUMENTS

The last part of Dr. Willis' chapter focuses on forensic assessment tools. Clearly they are needed. Just as clearly they do not exist, although the Instrumental Activities of Daily Living (IADL) Measure has important uses (Fillenbaum, 1985). However, there are dangers in the clinical application of tools. Most tools would probably have checklists, which can be dangerous because of the human tendency to overrely on them by mechanically filling in the blanks (Kapp, 1990). Moreover, checklists fail to consider individuality and the flavor of the person's unique situation. They also do not reflect fluctuations over time. These factors are critical for judicial determinations in tailoring guardianships and in monitoring these restrictive legal alternatives.

In her section on forensic assessment, Dr. Willis focuses on both self-reporting and objective tools. Self-reporting tools, despite their economy, are deeply flawed because elders tend to overestimate their abilities. Critical functions needed for independent management, as cited earlier in this response (i.e., money management and medication management), are exactly the areas where older adults tend to overestimate their abilities, according to Willis.

Some objective functional ability tools have been developed, but their focus on presenting the elder with a specific task to complete appears to be time consuming and onerous for the elder. A better way needs to be developed. Further, as mentioned by Dr. Willis, we also need tools to assess the environmental resources, both formal and informal.

CONCLUSION

This response to Willis' chapter has considered the various standards that have been used in determining if guardianship should be established, particularly as they relate to everyday competencies. Optimistically, we can look forward to sophisticated assessment tools that are objective, humanistic, reliable, and easily administered in clinical settings. These tools will come about through the cooperative efforts of the disciplines that are concerned about guardianship. Willis is correct when she states that the foremost concern of the elderly is functional competence and independence. The legal and psychological communities have much to offer each other as well as elders in the development and application of criteria and standards which maintain the dignity of elders and provide objective guidelines to courts and others concerned with their well being.

NOTES

1. The terms *guardian* and *guardianship* are used in this chapter to mean a court-appointed surrogate decision maker. The term *conservatorship* is used in many states and may or may not have a similar meaning, although conservators are also court-appointed surrogate decision makers.
2. Probate code 1801.
3 *Ibid.*, 1871, and 1826.

ACKNOWLEDGMENT

The author wishes to thank Jeanine Lim, L.C.S.W., for her suggestions in the evolution of this response paper.

REFERENCES

Diehl, M., & Willis, S. L. (1991, November). *Relationship between psychometric measures of intelligence and measures of everyday problem solving in older adults.* Paper presented at the annual meeting of the Gerontological Society of America, San Francisco, CA.

Fillenbaum, G. G. (1985). Screening the elderly: A brief instrumental activities of daily living measure. *Journal of American Geriatrics Society, 33,* 698–706.

Frolik, L. (1990). Elder abuse and guardians of elderly incompetents. *Journal of Elder Abuse and Neglect, 2,* 31–56.

Grant, I. H., & Quinn, M. J. (in press). Guardianship and abuse of dependent adults. In G. H. Zimny & G. T. Grossberg (Eds.), *Guardianship of the elderly: Medical and judicial aspects.* New York: Springer Publishing Co.

Keith, P. S., & Wacker, R. R. (1992). Guardianship reform: Does revised legislation make a difference in outcomes for proposed wards? *Journal of Aging & Social Policy, 4*(3/4), 139–155.

Kapp, M. B. (1990). Evaluating decision making capacity in the elderly: A review of recent literature. *Journal of Elder Abuse and Neglect, 2,* 15–29.

Nolan, B. (1984). Functional evaluation of the elderly in guardianship proceedings. *Law, Medicine & Health Care, 12,* 210–218.

Nolan, B. (1990). A judicial menu: Selecting remedies for the incapacitated elder. *Journal of Elder Abuse and Neglect, 2,* 73–84.

Quinn, M. J. (1989). Probate conservatorships and guardianships: Assessment and curative aspects. *Journal of Elder Abuse and Neglect, 1,* 91–101.

Quinn, M. J. (1990). Elder abuse and neglect: Intervention strategies. In S. M. Stith, M. B. Williams, & K. Rosen, *Violence hits home.* New York: Springer Publishing Co.

Quinn, M. J., & Tomita, S. K. (1986). *Elder abuse and neglect: Causes, diagnosis, and intervention strategies.* New York: Springer Publishing Co.

Roth, L. H., Meisel, A., & Lidz, C. (1977). Tests of competency to consent to treatment. *American Journal of Psychiatry, 134,* 279–283.

Wolf, R. S., & Pillemer, K. A. (1989). *Helping elderly victims: The reality of elder abuse.* New York: Columbia University Press.

Wood, E. F. (1986, June). *Statement of recommended judicial practices.* Adopted by the National Conference of the Judiciary on Guardianship Proceedings for the Elderly of the American Bar Association and The National Judicial College, Washington, DC.

Commentary: Decision-Making Capacity in the Acutely Ill Elderly

Cheryl Dellasega
Michael Smyer
Lori Frank
Rae Brown

According to Professor Sherry Willis' chapter in this book, a multidimensional perspective is needed to accurately assess the competence or decision-making capacity of older adults. Willis has developed a model based on this premise, which incorporates both personal and situational variables, and proposes that competence exists on a continuum and is context-specific. Willis suggests that personal factors influencing competence include health status and cognitive skills (both learned and innate), while environmental context consists of the social and cultural aspects of the person's surroundings. If there is congruence between the individual's abilities and environmental demands, Willis argues, competence will be supported (Willis, this volume).

A recent statutory development, the Patient Self-Determination Act[1] has initiated a closer examination of competence issues in a specific group of older persons, those who receive formal health care services reimbursed by Medicare and/or Medicaid. Under the provisions of this law, which was passed in 1990 and implemented in 1991, ill elderly individuals who are being admitted to the hospital for treatment must now be informed of their right to make decisions about the degree and type of future medical care they wish to receive. Implicit in the law is an expectation of competence on the part of the older patient.

Admission to the hospital for treatment of a serious illness offers a dramatic case-in-point of the environment–person tension Willis has described. Elderly persons with health impairments will be challenged cognitively and physically by the demands of the hospital environment. The competence of these individuals has not been questioned or examined in either research or regulatory efforts. This chapter reports on a preliminary investigation that used components of Willis' model to explore how competence and decision-making abilities of ill older persons could be understood from within the hospital context.

Study Description

The decision-making abilities of 60 persons aged 65 and over who were entering community hospitals for treatment of an acute illness condition were assessed. The sample consisted of 29 males and 31 females with a mean age of 73.6 years. The major diagnostic categories subjects were being treated for included circulatory (i.e., cardiovascular), respiratory, and genitourinary (55%) disorders (see Table 3.3).

Instruments used to measure decision-making abilities were the Hopemont Competency Assessment Inventory (HCAI) (Edelstein, Nygren, Northrop, Staats, & Pool, 1993), and the Understanding of Treatment Disclosures (UTD) (Grisso & Appelbaum, 1992). Selected, medically relevant items from the Everyday Problems Test (EPT) (Willis & Marsiske, 1993) provided a measure of functional abilities, and the Mini-Mental State Exam (MMSE) (Folstein, Folstein, & McHugh, 1975) was a referent for mental status. For a brief description of these measures, see Figure 3.8.

TABLE 3.3 Sample Demographics

	N=60	Percentage
Age		
Mean	73.6	
Sex		
Male	29	48
Female	31	52
Marital status		
Married	37	62
Widowed	16	27
Divorced	1	<1
Unknown	6	1
Race		
Caucasian	5	95
African American	1	<1
Other	1	<1
Diagnosis		
Cardiovascular	13	22
Respiratory	10	17
Genitourinary	10	17
Musculoskeletal	5	8
Pain, bleeding, dehydration	5	8
Othe	17	28
Medications[a]		
Cardiovascular	59	98
Analgesics	44	73
Antibiotics	29	48
Psychoactive[b]	25	42
Antiinflammatory	20	33

[a]Based on the number of prescriptions.
[b]Sedative/hypnotics and psychotropics.

Subjects were measured within 24 hours of admission to the hospital, and again 1–9 days later. Family members who accompanied the subject to the hospital or who were identified by the subject were also contacted and interviewed using the Relative Rating Scale developed for this study (Frank & Smyer, 1992) to gather data on their perceptions of the subject's competence.

11 items
gross measure of cognitive function
time to administer: 5-10 minutes

Everyday Problem Test (EPT)
(Willis, 1992)

5 items
measure of ability related to IADLs
"cued" responses recorded
time to administer: approximately 10 minutes

Understanding of Treatment Disclosure (UTD)
(Grisso & Appelbaum, 1992)

2 components: uninterrupted disclosure and element disclosure
measures ability to manipulate and recall information
time to administer: approximately 5-10 minutes

Hopemont Capacity Assessment Inventory (HCAI)
(Edelstein, 1992)

23 items
measures ability to understand medical information
in scenario format
time to administer: approximately 10 minutes

Relative Rating Scale
(Frank & Smyer, 1992)

33 items
measures relatives' perceptions of subject's function
time: approximately 5 minutes

Figure 3.8.   Mini-Mental state exam. From Folstein, Folstein, & McHugh, 1975.

The findings reported here relate to assessment of competence from the perspective of Willis' model. In particular, those results which describe the older adult's overall performance on study measures and ability to receive and process information from within the hospital context and while acutely ill will be presented.

Background

The Patient Self-Determination Act (PSDA),[1] part of the Omnibus Budget Reconciliation Act of 1990 (OBRA, 1990), was implemented by federal mandate on December 1, 1991. The act requires that all Medicare and Medicaid health providers (including hospitals, nursing homes, hospices, home health agencies, preferred provider organizations, and health maintenance organizations) provide patients with information about their legal rights regarding medical treatment decisions (American Bar Association [ABA], 1991). Specifically, patients are to be informed about their right to accept or refuse treatment and their right to establish advance directives (such as living wills or health care powers of attorney) in accordance with state law. For a summary of the PSDA statutory requirements, see Figure 3.9.

The intent of the PSDA was to encourage forethought and documentation about treatment choices. Implementation of the statute varies from state to state and thus the information given to patients is often state-specific (Teno, Sabatino, Parisier, Rouse, & Lynn, 1993).

Information on self-determination is to be provided at the time of admission to the institution, or upon enrollment in a health plan. In addition, the health care provider must make a note in the patient's medical record about whether or not the patient has issued an advance directive.

In 1988, Kapp questioned whether the effects of "illness and institutionalization" limited the ability of elderly nursing home residents to make choices (p. 669). In 1991, the PSDA was implemented without an answer to this question. Consequently, older persons entering hospitals or nursing homes must be given information about self-determination, and may even be encouraged to take action on it. No one really knows if they are competent to perform such a task at this point in time.

Willis' discussion of factors that determine competence are particularly relevant for acutely ill elders in the post-PSDA era. First, older adults constitute the majority of the hospital population, and are the group primarily affected by this act. Second, both intrapersonal conditions, such as physical illness, and environmental factors, such as the hospital atmosphere, will have a direct impact on an elder's cognitive function in this situation. A single criterion, such as medical diagnosis or age, will not provide a true picture of the decision-making capacity of these individuals. Therefore, determination of competence, which includes the ability to make decisions in natural contexts (Willis, 1993), must be based on multidimensional evaluation of mental and physical function.

Effective December 1, 1991, OBRA, 1990 requires hospitals, nursing facilities, home health agencies, hospice programs, certain HMOs and other prepaid organizations participating in Medicare and Medicaid to:

1. Establish written policies and procedures for implementing patients' rights to make decisions concerning their medical care.
2. Provide all adult patients written information on (i) their rights under state law (whether statutory or decisional law) to make decisions concerning their medical care, including the right to execute an advance directive, and (ii) the provider's policies to implement those rights.
3. Document in the patient's medical record whether or not the patient has an advance directive.
4. Comply with state law requirements for advance directives.
5. Provide for education of staff and the community on advance directives.

Figure 3.9.   Statutory requirements regarding advanced medical directives.

INTRAPERSONAL CONSIDERATIONS IN APPLYING THE COMPETENCE MODEL TO ACUTELY ILL ELDERS

Acute Illness

Many age-related changes lead older adults to respond to acute illness differently than their younger counterparts. A reduced ability to tolerate and adapt to severe physiologic stress leads to longer recovery times, and more complex hospital stays (Murray et al., 1993). While ill, many elderly patients suffer even greater declines in functional status than their younger counterparts and require longer lengths of stay for treatment of the same condition (Inouye et al., 1993).

More germane to competency considerations, delirium, a transient and potentially reversible alteration in mental status, affects 30%–50% of all older hospital patients (Foreman, 1992; Levkoff, Cleary, Liptzin, & Evans, 1991). A prominent clinical feature of delirium is the fluctuation of symptoms, which may create the very "window of lucidity" (p. 15) referred to by the American Bar Association in their translation of the PSDA for clinicians (ABA, 1991).

A. Reduced ability to maintain attention to external stimuli (e.g., questions must be repeated because attention wanders and patient is unable to appropriately shift attention to new external stimuli).

B. Disorganized thinking, as indicated by rambling, irrelevant, or incoherent speech.

C. At least two of the following:
   (1) reduced level of consciousness, e.g., keeping awake during examination;
   (2) perceptual disturbance: misinterpretations, illusions, or hallucinations;
   (3) disturbance of sleep-wakefulness cycle with insomnia, or hallucinations;
   (4) increased or decreased psychomotor activity;
   (5) disorientation to time, place, or person;
   (6) memory impairment, e.g., inability to learn new material, such as the names of several unrelated objects after 5 minutes, or to remember past events, such as history of current episode of illness.

D. Clinical features develop over a short period of time (usually hours to days) and tend to fluctuate over the course of a day.

E. Either (1) or (2):
   (1) evidence from the history, physical examination or laboratory tests, of a specific organic factor (or factors) judged to be etiologically related to the disturbance;
   (2) in the absence of such evidence, an etiologic organic factor can be presumed if the disturbance cannot be accounted for by any nonorganic mental disorder, e.g., manic episode accounting for agitation and sleep disturbance.

Figure 3.10. Delirium as specified in the DSM-III-R.

Many studies have documented the multiple adverse consequences of this condition, and recently Francis, Martin, & Kapoor (1990) questioned whether delirious hospitalized elders are ever able to return to their premorbid level of function. In looking at the DSM-IIIR criteria for delirium (Figure 3.10), it is clear that persons with this condition are not prepared to make major treatment decisions.

While the MMSE is not a measure of delirium, it does give a reliable indication of cognitive abilities. In our subjects, the mean score on the

MMSE was quite high (26.7, s.d. +3.2), but does not rule out the presence of delirium, which can be very transient. The MMSE scores suggest that at the time of admission these patients had cognitive abilities which were relatively intact. It should be noted, however, that patients who were medically unstable were automatically excluded from participation.

Scores on the other instruments were below available normative data. Compared to an unimpaired elderly sample (Willis & Marsiske, 1993), our subjects performed poorly on the EPT. Percent correct scores on the easy and medium EPT items ranged from 60% to 93%; scores on the difficult items ranged from 40% to 73%. In contrast, Willis' subjects were able to correctly answer over 90% of the easy items, over 80% of the medium items, and over 70% of the difficult items.

Normative scores for the UTD are based on a sample that excluded subjects over age 65 (T. Grisso, personal communication, 1993). Our subjects scored below the controls for all portions of the UTD: 4.9 versus 6.6 for the uninterrupted portion; 7.0 versus 8.3 for the element disclosure recall portion; and 6.7 versus 8.7 for the element disclosure recognition portion.[2] The absence of normative data for subjects over 65 makes comparisons difficult, however.

Pharmacology

In addition to various treatments that may be prescribed to address the elder's acute condition while she or he is hospitalized, it is likely that numerous medications will be ordered. The iatrogenic effects of pharmacotherapy on older patients are well known, and have the potential to adversely influence cognitive abilities (Spore, Horgas, Smyer, & Marks, 1992).

In our study, medication data were available for 40 (67%) of the subjects. An average of 6.1 medications were ordered per patient, with a range of 0–14. When broken down into regularly scheduled and *pro re nata* (as necessary) prescriptions, an average of 4.8 (range 0–6) and 1.6 (0–8) medications were ordered, respectively. Total number of medications (both regularly scheduled and prn) was negatively correlated with MMSE score ($r=-.452$, $p=-.004$), Hopemont score ($r=-.453$, $p=-.007$), relative rating score ($r=-.594$, $p=-.054$), and the EPT ($r=-.309$, $p=.056$).

We also identified subjects who had received a psychoactive medication (i.e., sedative/hypnotic or psychotropic), and compared performance for these subjects with the other subjects who did not receive such drugs. Subjects on psychoactive medications had significantly lower MMSE scores ($t = -2.3$, $p < -.05$), and were taking more medications on average (9.8 versus 4.6, $p < .05$) than the other subjects.

Adverse effects of medications on the functional and cognitive mental faculties of older persons have been described previously (Magaziner, Cadigan, Fedder, & Hebel, 1989; Smyer & Downs, in press). This is a relevant issue here, particularly for the 13 patients who received psychotropic agents.

Summary: Intrapersonal Considerations

Considering choices and making decisions are important components of competency. Willis and Schaie (1993) have identified the intraindividual conditions needed for engaging in everyday decision making, which include not only knowledge and understanding, but appropriate mental skills.

For the acutely ill in our study, the decision-making process related to PDSA would involve receiving and processing information about advance directives. To carry out this process successfully, individuals would need to have intact higher level mental abilities, an adequate knowledge base about advance directives and self-determination, an understanding of their current circumstances, and recognition of personal beliefs, values, and preferences. Finally, the elder would need to be able to integrate all the previous dimensions.

The presence of physical illness, with or without delirium, in conjunction with multiple medications and other treatments, can cause an older adult to experience temporary or permanent incapacities which limit the ability to make decisions. These conditions can also, in turn, influence the elder's response to environmental demands, ultimately affecting competence.

ENVIRONMENTAL CONSIDERATIONS IN APPLYING THE COMPETENCE MODEL TO ACUTELY ILL ELDERS

According to Willis, the external environment is composed of situations to which an elderly person must respond (Willis, 1993). She suggests that we know little about dimensions of the environment that foster or inhibit competency for older persons. In this study the influence of the physical and social environmental context on individual competence is an important consideration.

The Physical Hospital Environment

Although hospitals are meant to provide a therapeutic environment, they are, in fact, dangerous places for the elderly. Falls, incontinence, and cognitive impairment are more frequent in the older patient, and often lead to serious consequences (Hogue, 1992; Wyman, 1992; Foreman, 1992). In their replication study of adverse outcomes for hospitalized elders, Foreman, Theis, & Anderson (1993) documented that these events occurred for over half of their subjects.

Willis and others discuss the role of environmental complexity in cognitive performance. For example, the structure of an individual's environment will influence competence (Willis, 1993; Grisso, 1986); consequently, functional behavior will vary across environments. The hospital environment, which is unfamiliar and places many external demands on residents, has the potential to exert a profound negative effect on older patients. Initiation of hospitalization is likely to present the older adult with substantial environmental complexity.

Lawton's model of environmental press (Lawton & Nahemow, 1973) suggests that environmental demands directly and indirectly influence individual functioning. In addition to very real physical hazards confronting the elderly hospital patient, demands for cooperation and compliance while in residence may exceed his or her fragile personal resources. Consequently, the ability to make even the simplest decisions or process basic information can be overshadowed by the elder's need to respond to and cope with an intense, unfamiliar environment in an atmosphere of crisis (LaPuma, Orentlicher, & Moss, 1991). The artificial nature of the hospital environment also makes it difficult to determine if an elder's function on any given day represents a true picture of underlying premorbid abilities.

Health Care Providers

In the hospital setting, health care providers are an important aspect of the physical and social environment, and their role in fostering the functional and cognitive abilities of older patients can be profound. However, Willis has pointed out that little is known about criteria employed by professionals to make judgments about an elder's capabilities in the clinical setting. Previous studies (Dellasega, 1992; Palmateer & McCartney, 1985) have demonstrated that both nurses and physicians may be unaware of the true mental abilities of ill elderly persons, an ignorance which could lead to inappropriate interactions.

As part of our study procedures, we asked the hospital nurses to give permission for the initial contact between the research assistant and potential subject. The nursing profession has a long history of nurturing and protecting patients, and we found that this orientation often influenced their perceptions of a patient's ability to participate in our research. More than one research assistant (who were all nursing students) was told by a nurse that a particular elder would probably not be interested or able to participate, only to discover the opposite was true.

Although we did not collect any data on these nursing evaluations, the perceptions of key health care professionals about an elder's cognitive and functional abilities should be explored further, as should the subsequent care these individuals provide. "Sheltering" an elderly patient from additional environmental demands may be beneficial; underestimating his or her abilities may not.

Recent discussions suggest that there may be greater involvement of health care professionals in making judgments about the decision-making abilities of older persons in the future (Moreno, 1993), further escalating the need for investigation in this area. Even if the role of professionals does not increase in this regard, Kapp (1988) has pointed out that families and health care providers are already making many decisions for older persons before the legal system becomes involved.

Families

Another unexplored aspect of the social environment is the elder's family. Family members are an important part of the decision-making process for most older adults in any circumstance. Even when elderly individuals make their own decisions, family members are often intimately involved in the deliberations (Teno et al., 1993). However, little is known about the criteria or processes relatives use in assisting with or making major treatment decisions, such as those emerging from the PSDA.

As a part of our study, we attempted to gather information from

family members on their perceptions of the older adult who was participating in our research. Using a self-rated, forced choice questionnaire
we asked one relative, identified either on the patient's chart or by the
patient, to rate the patient's competence in a variety of activities derived
from Willis' identified essential IADLs. Although our sample size was
limited ($N=17$), it revealed that family members did have accurate perceptions about the decision-making abilities of their older relative, with
significant positive correlations reported between their ratings and the
MMSE ($r=.60$, $p < .05$), the HCAI ($r=.65$, $p < .05$), and the EPT
($r=.53$, $p < .05$). Relative ratings also correlated positively and significantly with the recognition component of the UTD ($r=.50$, $p < .05$).

Information

In 1992, the PSDA directly affected all older adults entering institutions
such as hospitals and nursing homes[3] the very individuals who comprised
our study sample. Since the law requires that patients be given information about their right to make treatment decisions, it was relevant for us
to explore how this process was implemented in the study sites. The
format for presenting information to ill elders influences their subsequent
ability to receive and process it (McGuire, 1993). We were particularly
interested in exploring how acutely ill elders responded to environmental
input, so we examined this issue using two different strategies. First,
we looked at the format of PSDA information presented to patients on
admission to the test site hospitals, and then we examined the ability of
subjects to process different information formats as contained in the
UTD.

We discovered that, in the hospitals used for data collection, information about the PSDA was routinely given at the time of admission.
The format of the information was all written, with verbal elaboration
provided only if the patient requested it. The printed materials consisted
of a total of nine different documents which contained textual information
describing the PSDA. Graphics were used minimally, and individual
documents were several pages long. Sample forms of advanced directives
were included with these materials. The information distributed to these
patients was almost always prepackaged and developed by professional
organizations concerned with legal matters.

A computer analysis using the program, *Rightwriter*, of the content of all documents given to patients revealed that the readability level of the materials was 12th grade. The strength index, an overall measure of effectiveness, was .14 (highest possible score is 1.0) and resulted from a writing style that depended on passive voice, lengthy, wordy sentences, unfamiliar words, abbreviations, and slang. A list of 186 difficult words was generated.

Additional analysis of the written patient information by a literacy expert revealed that many other format-related and presentation problems existed, such as: small type, insufficient white space and graphics, too much detail and complexity per page, and too many concepts covered per page. The expert concluded: "Based on my review, neither the older adult patients to whom the information is targeted nor their caregivers (spouses, children, etc.) will be very successful in understanding the materials." (B. Van Horn, personal communication, 1993).

The second strategy used to explore how information may be received and processed was administration of the UTD. This instrument gives the subject information about treatment decisions in contrasting formats. In the *uninterrupted disclosure condition*, the subject reads along as five paragraphs about ischemic heart disease are read aloud, and is then asked to recall and paraphrase information from the passage. In the *element disclosure condition*, the subject is read one paragraph at a time, and asked to immediately recall and paraphrase. The element disclosure condition also contains a recognition task in which, following reading of the target paragraph, the subject is asked to indicate whether four sentences, which are read aloud one at a time, contain the same information as the paragraph.

The element disclosure portion makes fewer demands on memory, and thus the expectation is that the scores on this portion will be higher. This was, in fact, the case with our sample. Most of our subjects (73%) performed better on the recall task in the element disclosure portion than on the uninterrupted disclosure portion ($p < .05$). Within the element disclosure section, performance on the recognition task was the same or higher than performance on the recall task for nearly half of the subjects (49%). This response pattern differed from the performance of younger adult subjects on these tasks, for whom the mean recognition score is higher than the mean recall score.

Summary: Environmental Considerations

Although the hospital environment did not seem to exert a negative influence on the decision-making abilities of our subjects, we lack prehospital comparison data which might have explained this finding. We also do not know the extent to which environmental supports were more or less available for patients being admitted to our study hospitals, but it is apparent that our subjects were functioning at a fairly high level.

From this perspective, Willis' question about the contribution and influence of people who shape the enviromental context to enhance or inhibit competence is important to consider. We did not collect data on the health care professionals' opinions of our subjects' cognitive and functional abilities. However, family members seemed to have good understanding of their relative's capabilities. The degree to which these members then buffered the elder from stressful demands of the hospital environment or supported their current abilities is not known.

Our study suggests that the ability of ill, older persons to receive and process input from the environment may be enhanced by providing information in small segments and soliciting frequent recall. One-to-one verbal interaction, although more costly, may be easier for ill elders to receive and process than written information, and should be explored further.

METHODOLOGIC ISSUES

Several methodologic issues arose in the course of our study which are relevant to the assessment of competence. These related to both the acute care setting and the subjects themselves.

Research involving hospitalized patients can be difficult for many reasons unrelated to the study's design or procedures. The major obstacle confronting us as investigators was the fact that our potential subjects were acutely ill, and may have declined to participate in data collection sessions for this reason. In fact, the most common reason given for nonparticipation was "I'm too tired." It was ironic that researchers were expected to solicit the interest and voluntary cooperation of potential subjects; these same individuals are automatically confronted with information on the PSDA, whether they wish to receive it or not.

Overall, our response rate was 30%, which, although low, is acceptable when considering the group under study. It was not surprising to find that those persons who agreed to be part of the investigation had MMSE scores which were actually quite high, and of a limited range.

Rather, this result suggests that an elite group exists even within the ill elderly. A larger, more representative sample, if possible to obtain, would most likely reveal a wider range of ability levels.

The high MMSE scores ($M=26.7$) achieved by subjects in this study, in combination with lower scores on tests of higher order cognitive skills, is consistent with previous studies. That is, the MMSE was able to screen gross cognitive function, but did not pinpoint specific deficits. Specifically, our study suggests that the MMSE does not capture cognitive domains that support functional competence.

Other difficulties associated with assessing acutely ill elders was the need to work around the complex hospital routine that was often "procedure dense" and left patients with little free time. This routine was often so exhausting for patients that they preferred to spend their "down time" resting, rather than participating in a complex research study. This situation became especially problematic when subjects were approached again a few days after admission and asked to complete the same instruments a second time. Consequently, relatively few subjects (47%) participated in both phases of data collection.

SELF-DETERMINATION AND HOSPITALIZED ELDERS

Willis & Schaie (1993) believe that a hierarchy of abilities exists in relation to competency. At the point of the pyramid, higher order cognitive tasks, such as processing information and making decisions, may be envisioned. Considering medical treatment options and issuing advance directives are good examples of higher order tasks. The well elderly person is likely to find this type of decision-making challenging, while for those who are impaired by illness and situated in an unfamiliar environment it may be impossible. Accurate determinations of whether this capacity exists requires more time and professional expertise than is likely to be available during the hospital admission process.

Although the subjects in this study scored well on the MMSE, indicating a fairly high level of baseline cognitive and functional ability, they were less consistent on more sensitive measures of decision-making abilities, such as the UTD. Our observations also suggest that functional status, that is, ability to respond to written materials evoking IADL tasks, may not tap the same dimension of cognition as complex decision-making choices about treatment alternatives.

In addition to objective measures of function such as the EPT, special strategies for assessing the ability of ill elders to receive and process information and make decisions across time and in different contexts must be developed and put to use. Willis has described the changing nature of competence, and points out that cognitive and functional abilities fluctuate across time and environments; she notes that follow-up assessments are therefore crucial for proper guardianship management. Our data suggest that assessment of decisional capacity could also be improved by repeated assessment. Since physical illness and/or delirium can lead an individual to appear incompetent while hospitalized, a measure of pre-illness function, if available, is also likely to provide more accurate information on the elder's true abilities. Willis' model provides a framework for comprehensively assessing personal and contextual variables that have the potential to influence competence. Consideration of the congruence between the individual's internal resources and the environment's external demands provides a more dynamic understanding of competence than solitary criterion measures such as age or function.

The competence model developed by Willis also provides direction for future research efforts in this area. Methods for assessing environmental characteristics which enhance or detract from the elder's inherent abilities during hospitalization is one such issue. Another potential research topic is a description of the health care providers' and family members' roles in promoting competence. Likewise, alternative methods for providing information in accordance with the PSDA requirements should be evaluated.

CONCLUSIONS

The effects of both illness and iatrogenesis can challenge the cognitive and functional abilities of older adults. A resulting state of impairment can be temporary, with full resolution occurring when the patient recovers from the acute illness. These circumstances make it particularly important to consider the influence of intraindividual factors on the ability of hospitalized elders to engage in receiving and processing information.

Physical and psychosocial aspects of the acute care environment also have the potential to contribute to or detract from an elder's ability to carry out essential and complex activities. Sensory overload and relocation stress may reduce capacity, while relief from pain and distress and relinquishing oneself to the care of another may enhance it.

Although competence theoretically is assumed for all adults, in the absence of a definitive legal determination of incompetence, this assumption is often violated in practice for the elderly in treatment settings; concerned others make decisions for them. Therefore, the presence of surrogate decision makers and their perceptions and attitudes about an elder's competence is another important aspect of an acutely ill elder's environment. Although family members are usually implicitly accepted as surrogate decision makers in health care settings (Kapp, 1992; p. 33), little attention has been paid to their perceptions about an ill elder's abilities.

Health care providers are also a component of the acute care environment with great impact on the behavioral competence of elderly patients (Baltes & Wahl, 1992). If providers accurately evaluate an elder's abilities and structure their interventions accordingly, a supportive and therapeutic environment can be created. However, if professionals are inaccurate in their judgments, they may directly or indirectly influence the elder's performance by excluding him or her from decision making, or presenting information in a form that is difficult, if not impossible, to process.

Determining the competence of physically ill elders who are hospitalized for treatment of an acute condition is a challenging task for both clinicians and researchers. These individuals can be considered cognitively challenged, but in ways that differ from the normal aging individual or persons with chronic forms of cognitive impairment.

At the same time, hospitalized older adults are the very group of individuals the PSDA will affect the most. The law mandates that all adults entering the hospital setting must, at minimum, receive information about advance directives. Our study suggests that for the acutely ill older adult, current implementation of the requirement uses what may be the worst possible strategy for implementing the spirit of this legislation.

NOTES

1. Patient Self-Determination Act, Omnibus Budject Reconciliation Act of 1990, Pub. L. No. 101–508 §4206, 4751.

2. Our scoring for one of the five element disclosure recognition questions differed slightly from that used by the instrument's authors; this difference may therefore be slightly exaggerated as a result.
3. Federal Register. (1992). Rules and regulations 57 (45). Mar 6: 8194–8204.

REFERENCES

Baltes, M., & Wahl, H. W. (1992). The dependency-support script in institutions: Generalization to community settings. *The Gerontologist, 7*, 409–418.

American Bar Association (1991). *Patient self-determination act: State law guide*. Washington, DC: American Bar Association Commission on Legal Problems of the Elderly.

Dellasega, C. (1992). Home health nurses' assessments of cognition. *Applied Nursing Research, 5*(3), 127–133.

Edelstein, B., Nygren M., Northrop, L. E., Staats, N., & Pool, D. (1993, August). *Assessment of capacity to make medical and financial decisions*. Paper presented at the 101st annual convention of the American Psychological Association, Toronto, Canada.

Folstein, M., Folstein, S., & McHugh, P. (1975). Mini-Mental State: A practical method for grading the cognitive state of patients for the clinician. *Journal of Psychiatric Research, 12*, 189–198.

Foreman, M. (1992). Acute confusional states in the hospitalized elderly. In S. Funk, E. Tornquist, M. Champagne, and R. Wiese (Eds.), *Key aspects of elder care* (pp. 262–277). New York: Springer Publishing Co.

Foreman, M., Theis, S., & Anderson, M. (1993). Adverse events in the hospitalized elderly. *Clinical Nursing Research, 2*, 360–370.

Francis, J., Martin, D., & Kapoor, W. (1990). A prospective study of delirium in hospitalized elderly. *Journal of the American Medical Society, 263*, 1097–1101.

Frank, L., & Smyer, M. (1992). *Relative rating scale*. Unpublished questionnaire.

Grisso, T. (1986). *Evaluating competencies: Forensic assessments and instruments*. New York: Plenum.

Grisso, T., & Applebaum, P.S. (1992). Understanding of treatment disclosure. Worcester, MA: University of Massachusetts Department of Psychiatry.

Hogue, C. (1992). Managing falls: The current basis for practice. In S. Funk, E. Tornquist, M. Champagne, & R. Wiese, (Eds.), *Key aspects of elder care* (pp. 41–57). New York: Springer Publishing Co.

Inouye, S., Wagner, D., Acampora, D., Horwitz, R., Cooney, L., Hurst, L.,

& Tinetti, M. (1993). A predictive index for functional decline in hospitalized elderly medical patients. *Journal of General Internal Medicine, 8*, 645–652.

Kapp, M. B. (1988). Decision making by and for nursing home residents. A legal view. *Clinics in Geriatric Medicine, 4*, 667–679.

Kapp, M. (1992). Geriatrics and the law: Patient rights and professional responsibilities, (2nd ed.). New York: Springer Publishing Co.

LaPuma, J., Orentlicher, D., & Moss, R.J. (1991). Advance directives on admission: Clinical implications and analysis of the Patient Self Determination Act of 1990. *Journal of the American Medical Association, 266*, 402–405.

Lawton, M. P., & Nahemow, L. (1973). Ecology and the aging process in C. Eisdorfer & M. Lawton (eds.), *The psychology of adult development and aging*. Washington, DC: American Psychological Association.

Levkoff, S., Cleary, P., Liptzin, B., & Evans, D. (1991). Epidemiology of delirium: An overview of research issues and findings. *International Psychogeriatrics, 3*(2), 103–113.

Magaziner, J., Cadigan, D., Fedder, D., & Hebel, J. R., (1989). Medication use and functional decline among community-dwelling older women. *Journal of Aging and Health, 1*, 470–484.

McGuire, L. (1993, November). Doctor's orders: *Adults' one month retention of medical information*. Paper presented at the 46th Annual Meeting of the Gerontological Society of America, New Orleans, LA.

Moreno, J. (1993, January–February). Who's to choose? Surrogate decision-making in New York State. *Hastings Center Report, 23*, 5–11.

Murray, A., Levkoff, S., Wetle, T., Beckett, L., Cleary, P., Schor, J., Liptzin, L., Rowe, J., & Evans, D. (1993). Acute delirium and functional decline in the hospitalized elderly patient. *Journal of Gerontology, 48*(5), M181–M186.

Palmateer, L., & McCartney, J. (1985). Do nurses know when patients have cognitive deficits? *Journal of Gerontological Nursing, 11*(2), 6–16.

Rightwriter. (1990). Macintosh Versin 3.1. Sarasota, FL: Rightsoft Inc. (Computer program).

Smyer, M. A., & Downs, M. G. (in press). Psychopharmacology: An essential element in educating clinical psychologists for working with older adults. In B. Knight, L. Teri, J. Santos, and P. Wohlford (Eds.), *Applying geropsychology to services for older adults: Implications for training and practice*. Washington, DC: American Psychological Association.

Spore, D., Horgas, A., Smyer, M., & Marks, L. (1992). The relationship of antipsychotic drug use, behavior, and diagnoses among nursing home residents. *Journal of Aging & Health, 4*, 514–535.

Teno, J. M., Sabatino, C., Parisier, L., Rouse, F., & Lynn, J. (1993). The impact of the Patient Self-Determination Act's requirement that states describe law concerning patients' rights. *The Journal of Law, Medicine & Ethics, 21*(1), 102–108.

Willis, S., & Marsiske, M. (1993). *Everyday Problems Test manual.* University Park, PA: Pennsylvania State University.

Willis, S., & Schaie, W. (1993). Everyday cognition: Taxonomic and methodological considerations. In J. M. Puckett & H. W. Reese (Eds.) *Lifespan developmental psychology: Mechanisms of everyday cognition.* Hillsdale, NJ: Erlbaum.

Wyman, J. (1992). Managing incontinence: The current bases for practice. In S. Funk, E. Tornquist, M. Champagne, & R. Wiese (Eds.), *Key aspects of elder care* (pp. 135–154). NY: Springer Publishing Co.

Older Adults' Decision-Making
and the Law - Smyer, M.,
Schaie, W. & Kapp, M, (eds)
Springer Pub. Co. NYC, NY
1996.

CHAPTER 4

Resolving Ethical Dilemmas Arising from Diminished Decision-Making Capacity of the Elderly

Elias S. Cohen

E thical issues in the context of old age have been the subject of systematic inquiry only recently. In one of the earliest articles in the gerontological literature, Warren Reich drew attention to the special dilemmas confronting investigators conducting research involving elderly human subjects (Reich, 1978). At that time, he addressed problems arising in anti-aging research, health problems which render the elderly vulnerable to excessive selection as research subjects, issues of competence and voluntary consent by the elderly, problems arising from surrogate decision making, and special issues for research on the institutionalized elderly.

Since then there has been a spate of books and a growing literature addressing various ethical issues concerning old age and old people (e.g., "Aging and disabilities," 1992; Kapp, Pies, & Doudera, 1985; Lynn,

1986; Callahan, 1987; "Autonomy and long term care," 1988; Homer & Holstein, 1990). However, the literature is sparse in terms of applied ethics and techniques of ethical analysis in the resolution of ethical dilemmas.

Fletcher, Quist and Jonsen (1989) viewed ethics consultation more in the context of conflict negotiation and resolution than in a context of dilemma resolution (see also Moody, 1988). Relatively little help was offered by way of a protocol or set of protocols which might assist the practitioner confronting bona fide ethical dilemmas.

More useful, albeit in a narrower substantive context (not specifically addressing old age) is Walton's (1983) volume of case studies involving withdrawal of life support. Of particular interest are his discussion of ethical theory and his presentation of case studies complete with both medical records and the ethical conflicts and dilemmas presented. This chapter hopes to offer some modest suggestions to assist ethical analysis of ethical dilemmas. It also seeks to sharpen the focus on *ethical*, as opposed to other, issues.

SOME INTRODUCTORY CONSIDERATIONS

Ethical Issues Distinguished

Resolving ethical dilemmas requires that we understand (a) the nature of ethical issues, (b) how to distinguish ethical problems and analysis from legal issues and analytical methods, (c) the environment—social, physical, economic and temporal—in which the dilemmas arise, and (d) the elements of ethical analysis that assist in arriving at resolution of ethical dilemmas.

Ethical issues are those which concern what *ought* to be done in certain circumstances. Legal issues are those which concern what *must* be done. "Must" always carries the implication that, ultimately, the police power of the state can be invoked. One wag has suggested that all taxes are collected at the point of a gun. I *ought* to tell the truth to my children, my colleagues, my relatives, and even to strangers in a bar (or a senior citizens center). I *must* tell the truth when under oath in court, when engaging in certain sales, when labeling foods, drugs, and devices, that is, when society has declared through a law-making process that I must do so or suffer the consequences, which can be enforced by the police.

The line between legal and ethical obligations is not always immediately apparent. A few examples may illustrate the point:

- There is an ethical obligation by professional providers to provide care and treatment (medical, social, and/or psychological) to the ill and disabled in accordance with the state of the art and congruent with the extension and/or maintenance of maximum autonomy for the patient/client. This is an obligation quite different from the practical limits on the duty of care owed by practitioners to their patients/clients imposed by statute or the law of negligence.

- There is a moral obligation on the part of guardians, conservators, or other fiduciaries responsible for the estate of an incompetent (or incapacitated) person to protect, maintain, maximize and access the inchoate estate.[1] There is no legal obligation imposed upon attorneys, guardians, or conservators charged with managing estates, or providing counsel to competent individuals for that matter, to assure that everything is done to protect, maintain, maximize and access the inchoate estate.[2]

- For service providers and advocates, there is a moral obligation to engage the most creative and effective use of any and all legitimate tools to secure benefits and services for individuals and groups they represent and who may be eligible for such benefits and services. These tools might include techniques of litigation, public exposure, negotiation, and education of clients in techniques of self-help. There is no legal obligation to undertake such efforts.

- There are ethical obligations of scholars and teachers to pursue and explore the validity and rationality of what may be generally accepted principles and assumptions such as the "least restrictive alternative" (as opposed to the "most liberating alternative") or the notion that refusal to consent to medical treatment raises the rebuttable presumption of incompetence or incapacity while consent never raises the presumption.

- Finally, in the context of this volume, it is necessary to raise questions about the moral obligations of guardians and conservators (even beyond those set forth in the discussion about inchoate estates). There is a moral obligation, I would suggest, for guardians and conservators to maximize the exercise of autonomy of incompetent or incapacitated persons—an arena in which law has little to say or offer until there is the imposition of physical restraints on liberty, imprisonment, or deprivation of due process. Yet, there is little in the literature or in practice that speaks to this kind of moral obligation.

The distinction between legal obligations and ethical obligations is important because there is very considerable confusion about it. So much of the *sturm und drang* over "death with dignity," "pulling the plug," and surrogate decision making is a discussion about what the law is or is not, and what some people would like the law to be or not to be. In fact, most of what is referred to so-called ethics committees involves explorations of what legal obligations may govern rather than what the moral obligations are and how those may be effected. This is no less true in the legal profession than in society in general. What is referred to as legal ethics is actually the study of how the disciplinary codes of bar associations are applied. In point of fact, breaches of the disciplinary codes can result in disbarment and suspension from the practice of law, sanctions which can and will be enforced by the police power of the state. Virtually all continuing legal education on legal ethics is continuing education in what the boundaries of legal requirements are in the practice of law.

Furthermore, there is widespread confusion, which carries over into practice, over what constitutes obedience to law. Is it sufficient to secure an advance directive (or a consent to perform surgery or other treatments) on a written document in order to meet requirements of the law governing advance directives or informed consent? Is it ethical to secure these instruments in the manner in which they are secured in 98% of the hospitals and long-term care facilities in the United States? Are these documents sufficient to rely upon in the event of legal challenge? Is it ethical to rely upon and to proceed on the basis of a document secured—in the customary fashion—by the admitting clerk?

Over the ages there have developed ethical principles which offer powerful guidelines to the conduct of human activity. These principles have gained their currency through the refinements and analyses of philosophers, divines, scholars, lawyers, writers, judges, common folk, politicians, scientists, and poets. The principles have always been the forerunners of the great civil rights documents of the ages—ancient and modern (Cohen, 1992). This is true whether we discuss truth telling, respect for persons, beneficence or nonmaleficence, just distribution, or any other ethical principles.

Ethical dilemmas arise when two or more principles are in conflict, and when there is no method or procedure in place that yields a clear declaration of legal rights to resolve the conflict. When they do arise, it is necessary to proceed as systematically as one would in seeking resolution of a legal conflict.

Systematic approaches, however, do not mean we must confine ourselves to the same rules of resolution. For the most part, legal conflict is resolved on a binary basis—people are guilty or innocent, sane or insane, competent or incompetent (even in jurisdictions which permit parsing a person's capacity into segments). The law does not deal well with issues at the margins. It relies heavily upon formalisms and documents. Cases proceed burdened with rebuttable presumptions or absolute presumptions (like the legal incompetence of a four-year-old). As we shall see later, resolution of ethical problems proceeds somewhat differently albeit, one hopes, no less rigorously.

Ethical Considerations in Singling Out the Elderly

When we single out groups for special treatment, positive or negative, ethical antennae tingle. To what extent are we verging on the edge of paternalism (Cohen, 1985)? Protective legislation, for example, for women, may be ostensibly beneficent, but may also be disrespectful of female persons (*Muller v. Oregon*, 1908) or may unjustifiably burden male persons. The history of protective legislation for women includes attacks using both principles (i.e., respect for persons and just distribution). In the case of people of color, once regarded as capable of being property available for sale or trade, it was ethical arguments of respect for persons which joined the debate ultimately resolved in war. Similar questions of respect and just distribution are raised when the elderly are singled out.

What about the distinction drawn between the elderly and the rest of the population? There are, of course, all sorts of legal distinctions drawn—pro and con—ranging from senior citizen discounts and special prices, to special tax treatment, and, from time to time, outright discrimination on the basis of age (although less and less than formerly). However, it is in the "ought" area that we should explore the ethical rectitude of special attention to the elderly. How long do you think we might get away with a session entitled "Resolving Ethical Dilemmas Arising from the Diminished Decision-Making Capacity of Women", or "of Negroes", or "of Indians"?

Why single out the elderly at all? Are the ethical and legal problems of diminished decision-making capacity of the elderly different from those of other adults? Or does the fact of higher incidence rates of dementia justify singling out the elderly from others? And if so, will ethical analysis support the conclusion?

I raise the issue not to criticize, for I have done as much and worse in papers, speeches, and other utterances. I raise it, rather, to illustrate the care we must take in the exercise of beneficent scholarship, service, lawyering and citizenship.

Etiology Makes a Difference

With the issue of distinguishing the elderly from others still in mind, it may be useful to consider how diminished decision-making capacity arises in the elderly. In no particular order of importance we list the following:

- cerebral vascular accidents (stroke)
- dementia (reversible and irreversible)
- depression
- head trauma
- intracranial tumors
- mental illnesses of various types
- mental retardation
- multiple infarct
- nutritional and metabolic disorders

All of the above are cited as possible causes of dementia (Office of Technology Assessment, 1987). Diminished capacity, on the other hand, which include full-blown dementias (or pseudodementias), is a broader term. In addition, diminished capacity may reflect:

- congenital developmental disability

- insufficient understanding or comprehension because of language, background, experience, or medical naivete
- physical weariness or exhaustion
- prejudice about the disease, treatment, or prognosis
- personality factors, such as submissiveness, insecurity, pugnacity, animosity, dependency, and others

Etiology may make a difference in assessing a given situation. Reversibility of a condition, time required for adjustment or treatment, and even time for diagnosis may vary with the basis of the diminished capacity, as we shall see as we look at some cases.

SOME ETHICAL DILEMMAS

Example 1. Prior to or just at the time of admission to a long-term care facility, Mary Jones executed an advance directive which set forth in some specificity what procedures she wanted done or withheld under certain circumstances. Now, nine years after the execution of the advance directive some of those circumstances have arisen. What ought her caregivers (or agent) to do relative to those nine-year-old instructions?

Example 2. Same facts as above, but during the last month Ms. Jones has been hospitalized. At times she has been stuporous and unclear while at other times she has been reasonably well oriented to time, place, and person. She has seemed to change her mind concerning treatment at least three times during this hospital stay. Given these circumstances, what ought the caregivers/agent to do?

Example 3. Same facts as in the example above, except that some of the expressed wishes are very consistent with the advance directives, although a few are not. In fact, the patient's actions relative to treatment, medications, and taking nourishment appear to be contrary to her verbal expressions, which are consistent with the directive. What then? Imagine a variation in which communication disabilities are involved. Then there would be no verbal confirmation, only actions that seem to contradict the advance directive. What now?

Example 4. The resident of a nursing home has slipped into a state of nonresponsiveness to voice, although there is some response to touch. Six months earlier the patient had a jejunostomy tube inserted for feeding. There is no advance directive and nobody in the family can recall ever having had a direct conversation with the patient about matters concerning advance directives. The nursing staff turns to the family for direction. The family members (and for that matter, the patient) had no agreement on their religious beliefs. If anything, there is conflict. How does the staff get direction?

Example 5. The patient has just been told that she has lymphoma. She responds clearly that she wants no treatment. "After all," she says, "when you have cancer, it's all over." She then proceeds to recite a list of friends and family who have died from cancer over the last 22 years. She wants nothing to do with any explanations, conferences with oncologists, physicians, nurses, or social workers on this topic. In fact, there is some reason to believe that the prognosis is good, provided treatment is initiated. What ought the physician or staff do? Should ethical considerations be different if the cancer is metastasized and the patient insists upon a full range of treatments, CAT scans, MRI exams, biopsies, and other procedures when the medical judgment is that such treatment and/or diagnosis is futile? Is good or poor judgment a measure of undiminished or diminished capacity?

Example 6. The 78-year-old patient has suffered a cerebrovascular accident (CVA) with a residual hemiplegia. Prior to the CVA, the patient was an active gardener, but not necessarily athletic. Prognosis for independent living is good, provided that the patient proceeds with rehabilitation therapy, including serious efforts to learn the techniques of independent living. Widowed, the patient has one adult child in the same city and two who live in different towns 250 and 300 miles away. Over the lifetime, the patient has suffered three or four bouts of major depression with good recovery following each. Now the patient gives good evidence of another episode. Although reasonably oriented to person and place, orientation in time seems to be a problem, as does memory. In any event, the patient is listless, almost mute, uninterested in treatment or rehabilitative therapy, probably legally competent, and unwilling to provide consent to treatment and/or therapy. What does the hospital staff do in this situation? What do relevant caregivers do: in a rehabilitation facility? a nursing home? in the patient's daughter's home 300 miles away? To whom does an agency, physician, or home health care provider respond? How far does one go in treating the depression? How heavy-handed do caregivers become?

What are the ethical dimensions of delay? How long can we avoid respecting the patient's wishes while we seek to "educate" the patient to better understand the likelihood of returning to active life in spite of hemiplegia?

RESOLVING ETHICAL DILEMMAS

The resolution of ethical dilemmas requires the creation of protocols that include the following elements:

1. powerful fact gathering with particular attention to decisional versus executional autonomy;
2. knowledge of preferences, values, and perceptions of parties expressing an interest;
3. clear articulation of competing interests—including the interests of advocates;
4. a projection of outcomes from alternative courses of action;
5. alternative characterizations of the problem;
6. analysis: deliberate assessment of how the facts, values, and interests reflect ethical principles such as beneficence/nonmaleficence, distributive justice, respect for persons, and truth telling.

The logic of ethical analysis is not the logic of mathematical algorithms, which inevitably yield certain results. Rather, it is a dialectical form of the logic, with dialog leading to a synthesis of ideas.

As in legal analysis, although in far less structured a way, ethical analysts have to sort out which facts are relevant and which are not; whose interests are at stake, and what the stakes are; how the interests will be affected by particular courses of action, and how the application of ethical principles affects the choices made by parties with relevant interests.

When we encounter ethical dilemmas, the typical approach, more often than not, is informal rather than formal—ethics committees notwithstanding. It is the exception, rather than the rule for anyone to attempt an "ethical brief." And on those occasions when some dialog occurs, it is, more often than not, concerned with the legal issues of what is permitted and what is forbidden under the law as it is currently expressed and understood.

Essential elements of a protocol for resolution of ethical dilemmas are suggested under the headings that follow.

Fact Gathering

As in the assessment of legal disputes, systematic fact gathering is crucial. The facts that are collected, however, may be somewhat different from what we might collect in the course of exploring a legal problem. In any situation, fact gathering includes the following:
- statement of the current issue—consent, advance directive, measures of legal competence, eligibility for service or benefits, etc.
- facts related to health status, intellectual functioning, physical capabilities, facts relating to danger to self or others, current living situation, social engagement, and behavior
- facts setting forth the parties involved and at interest
- facts which led to the apparent ethical dilemma
- history of behaviors and intellectual positions over the adult lifetime reflecting values, or positions on issues relevant to the current dilemma

Knowledge of Preferences, Values and Perceptions of All Parties

Probing preferences, values and perceptions requires something different from collecting facts. Finding out what people believe, what people hold dear, their notions of justice and fairness, and how they may have operationalized those notions during the lifetime yields understanding about how people exercise autonomy, and measure their relationships and their self value.

Articulation of Competing Interests

Systematic identification and statement of competing interests is not to favor one or the other party. Rather, it is to recognize that interests may be different and that pursuing different interests can lead to different results. Understanding that there may be different interests makes it possible to explore alternative outcomes. *Interest analysis* begins with taking the facts about who has an interest in the situation and stating as precisely as possible what that interest is or might be. This permits us to weigh interests of parties against each other in terms of ethical principles. The interest analysis necessarily pursues various outcomes for parties with different interests when projected outcomes are set out. Sometimes, interest analysis points up *legal* obligations that short circuit the ethical dialog.

Projection of Alternative Outcomes

Related to fact gathering, but "softer," is the process of prognostication—a careful statement based upon the best information available about what happens in the future if this or that course of action (including inaction) is pursued. For purposes of assisting resolution, it is also necessary to indicate how reliable the prognostication is in the given case. Playing out the "what if" game is essential to the dialectic of ethical analysis. All of the foregoing permits the analyst to test the result of alternative pursuits against ethical principles. Presumably, careful weighing of those results can lead the analyst to the "least worst" or "most best" resolution of the dilemma.

Characterization of the Dilemma

At the point at which we have set forth the facts, the prognoses, and the interests, we can begin to characterize the dilemma in terms of the ethical principles that appear to be in conflict. Is this a case of conflict between respect for persons and just distribution, or between truth telling and beneficence, or any other set of conflicts? We must try to articulate what appears to be maleficent, or how burdens and benefits are distributed, so that we can attempt to weigh the importance of each.

Assessment of how Facts, Values and Interests Reflect Principles

This step forces us to seek agreement among those confronting the dilemma about the weights we are assigning. Are we able to sort out our personal prejudices and preference and distinguish them from what we believe to be the relevant consensus about what is consistent with the principles?

From a procedural point of view, what is necessary to maintain pressure to move toward conclusions and answers to our questions is the presence of a wise interlocutor, who can narrow the issues and move the dialectical discourse to the highest level of synthesis available at the time. And, I suspect, it is also necessary to understand when it may be appropriate to muddle through and avoid imputing clarity when, in fact, clarity may not exist.

Following the procedure will not produce satisfactory resolution in every situation any more than legal analysis and procedure produce satisfactory resolution of legal conflict in every situation. What it will do, however, is assure that hard questions have been addressed systematically by taking into account the relevant factors involved in seeking resolution. That, of course, is a moral imperative imposed upon all of us who undertake to help people in need of help.

NOTES

1. Inchoate estate is a term that defines the capital value of benefits to which an individual may become eligible at some future time, or for which he/she may be eligible under certain conditions. For example, an individual may be eligible for Medicaid benefits on the basis of income but ineligible because of ownership of nonresident property or other assets which exceed regulatory limits. If the Medicaid benefits, purchased on the open health insurance market, would cost $2,000/

year, capitalizing that cost at 6% would suggest an inchoate capital account (estate) of $33,000. Examining the panoply of benefits which a poor person (however that may be defined in law covering health care, social services, nutrition programs, income maintenance, rehabilitation, etc.) and capitalizing the value of those benefits yields a figure (admittedly a legal fiction) which might be termed the inchoate estate. This inchoate estate deserves as much protection as an estate in which an individual has an unfettered and unconditional ownership interest.

2. An analog following the same reasoning suggests a moral obligation on the part of public social service and income maintenance administrators, supervisors, and workers to aggressively seek out and assist all eligibles for health, welfare, and income benefits to secure the benefits for which they are eligible.

REFERENCES

Aging and disabilities: Seeking common ground. (1992). *Generations, 16*, 1.

Autonomy and long term care. (1988). *The Gerontologist, 28* (Suppl.), 3.

Callahan, D. (1987). *Setting limits*. New York: Simon and Schuster.

Cohen, E. S. (1985). Autonomy and paternalism: Two goals in conflict. *Law, Medicine and Health Care, 13*(4), 145–150.

Cohen, E. S. (1992). What is independence? *Generations, 16*, 1, 49–52.

Fletcher, J. C., Quist, N., & Jonsen, A. R. (Eds.), (1989). *Ethics consultation in health care*. Ann Arbor, MI: Health Administration Press.

Homer, P., & Holstein, M. (Eds.). (1990). *A good old age?* New York: Simon and Schuster.

Kapp, M. B., Pies, H. E., & Doudera, A. E. (Eds.). (1985). *Legal and ethical aspects of health care for the elderly*. Ann Arbor, MI: Health Administration Press.

Lynn, J. (Ed.). (1986). *By no extraordinary means*. Bloomington: Indiana University Press.

Moody, H. (1988). From informed consent to negotiated consent. *The Gerontologist, 28*, (Suppl.), 64–70.

Muller v. Oregon, 208 U.S. 412 (1908).

Office of Technology Assessment (1987). *Losing a million minds*. Washington, DC: U.S. Government Printing Office.

Reich, W. T. (1978). Ethical issues related to research involving elderly subjects. *The Gerontologist, 18*, 326–337.

Walton, D. N. (1983). *Ethics of withdrawal of life-support systems*. Westport, CN: Greenwood.

Commentary: The Role of Values in Influencing Ethical, Legal, and Policy Decisions

Gene Cohen

Elias Cohen's chapter on "Resolving Ethical Dilemmas Arising from Diminished Decision-Making Capacity of the Elderly" delineates several key points and perspectives. His differentiation of ethical issues (what ought to be done) from legal issues (what must be done) is useful and important. He reminds us that the line between ethical and legal issues is not always apparent, and later he emphasizes the critical role of powerful fact finding and knowledge in resolving ethical dilemmas. What should also be recognized is the key role of values—not only in blurring the line between ethical and legal issues, but in influencing both ethical deliberations and legal/policy developments. Here, too, the absence of adequate fact finding and knowledge can adversely affect formulations and conclusions to the disadvantage of older persons, their families, and society alike.

Particularly during difficult economic times, values are challenged or enter into flux. Increased media portrayals of older persons as "greedy geezers'' or burdens for society reflect such stirring, as do references to intergenerational conflict which depict older adults creating problems and resentment in younger persons. We/they portrayals of the young versus the old in this regard are curious indeed—especially since the elderly are one minority group everyone aspires to join, given the alternatives. Contrary to mischievous and exaggerated descriptions of a fundamental and growing tension between the different age groups, research on families reveals that younger family members remain strongly committed to helping older loved ones achieve or maintain well being (U.S. Congress, Senate Special Committee on Aging, 1991).

False analogies or misinformed perspectives often pop up in discussions about what society ought to consider in the realm of personal as well as societal policy options. One such example is the suggestion that contemporary society might learn from ancient societies or less advanced species that purportedly exercised "benign neglect" toward older members who became too frail or dependent. But let⁴s look at more recent data on the Neanderthals—long regarded as one of the most "brutish" of early hominid-like species. Findings from anthropological research on fossil bone discoveries have revealed a significant number of Neanderthal bones and skeletons showing signs of severe impairment, such as withered arms, healed but incapacitated broken bones, tooth loss, and sever osteoarthritis. Only care by young Neanderthals could have enabled such older members to stay alive to the point of such incapacitation. More fundamentally, it means that a significant number of Neanderthals were allowed and helped to reach old age. Were they not assisted by younger members of their tribes, they would have succumbed much earlier to a hostile environment, dying much sooner from the complications of frailty. Their frailty made them dependent, again suggesting support beyond tolerance from their community (Diamond, 1989). Hence, one of the most "brutish" of species was supportive and protective of its frail, dependent older members; the old of their community were valued.

Back to the present: Myth and misinformation today center around supposedly staggering costs that older persons incur from purportedly heroic interventions to save them at the end of life (Cohen, 1994a; Cohen, 1994b). These myths and data distortions confound legal and policy debates and confuse ethical deliberations.

LAST-YEAR-OF-LIFE MEDICAL COSTS
IN THE CARE OF THE ELDERLY

The characterization suggests that with increasing age persons incur greater and greater medical costs in their last year of life. Such views feed into debates on whether or not to ration treatment based on a certain cutoff age. But a major confounding factor is at work here—namely, last-year-of-life medical costs in general are confounded with last-year-of-life medical costs for the elderly. In fact, the major categories of medical costs on which we typically focus—hospital costs and physician costs—exhibit steep declines in the over-80 age group as compared to those aged 65–79, as well as those under age 65 (Scitovsky, 1989). Scitovsky found that hospital costs in those over age 80 in their last year of life were less than half of those for the other age groups, while hospital costs for the 65–79 age group were similar to those under age 65. Where costs go up are in the nursing home and home health categories–the low-tech or no-tech care categories, in contrast to the heroic interventions arena. Even when combining acute medical care costs and nursing home costs, the bill is not higher for the last year of life in those over age 80 than for the younger age groups. Note, too, that census data reveal that in 1989 there were 34% more deaths in the under-65 age group than in those over age 85 (Taeuber, 1992).

HEROIC, HIGH-TECH, FUTILE INTERVENTIONS
FOR THE OLD-OLD

Individual anecdotes are too often amplified as if they represent a population group in the aggregate. In other words, misinforming media portrayals of individual cases of an older person in a largely vegetative state receiving aggressive, high-tech medical treatment are offered as data documenting a national trend. In the aggregate, this is a gross distortion. Scitovsky (1989) found that functional status, rather than age, influenced the aggressiveness and expense of interventions. In other words, aggressive treatment was most common among those with good functional status and a good prognosis for improvement and recovery–particularly among the young-old and those under age 65.

A related study compared health care costs for those age 65 to 74 in their last year of life with those 65 to 74 not in their last year of life; costs for the former were 285% higher than the latter (Temkin-Greener, Meiners, Petty, & Szydlowski, 1992). In marked contrast, those age 85 and older in their last year of life incurred costs only 35% higher than those the same age not in their last year of life. These data, too, illustrate that with increasing age, acute care costs associated with high tech interventions go down–not up.

More recent data also demonstrate that clinical outcome is influenced primarily by the magnitude of illness rather than by age (Chelluri, Pinsky, Donahoe, & Grenvik, 1993). Research comparing the young-old (65–74) with those 75 and older found that age made no difference in length of hospital stay, mortality at 1 year, or hospital charges. Most patients in both age groups rated their quality of life as adequate and indicated that, if necessary, they would want to receive intensive care again under the same circumstances.

DISABILITY AND AGING

Another assumption in the absence of data is that the increasing number of older persons in our society brings a comparable, if not greater, rise in the prevalence of disability. A recent analysis of data from the National Long-Term Care Surveys revealed a different finding. Between 1982 and 1989, the population age 65 and over grew by 14.7%, but during that same period the number of persons who were chronically disabled and institutionalized rose by only 9.2% (Manton, Corder, & Stallard, 1993). Such data illustrate the important difference between age and cohort factors that influence health, as new cohort groups are approaching later life with both better heath habits and higher levels of overall functioning.

Moreover, popular assumptions apart, disability is not primarily a problem of older adults; most adults living in the community with serious disability are under age 65, according to a study utilizing 20 years of Medicare and Medicaid data, which found the number of severely disabled adults aged 18 to 64 living outside institutions to be more than twice the total of all chronically ill and severely disabled persons aged 65 and older residing in nursing homes and elsewhere (Binstock, 1992; Gornick, McMillan, & Lubitz, 1993).

FEDERAL VERSUS NATIONAL
(LOCAL, STATE, AND FEDERAL TOGETHER) COSTS

Another shot from the hip that is off the mark is the criticism that so much (30%) of federal monies go to programs for the elderly. Anyone who feels compelled to make this complaint should place the issue in the right context. To focus only on federal expenditures provides an incomplete picture. The issue is not federal dollars, but national dollars; take into consideration local and state expenditures along with federal outlays. Keep in mind that the significant growth of the older population is a recent historical phenomenon. In the past, local, county, and state governments committed most of their funds to programs for children (e.g., education), to public safety (e.g., police and fire departments), and to a range of other areas (e.g., recreation) that affected younger adults much more than the elderly. By the time of the demographic revolution, these nonfederal governments across the nation had limited funds left to devote to the needs of older Americans. This left mainly the federal government as the body that could best provide the necessary new resources—the backup role being one of the traditional roles of federal agencies.

In the state of Arkansas, for example, where 15% of the population is 65 years of age and older, only about 11% of state funds (not including federal grants and reimbursements) go to the two major programs for older adults—Medicaid payments for the elderly and the Division of Aging and Adult Services. In Wisconsin, with 13.3% of its population age 65 and older, only 3.5% of state revenues are allocated to comparable budget areas. In New York and Massachusetts, which have approximately the same proportions of older persons, the percentages of state funds going to Medicaid and each state office on aging are about 8.3% and 4.8%, respectively. (All of these data were obtained via personal communications with state officials working in the area of aging and/or budget in each of the states mentioned.)

Hence, a much more accurate picture of national public expenditures for the elderly is presented when figures on state, county, and local expenditures for the elderly are provided in addition to federal outlays. Diatribes about intergenerational equity then receive an important reality check.

OLDER PERSONS—A NATIONAL RESOURCE
VERSUS BURDEN

Finally, it should be recognized that while so much discussion focuses on problems that older persons face and the costs that are incurred in dealing with these problems, the elderly are assuming a growing number of roles that reflect their contributions as a national resource. From extensive community volunteer work, to providing child care for grand-children whose working parents cannot afford hired assistance, to financial transfers to younger members in the family, older persons are playing diverse and support-giving—in contrast to support- receiving—roles. This is a characteristic of a new cohort of older adults that has emerged in American society as well as worldwide.

Older persons today are in the aggregate healthier, more affluent, and better educated that ever before. For example, consider the change in educational level in the second half of the 20th century alone. In 1950, the median number of years of school for the 65-and-older age group was 8.3—less than a high school education; by 1989, that number had risen to 12.1 years—more than a high school education (U.S. Congress, Senate Special Committee on Aging, 1991). Such changes influence the decision-making capacity of elderly individuals and the decisions that society makes about older adults. A more balanced picture of the abilities and contributions of older persons—focused beyond the problems and burdens they and their families confront—can help balance societal debates on policies that will affect the lives of older Americans. Similarly a more informed understanding of the nature, course, and costs of disease and disability in later life will reduce the risk of unfounded conclusions that can subtly influence values and, in turn, ethical dilemmas at the levels of both society and the older individual.

REFERENCES

Binstock, R. H. (1992). The oldest old and "intergenerional equity." In R. M. Suzman, D. P. Willis, & K. C. Manton (Eds.), *The oldest old* (pp. 394–417). New York: Oxford University Press.

Cohen, G. D. (1994a). Journalistic elder abuse: It⁴s time to get rid of fictions, get down to facts. *The Gerontologist, 34,* 399–401.

Cohen, G. D. (1994b). Health care at an advanced age: Myths and misinformation. *Annals of Internal Medicine, 121,* 146–47.

Diamond, J. (1989). The great leap forward. *Discover, 10,* 50–60.

Gornick, M., McMillan, A., & Lubitz, J. (1993). A longitudinal perspective on patterns of Medicare payments. *Health Affairs, 12,* 140–150.

Chelluri, L., Pinsky, M. R., Donahoe, M. P., & Grenvik, A. (1993). Long-term outcome of critically ill elderly patients requiring intensive care. *Journal of the American Medical Association, 69*(2), 3119–3123.

Manton, K. G., Corder, L. S., & Stallard, E. (1993). Estimates of changes in chronic disability and institutional incidence in the U.S. elderly population from the 1982, 1984, and 1989 National Long Term Care Survey. *Journal of Gerontology: Social Sciences, 48* (2), S153–S166.

Scitovsky, A. A. (1989). Medical care in the last twelve months of life: The relation between age, functional status, and medical care expenditures. *The Milbank Quarterly, 66*, 640–60.

Taeuber, C. M. (1992). *Sixty-Five Plus in America*. Washington, DC: U.S. Department of Commerce Bureau of the Census.

Temkin-Greener, H., Meiners, M.R., Petty, E.A., & Szydlowski, J.S. (1992). The use and cost of health services prior to death: A comparison of the Medicare-only and the Medicare-Medicaid elderly population. *Milbank Quarterly, 70*, 679–701.

U.S. Congress, Senate Special Committee on Aging, American Association of Retired Persons, Federal Council on the Aging, & U.S. Administration on Aging. (1991). *Aging America* (DHHS Publication No. FCOA 91-28001). Washington, DC: U.S. Government Printing Office.

CHAPTER 5

Alternatives to Guardianship: Enhanced Autonomy for Diminished Capacity

Marshall B. Kapp

here are an increasing number of older individuals today with some degree of mental impairment in their ability to engage in rational decision making processes and to reach and communicate autonomous, authentic choices concerning financial and personal (including medical) matters. Other chapters in this volume have dealt with the assessment and measurement of this impairment. This chapter, by contrast, is concerned with part of the "So what?" question, namely, the social strategies that must be developed and implemented to protect a person from harm without excessively intruding on his or her autonomy, once he or she has been assessed as having impaired decisional capacity. This chapter concentrates particularly on the role of service providers' perceptions about potential exposure to legal liability as a major barrier to the effective, timely development and implementation of those social strategies.

Some older persons with impaired capacity are subjected to formal guardianship or conservatorship proceedings (Hightower, Heckert, & Schmidt, 1990; Schmidt & Peters, 1987). A court officially declares the older person legally incompetent and appoints someone else as the guardian or conservator with legal authority to make decisions on behalf of the ward. Sometimes there is no meaningful choice about this course of action, because less intrusive alternatives have been tried and have failed, for example when the party in a position of trust abuses or exploits the impaired person.

A number of policy considerations, however, argue against overuse of this formal legal mechanism. Guardianships frequently are expensive, time consuming, and emotionally tumultuous; they may result in unnecessary deprivation of basic civil liberties. Yet, in many cases, they provide the ward with little meaningful protection against abuse and exploitation (American Bar Association, 1989). A much fuller exposition of the subject of guardianship is provided in Penelope Hommel's chapter in this volume.

In developing alternatives to guardianship, society must balance the ethical principles of self-determination, on one hand, and nonmaleficence (preventing self-harm) and beneficence (doing good), on the other. Optimal methods will minimize external intrusion into the individual's freedom and autonomy, while safeguarding from potential harms of impaired personal and financial decision making.

Much recent attention has been paid to exploring and developing viable alternatives to plenary (complete) guardianship of indefinite duration that strike an acceptable balance between protection and independence (Stiegel, 1992). Increasingly, the courts have relied more on these less restrictive and intrusive alternatives to guardianship for older individuals with compromised cognitive and emotional abilities. There have been no comprehensive evaluations of the effectiveness of alternatives. However, substantial anecdotal evidence suggests a serious impediment to the development and implementation of such guardianship alternatives: anxiety concerning potential exposure to legal liability in the event of harm to the older person.

This chapter reports on a recently completed project that examined the legal, administrative, and policy forces that affect development and implementation of alternatives to guardianship. Some factors encourage unduly conservative behavior in pursuing alternative-to-guardianship activities. Others discourage professionals, volunteers, and proprietary and community agencies from undertaking activities that might reduce, divert, prevent, or delay the need for formal guardianships. The principal barriers are: (a) fear of lawsuits brought by the older individual or his or her family members against the service provider and (b) difficulty in obtaining and/or affording professional liability insurance to indemnify and defend professionals, volunteers, and agencies in the event of a lawsuit questioning the appropriateness of their activities undertaken to forestall or eliminate the need for formal guardianship.

This chapter will begin with a definition of alternatives and a discussion of specific approaches—case management, adult protective services, and money management. In the second section, the powerful impact of liability perceptions on alternatives is considered. The third section places these perceptions in legal and historical context. Finally, a concluding section offers suggestions for next steps.

ALTERNATIVE-TO-GUARDIANSHIP SERVICES

As used in this chapter, *alternative-to-guardianship services* (AGSs) comprises a broad and diverse landscape. The term is widely used to represent a host of legal tools, social services, benefit programs, and residential options that enhance or maintain a cognitively or emotionally impaired older person's individual autonomy. These approaches share a common goal: to delay or avoid the deprivation of civil rights and liberties, loss of control, and financial and emotional costs associated with formal plenary guardianship. An AGS may also divert from the guardianship system older persons who do not meet the applicable legal criteria for guardianship but who might be at risk of guardianship imposition anyway if not assisted with certain aspects of living.

Guardianship alternatives can be categorized using several criteria. Factors relevant to the agent include (a) the type of sponsoring entity, (b) the qualifications, educational background, and credentials of service providers, and (c) the form of support offered by the provider. An older person or family member seeking AGSs may face a perplexing assortment of public and private sector care providers, many of whom may offer similar types of services, even though they commonly come from professions as diverse as financial planning, social work, gerontology, counseling, or nursing. Some providers are professionally licensed and credentialed and/or are members of newly emerging national or regional professional associations, while other providers work independently, without being subject to any type of licensure, supervision, or regulation. In many geographic areas, prospective clients and their families must choose from among a nonprofit agency, a proprietary business, and an individual private practitioner who offer similar specialized services for older persons and their families.

Other common distinguishing factors concern the mechanism of support: whether the alternative was (a) planned or unplanned, (b) provided by a formal or informal support system, or (c) a more or less restrictive form of legal intervention. Legal tools such as durable powers of attorney (including those specifically for health care), living wills, voluntary money management services, preselected housing options, and trust and joint property arrangements are methods by which a presently competent person can plan for potential future incapacity. On the other hand, alternatives such as representative payee arrangements, court-directed business transactions, and limited or total guardianships are proxy decision-making mechanisms that tend to occur in lieu of planning.

Volunteer services are also an integral part of many AGSs and programs. Some programs operate primarily according to a volunteer assistance model, rather than relying on a staff of paid professionals. Many (although not all) service providers report that volunteer services provide a method for serving a greater number of clients on a more individualized basis, can reduce programming costs, and may make a service attractive to potential funding sources.

A growing number of older adults, often at the recommendation of service providers, are beginning to take advantage of several techniques that can help them preserve autonomy and independence, prepare for future incapacity, and possibly delay or avoid guardianship. Examples of such techniques include case management (Rose, 1992), adult protective services (Kapp, 1983), money management, durable powers of attorney, trusts, and representative payees.

Case Management

Case management is sometimes known as "coordinated care" or "geriatric care management." If successful, case management maximizes an older person's independence and autonomy through two, related functions: comprehensive assessment of the individual's needs and coordination of services to assure the older person's highest practical level of self-sufficiency.

Eligibility criteria may vary across different types of case management providers (e.g., private fee-for-service geriatric care managers, state and federal public case management services, and nonprofit organizations). Some may give certain types of older adults priority during the application process. Others may have basic program eligibilities based on factors such as age, level of impairment, place of residence, income, or status of the elder's existing support network.

After acceptance as a client, initial screening and assessments identify the older person's medical, personal care, cognitive, psychological, financial, and social support needs. This information is used to develop a comprehensive care plan, often coordinated in conjunction with the elder's physician, outlining the recommended services required to enable the older person to live as independently, yet safely, as possible. Often, the older person's family is heavily involved in this process.

Case managers are responsible for coordinating the care plan services. Legal referrals or help in obtaining government subsidies and entitlements are a component of some coordinated care services. Information and referrals may be given for obtaining medical care and equipment, transportation, in-home care, adult day care, and community or home-delivered meal service. Case managers face challenges in finding alternative ways for older people with limited resources to access affordable services. Finally, follow-up services are normally an integral part of case management. Ongoing monitoring helps ensure the effectiveness of the care plan, as well as alerting the case manager to changes in the client's condition or family needs that might warrant care plan modifications.

Case management arrangements may be a part of a guardianship arrangement. They may also be used without a guardianship setting. Thus, case management may be an effective mechanism for delaying or avoiding formal guardianship, or it may result from or contribute to imposition of guardianship.

Adult Protective Services

Adult protective service providers may engage in a wide range of preventive, supportive, and surrogate services. This may include the coordinating and delivering of a variety of health and social services, as well as seeking appointment of a substitute who will accept some or all of the elder's decision-making authority. Vulnerable elderly people, at risk of abuse, neglect and exploitation, may be able to live independently longer with the availability of protective services such as information and referral, consultation and counseling, money management, health services, social services, personal care, and advocacy and protection. Adult protective services may also include surrogate decision-making authority via power of attorney, guardianship, and special court orders or involuntary commitment proceedings against elders who need, yet refuse to accept voluntarily, critically needed services such as property management, public assistance, nursing home placement, or other institutionalization.

Under their *parens patriae* and police powers, states may intervene on behalf of citizens who can no longer care for or protect themselves or whose conduct poses a danger to others. As noted in Sabatino (this volume), state laws vary as to when imposition of such supportive or preventive action may be warranted, even over a citizen's objections.

In the past, public attention has been given in large part to criticizing a state's choice to intervene unilaterally in the life of an objecting elder. However, criticism does not necessarily take into account the fact that, ordinarily, protective services are willingly and gratefully accepted by the older client (Kapp, 1983). Nevertheless, there is a huge practical and philosophical distinction between voluntary and involuntary adult protective services (Schmidt, 1986; Schmidt & Miller, 1984).

Unfortunately, in many instances adult protective services agencies are characterized by extremely limited resources and large caseloads shouldered by overworked staffs. Such limitations may prevent the agency from doing much for older clients beyond immediate crisis management.

Money Management and Representative Payee Services

Recent estimates conclude that between 5% and 10% of all community-based older people (65+) need some form of assistance with money management (Wilber & Buturain, 1992). Contributing factors include changes in elder's marital status and social circumstances; accidents, illnesses, and physical limitations; dementia and other mental impairments; sensory losses and impairments; and combinations of other social, physical, and psychological changes related to the aging process. In the past, family members or other caregivers, rather than social service agencies, tended to perform the daily financial tasks required by the frail elderly (White, 1989). In many cases, this pattern still occurs.

Today, however, an increasing number of nonprofit and proprietary organizations, as well as independent practitioners, offer clients some form of money management assistance on a free or a fee-for-service basis (Wilber & Buturain, 1993). Fees are usually determined by a sliding scale that is based on either the client's liquid assets and spendable income or on the value of the client's total estate and/or assets. A recent study indicates that money management services lack uniformity because they often develop in an ad hoc fashion as client needs are recognized (Wilber & Buturain, 1992). The types of financial services offered, funding sources, and staffing qualifications vary considerably, largely in response to the availability of community resources, the geographic setting, and the economic and social needs of elderly clients. Idiosyncratic historical factors in the development of a program also are important in shaping its character.

Further investigation is needed to document that daily money management actually acts as an effective diversionary, preventive, or substitutive factor for guardianship. At this point, the hypothesis about the effect of money management services in decreasing guardianship rates has not been proven conclusively. Indeed, one important study seems to point in the opposite direction (Wilber, 1991). At the very least, when money management services have been tried but prove inadequate to prevent eventual guardianship, we can be more confident that the individual really needed the guardianship, rather than an AGS alone.

LIABILITY PERCEPTIONS AND THEIR IMPACT

Fear of legal liability in the event of client harm inhibits the development and expansion of AGSs, and may exert a negative effect on guardianship services themselves. This section reports on a survey of provider and potential provider perceptions conducted as part of a Retirement Research Foundation-sponsored project (Kapp & Detzel, 1992).

In this project, an introductory letter was mailed to over 150 applicable state and federal aging-related agencies, proprietary businesses, and nonprofit organizations providing AGSs for older adults. Organizations were selected from a manual literature search for AGSs providers and a 1988 list compiled by the American Bar Association's Life Services Planning Project, which identified over 100 organizations throughout the country that provided specialized services to older persons, persons with disabilities, and families with an older or disabled dependent. Based on responses to this letter, 76 organizations were identified for a subsequent structured telephone interview. In addition, telephone interviews were conducted with key gerontologists, academics, and researchers in the field of aging. Personal, on-site interviews were conducted with more than 20 AGS providers, evaluators, planners, and funders, as well as with court officials, in four different jurisdictions.

Service Provider Liability Anxiety

Nearly all service providers (or would-be service providers) experience some degree of anxiety concerning possible legal liability. A typical comment in the study was that of the director of a midwestern statewide alliance on aging, who said that service providers in his state are "paranoid about liability. . . .In any type of service delivery, the second word out of everyone's mouth is, 'Can I get sued?'" An executive director of a senior citizen center in a western state expanded on this sentiment when explaining that there are two main hurdles to overcome in aging services: funding and liability.

A heightened level of fear of liability can result when a neighboring service provider is sued or threatened with a lawsuit. This was the case for the money management community in California, in the aftermath of the disintegration of a well-known and highly respected organization in the San Francisco area, Support Services for Elders, due to massive embezzlement by a trusted, longstanding employee.

However, in most cases, fear of liability appears to be generic and free-floating in nature. When pressed, service providers had difficulty articulating specific worries. Few were able to cite an actual case upon which they based their fears, and even fewer had been sued or personally involved in defending a legal action. According to one public guardian, "Confusion is running so high that we can't even talk about liability concerns. It is an unintelligent fear that is a cover for lack of available interventions and knowledge. . . .A general attitude exists that if we notice liability concerns, then our liability will increase."

Meeting an older client's needs often may be a very complex and challenging task. A care manager described feeling as if her job was full of "mini-minefields." Approaches to cases vary, even within the best social service system. The depth and quality of family involvement may affect choices made regarding treatment plans and care options. Different practitioners may approach a case in a different manner, thus resulting in potentially internally inconsistent practices within an agency. Services, treatment philosophies, and areas of expertise also vary from agency to agency.

In certain instances, issues may become convoluted as the interests of family members and the elder come into conflict. For example, such a problem might occur when a family caregiver who has lived with an older person faces the prospect of selling the elder's home to pay for medical or long-term care expenses. It may be in the best interest of the elder to have the home sold, but such a sale would also deprive the family member of a home.

Providers, too, can feel trapped in conflicts involving the balancing of autonomy and beneficence (Kane & Caplan, 1993). If, for example, an elderly client living alone begins to have difficulty remembering to shut off the stove, the agency may fear liability for the benevolent and protective act of unplugging the stove because the client may fall and injure herself while trying to plug it in again. Yet, on the other hand, a service provider deciding to take a stance that protects the client's autonomy and self-determination may fear liability for nonfeasance if it does nothing and the home burns down the next time that the woman forgets to turn off the stove.

Factors Contributing to Liability Anxiety

Anxiety about liability can come from many sources, some of which go beyond the realm of legal requirements and insurance-dictated practices. A majority of informants stated that the general litigious nature of today's society, plus heightened media coverage of isolated exorbitant damage awards or sensationalized accounts of alleged cases of human rights violations or malpractice by service providers, strongly influence their perceptions about potential legal liability. For some in the field, the mere prospect of facing the time, cost, and bad publicity associated with defending against a lawsuit (even a nuisance one) is nearly as inhibiting as the prospect of an actual finding of liability and awarding of damages.

Interviewees in the study indicated that they generally have no difficulty in obtaining access to legal advice. Attorneys regularly serve *pro bono* on agency boards and advisory committees. One nonprofit organization has recently hired an in-house legal counsel for technical assistance and advice. Other providers retain law firms or private practitioners, contract for legal consulting services, employ legal services developers, use the state attorney general's office as a resource, or direct questions to a local legal aid office.

Access to legal advice has both a positive and negative impact on the provider's perception concerning legal liability. A "go ahead and let them sue" mentality exists among a few providers having easy access to legal resources, particularly when legal defense is at no charge to the provider. Overall, lawyers appear to be not only helpful in solving legal issues pertaining to AGS, but equally adept at pointing those issues out— thus both enflaming and mitigating the service provider's level of liability anxiety.

Providers pointed out that increasing caseloads, declining funds, and reduced staffing play important roles in increasing anxiety about liability. Caseworkers, supervisors, and administrators are aware that decreasing personal contact with an elderly client is a by-product of an ever-increasing client caseload. This factor, when coupled with an undertrained and overworked staff, may create a high-risk situation ripe for staff's making mistakes or missing important details.

Liability perceptions also seem to hinge on the degree to which industry standards have developed, although such standards may have opposing effects. First, industry standards provide a "roadmap" for service providers to follow in many common situations. This gives the provider generalized guidelines that may help reduce liability anxiety. At the same time, however, strong industry standards also help define a legally objective measure against which the "reasonableness" of the service provider's behavior can be judged. This improves a plaintiff's chance to prove substandard care when the provider has deviated from the agreed upon measure, an essential element of any successful malpractice lawsuit.

Since many AGSs comprise a new and growing enterprise, service providers often are still unable to take advantage of established industry standards, ethical guidelines, or professional practice parameters that might assist them in determining reasonable, appropriate behavior. One provider commenting on the present lag in the broad-based acceptance and implementation of industry standards predicts, ''This is just the tip of the iceberg concerning alternative-to-guardianship liability. It is going to increase more and more as the profession defines and develops.'' Few providers, however, now understand that compliance with industry standards can supply a powerful defense to a claim of malpractice.

Another key liability anxiety factor appears to be what the provider personally has at stake. This might include the provider's reputation, business, personal assets, or career goals. The opportunity to obtain or afford adequate insurance coverage may mitigate financial concerns related to defending against many types of potential lawsuits. However, insurance coverage does not necessarily rid the provider of anxiety surrounding the possible loss of reputation or stymied career progress that may accompany charges of alleged wrongdoing.

The owner of a private case management service, whose business has been in existence for nearly seven years, summed it up: ''My fear is very real. My partners and I not only risk potentially losing our company, but our personal assets as well.'' Although the owners had run an ethical business for years, the informant described the terrifying thought that it could be destroyed almost overnight if the media obtained, augmented, and sensationalized claims of damaging or embarrassing activity. The owners would be left to deal with the aftermath of the negative press coverage and public impressions that would inevitably follow even a frivolous claim.

Finally, two interviewees believed that capable, autonomous, and informed elderly clients are better able to recognize substandard care or individual rights violations, and may therefore pose a greater risk of suing a service provider than their cognitively impaired peers. Likewise, family members, friends, or an outside advocacy network may assist in bringing legal action against service providers that abuse or exploit an elderly client. At least in some instances, it appears that consumer education and advocacy for the elderly, while playing a crucial role in protecting vulnerable older clients, may heighten provider liability anxiety by extending the provider's potential risk of exposure to legal action.

Provider Perceptions About Guardianships and Liability

A significant number of providers perceive court-approved transactions to be preferable to alternative substitute decision-making arrangements not falling under direct court supervision. Many service providers consider formal court arrangements such as guardianship or conservatorship to be safer than alternative service arrangements, particularly in high-risk situations. After handling a number of cases dealing with family infighting and potential abuse, one typical case manager concluded that her preference is always for court-appointed surrogates, instead of alternatives such as powers of attorney. This prevalent attitude creates serious implications for the autonomy of older persons, although some commentators might argue that autonomy is most fully protected against abuse and exploitation under the procedural due process model of formal guardianship.

Some of the service professionals providing either limited or plenary guardianship or conservatorship cited uneasiness over ambiguities in state guardianship or conservatorship statutes. Providers also wondered about liability associated with failure to adequately perform a statutory requirement (for example, a social worker's removing a ward from a dangerous living situation prior to obtaining, as required by state statute, court approval to change the ward's abode). Other service providers acting as financial and medical surrogate decision makers worried about liability issues that could emerge around the meaning of general statutory requirements, such as acting like a "prudent person" or in the "best interest" of the ward.

Third Party Fear of Liability

Perceived fear of liability not only impedes AGS providers and sponsors, but also deters other parties from acting on or honoring alternatives to guardianship. A number of physicians, health care facilities, and financial institutions are hesitant, or even refuse, to honor a validly drafted durable power of attorney instrument. This behavior is partly due to confusion surrounding the legal and practical ramifications of this new form of decision-making mechanism, especially in light of ambiguous state statutes. Government agencies such as the Department of Veterans Affairs and the Social Security Administration also refuse to honor powers of attorney, relying instead on representative payee programs or pushing for guardianship declarations.

Interviewees suggest that third-party reticence in honoring guardianship alternatives may serve as a smokescreen covering for other underlying problems, rather than rest on the pure liability concerns that many third parties profess. For example, some banks may be reluctant to invest the time required to determine the validity of an alternative-to-guardianship arrangement. The time, staff, and expertise required to check the documents can translate into additional costs for both the third party and the service providers, thus making it attractive to follow the "safer" route of honoring only standardized documents or formally sanctioned court relationships such as guardianships or conservatorships.

PUTTING LEGAL RISKS INTO PERSPECTIVE

To combat some of the mythology and anxiety about liability exposure that often acts as a barrier to the development and expansion of AGSs for older persons, it is important to place legal risks into some realistic perspective. This section examines litigation history and trends in this area and explicates possible defenses and positive risk management strategies.

Litigation History and Trends

No service provider wants to be sued. But substandard care, provider indifference, fraud, or blatant acts of disregard for the well-being of the elderly client may drive aggrieved clients to attorneys. Most would agree that many lawsuits emanating from such factual situations are warranted, and most reputable service providers even might encourage legal action against other service providers in these types of situations.

It is important for providers to realize that litigation against health or social service professionals or other private individuals providing alternative-to-guardianship assistance is extremely rare. Research has uncovered no published cases in which AGS providers for cognitively or emotionally impaired elderly clients were listed as defendants. However, health and social service providers working in fields outside of alternative-to-guardianship care have been sued.

These reported cases, as well as guardianship litigation, give clues about liability trends that may eventually filter down to those providing alternative-to-guardianship assistance for older clients. In most instances, these health and social service professional cases entailed allegations of flagrant disregard of the client's welfare, with reported litigation centering around issues such as sexual misconduct (*Horak v. Biris*, 1985), duty to protect clients from abuse and neglect *Jensen v. South Carolina Department of Social Services*, 1988), and firing employees for violating agency policies prohibiting personal or social relationships with clients (*Gonzales v. Palo Verde Mental Health Services*, 1989).

There are several possible reasons for the lack of lawsuits against AGS providers. Financial abuses of moderate-or low-income elderly are very infrequently detected and reported. Homebound elderly may be afraid or unable to report abuse, negligence, or exploitation if the wrongdoer plays a significant role in meeting some or all of the older person's basic needs, especially if the fulfillment of those needs helps to keep the elder out of an institution. Some elderly persons are extremely loyal to and protective of someone charged with their care. One service provider told of an older woman who was repeatedly exploited financially by another service provider in the community, but adamantly refused to take legal action for fear of getting the service provider in trouble with his supervisors.

A prospective elderly plaintiff also may encounter legal barriers to successfully pursuing a claim against a service provider. A physically, emotionally, or cognitively impaired plaintiff may not be a credible witness, especially when up against a more powerful, established community service provider. In calculating money damages, an injured retired person's retrospective and prospective lost wage amount is usually significantly lower than would be that of a younger injured or disabled worker. Other future damages also tend to be relatively low, since advanced age reduces life expectancy and thereby reduces potentially recoverable compensatory amounts. Due to these and other limitations, an elderly person may find it difficult to secure strong legal representation on a contingency fee basis.

There is speculation that this difficulty may be abating, at least for older nursing home residents who have been the victims of extreme abuse or neglect (Kapp, 1991). Some verdicts in this context in the past few years have included large awards, and the Association of Trial Lawyers of America now contains a separate subdivision for plaintiffs' attorneys who engage in tort litigation against nursing homes. This changing legal environment for older plaintiffs does not appear to have spread, though, beyond the nursing home at this point in time.

In 1987, only one case against a representative payee was referred to a United States Attorney's office for fraud prosecution, even though United States Department of Health and Human Services statistics indicate that over 4.4 million people had an appointed representative payee in that same year (Komlos-Hrobsy, 1989). Yet power of attorney, representative payee, and other fiduciary arrangements are still potentially risky to service providers because they allow a decision-making proxy to have control over an elderly client's income and assets. The danger of abuse or overreaching with vulnerable, elderly impaired clients who are dependent on the reliability, competence, and knowledge of the money controller is substantial.

Moreover, the commonly held service provider perception that guardianships are safer than alternative arrangements is also directly counter to current actual litigation trends. The mere fact of court authorization and oversight does not automatically eliminate all providers' legal concerns. In fact, quite the converse is true. Breach of fiduciary duty and misappropriation of estate funds resulted in personal liability and a recent judgment of over $177,000 against a private conservator and his wife (*Bryan v. Holzer*, 1991). Banks have become embroiled in litigation surrounding the charging of unreasonable conservatorship fees (*In re* Conservatorship of the Estate of Vaksvik, 1990) and negligence actions where a ward's funds held in trust by the bank were misappropriated by a former attorney/conservator (*Great Southern National Bank v. Mink*, 1991). Finally, service providers have been sued for initiating an involuntary temporary guardianship of an older person without sufficiently investigating the need for such action (*Goldman v. Crane*, 1989). Cases like these emphasize that service providers do not avoid liability risks by shunning less restrictive alternatives to guardianship consistent with the needs and resources of an older client.

A significant minority of service providers still engage in other expensive, peripheral tactics that actually are reactive attempts to avoid the financial and emotional costs associated with defending against lawsuits or threats of lawsuits (Kapp & Detzel, 1992). For example, some service providers report taking losses and writing off unpaid bills, even when they feel confident that they handled a client's affairs in a defensible and ethical manner, simply to silence or avoid threatening relatives who may cause legal problems. They also relate negotiating out-of-court settlements to avoid further litigation costs, even in the absence of real liability. (Such settlements are not reflected in legal databases.) In order to avoid possible liability, other providers regularly petition the court for specific orders, as a safeguard in questionable situations such as those involving ambiguous competency and medical and/or financial decision making.

These reactive responses show that although legal research found a virtual dearth of actual elder care alternative-to-guardianship litigation, service providers out in the trenches still perceive a need to take defensive postures to curb legal threats that could conceivably be brought by elderly clients and/or their family members.

Defenses and Risk Management Strategies

Many service providers are not familiar with potential legal defenses that could help mitigate some of their liability concerns. These include denial defenses ("I did not do what I am accused of doing," "What I did was not the direct cause of the injury you are claiming," or "You did not really suffer the injury you say you did") and affirmative defenses such as comparative or contributory negligence or assumption of risk on the plaintiff's part. Furthermore, many service providers are unclear as to the degree of protection afforded by state and federal sovereign, charitable, volunteer, and board immunity statutes.

Nearly all AGS providers engage in some form of deliberate risk management or use quality assurance techniques intended to mitigate liability concerns. The goals of risk management are to prevent harm and to avoid or lessen the danger of financial losses experienced by the organization as a result of legal liability. Quality assurance relates to risk management by focusing on directly assessing and improving the quality of care that the client receives from the provider. These strategies indicate a general dedication on the part of agencies and individual service providers to encourage safe actions that protect clients, staff, volunteers, and the total organization; reduce the possibility of damage or loss to real or personal property; and, ultimately, reduce the pervasive anxiety about liability that can inhibit development of new services and programs for older people or the continuation and expansion of existing services.

CONCLUSIONS

Providers of alternative-to-guardianship services, as well as the liability insurance industry, exhibit a pervasive, though largely uninformed, anxiety regarding the threat of potential liability for services delivered to elderly clients. Actual and imagined laws, voluntary professional standards, and customs have combined to inhibit many health and social service professionals, potential volunteers, governing boards, administrators of proprietary and community agencies, and insurance companies from performing or insuring activities designed to meet the needs of cognitively or emotionally impaired older persons without formal plenary guardianship.

The level of liability anxiety reported by AGS providers is significantly higher than the danger actually indicated by past litigation and insurance claims experience. Research has uncovered no reported judgments against AGS providers brought by or on behalf of older cognitively and emotionally impaired clients. However, the slow, yet steady, stream of lawsuits against guardians and health and social service professionals working in other capacities with different client populations continues.

In some ways, the accuracy of service provider and insurer perceptions is immaterial. Liability anxiety has already infiltrated service providers' business practices and has stymied providers' interaction with elderly clients and family members. Despite the lack of actual litigation, many elderly clients are being turned away because they are seen as possible legal threats to the service provider. Crucially needed services such as money management and transportation, as well as the volunteer components of some programs, are hardest hit by service providers who decide to mitigate potential losses by avoiding, eliminating, or limiting certain types of "riskier" areas of service delivery.

Many service providers are misguided in their naive assumption that guardianships are safer routes to follow than alternative arrangements. In fact, present case law thoroughly fails to support this assumption.

Liability anxiety also colors relationships between service providers and insurance carriers. Insurance premium costs remain prohibitive for some providers, and have depleted the meager financial resources of other service providers. The insurers' anxiety, reflected in a general past hesitancy to extend coverage to certain so-called high-risk service providers, today is masked behind escalating premiums appearing to have little relationship to actual litigation or claim-filing trends.

The high cost of obtaining liability insurance (a service providers' primary protection against selected risks) remains problematic, despite an insurance market that should allow service providers greater leverage in purchasing, upgrading, and renewing existing or new policies. Service providers' inability to effectively negotiate with insurers may, in part, stem from the fact that most service providers simply do not appear to understand their own insurance policy provisions, conditions, exclusions, and coverage amounts. Such lack of knowledge makes providers vulnerable and ill equipped to successfully bargain on their own behalf with insurance agents, underwriters, and carriers for favorable policy terms.

This does not mean, however, that service provider fear is totally unfounded. In theory, all service providers, employees, and volunteers remain potentially liable for negligent acts and omissions, as well as intentional misdeeds and breaches of contract. Nearly all service providers, therefore, correctly find it advantageous to use deliberate risk management strategies designed to reduce their anxiety about possible legal exposure.

Finally, service providers engage in a host of reactive techniques and defensive postures, such as writing off legitimate bills and negotiating out-of-court settlements with elderly clients and their families, even in the absence of fault. These defensive postures both contribute to, and reflect, liability anxiety and usually are counterproductive to the development and implementation of alternative modes of service delivery to the elderly.

All of these impediments, along with other legal, administrative, and policy barriers to effective service provision, must be overcome if service provider liability anxiety is to be kept in check at a more realistic level. An ambitious research, demonstration, and informational agenda to accomplish this aim is necessary. This agenda should move toward determining and replicating those societal changes (e.g., further immunity statutes, changes in insurance industry practices) and/or organizational interventions (e.g., in-service educational efforts, governing and advisory board structuring, formal risk management strategies) that are most effective in helping AGS providers and potential providers deal productively with the problem of liability anxiety. Vigorous implementation of the fruits of that agenda should, in turn, encourage service providers to remain on the forefront of designing and delivering vitally needed AGSs to older cognitively, emotionally, or physically impaired adults.

ACKNOWLEDGMENTS

This chapter is based on a project conducted under the sponsorship of the Retirement Research Foundation by the author and Joyce A. Detzel, JD, MA.

REFERENCES

American Bar Association, Commission on the Mentally Disabled and Commission on Legal Problems of the Elderly. (1989). *Guardianship: An agenda for reform*. Washington, DC: Author.

Bryan v. Holzer, 589 So.2d 648 (Miss. Sup. Ct. 1991).

Goldman v. Crane, 786 P.2d 437 (Colo. Ct. App. 1989).

Gonzales v. Palo Verde Mental Health Services, 783 P.2d 833 (Ariz. Ct. App. 1989).

Great Southern National Bank v. Mink, 590 So.2d 129 (Miss. Sup. Ct. 1991).

Hightower, D., Heckert, A., & Schmidt, W. (1990). Elderly nursing home residents' need for public guardianship services in Tennessee. *Journal of Elder Abuse and Neglect, 2*, 105–122.

Horak v. Biris, 130 Ill. App. 3d 140, 474 N.E.2d 13 (1985).

In re Conservatorship of the Estate of Vaksvik, 458 N.W.2d 339 (N.D. Sup. Ct. 1990).

Jensen v. South Carolina Department of Social Services, 297 S.C. 323, 355 S.E.2d 102 (Ct. App. 1988).]

Kane, R. A., & Caplan, A. (Eds.). (1993). *Ethical conflicts in the management of home care: The case manager's dilemma*. New York: Springer Publishing Co.

Kapp, M. (1991). Malpractice liability in long-term care: A changing environment. *Creighton Law Review, 24*, 1235–1260.

Kapp, M. (1983). Adult protective services: Convincing the patient to consent. *Law, Medicine & Health Care, 11*, 163–167, 188.

Kapp, M., & Detzel, J. (1992). *Alternatives to guardianship and the elderly: Legal liability disincentives and impediments*. Dayton, OH: Wright State University.

Komlos-Hrobsy, P. (1989). Representative payee issues in the Social Security and Supplemental Security Income programs. *Clearinghouse Review, 23*, 412–417.

Rose, S. (Ed.). (1992). *Case management and social work practice*. New York: Longman.

Schmidt, W. (1986). Adult protective services and the therapeutic state. *Law and Psychology Review, 10*, 101–121.

Schmidt, W., & Miller, K. (1984). Improving the social treatment model in protective services for the elderly: False needs in the therapeutic state. *Journal of International and Comparative Social Welfare, 1*, 90–106.

Schmidt, W., & Peters, R. (1987). Legal incompetents' need for guardians in Florida. *Bulletin of the American Academy of Psychiatry and the Law, 15*, 69–83.

Stiegel, L. (1992). *Alternatives to guardianship—Substantive training materials and module for professionals working with the elderly and persons with disabilities*. Washington, DC: American Bar Association Commission on Legal Problems of the Elderly.

White, M. (1989). *Daily money management: A brief overview*. Pasadena, CA: Huntington Memorial Hospital.

Wilber, K. (1991). Alternatives to guardianship: The role of daily money management services. *The Gerontologist, 31*, 150–155.

Wilber, K., & Buturain, L. (1992). *Daily money management: An emerging service in long term care*. Los Angeles: Andrus Gerontology Center, University of Southern California.

Wilber, K., & Buturain, L. (1993). Developing a daily money management service model: Navigating the uncharted waters of liability and viability. *Gerontologist, 33*, 687–691.

Commentary: Barriers to the Development and Use of Alternatives to Guardianship

Lori A. Stiegel

Professor Kapp's chapter on alternative-to-guardianship services (AGS) issues discusses thoroughly and well the fear of liability by service providers that impedes their development and promotion of AGS and, ultimately, the use of guardianship alternatives by older persons. Kapp identifies lack of adequate funding as the other major barrier to the development and implementation of alternative to guardianship services.

Fear of liability and inadequate funding, however, are only two of several obstacles inhibiting the widespread development and utilization of guardianship alternatives by the public. While these two barriers impede the institutional development of AGS, other obstacles suppress the public's use, and therefore its demand for formation and funding, of guardianship alternatives. These other hindrances include (a) lack of understanding of the nature and use of alternatives, (b) trepidation about and aversion to planning for possible incapacity, (c) lack of capacity to execute or benefit from guardianship alternatives, (d) gaps and failures in the alternatives themselves, (e) concerns about misuse or abuse of alternatives, and (f) third-party reluctance or refusal to follow alternatives. This chapter will discuss each of these barriers and offer some ideas for reducing them.

LACK OF UNDERSTANDING

A tremendous need exists for education of professionals and the public about alternatives to guardianship. The concept of alternatives to guardianship is relatively new to the law and is not widely understood. The use of guardianship alternatives is often still a matter of controversy among those lawyers who are aware of them; some lawyers think that guardianship should be used as a protective tool whenever someone lacks capacity, while others believe that guardianship should be used only as a last resort when alternatives are not sufficient. It is only in the past ten years, in large part due to the growth of the elderly population and the advent of the private practice of "elder law," that lawyers have been able to find and benefit from continuing legal education (CLE) programs and other training about guardianship and its alternatives. In the past four years, CLE courses and law texts addressing guardianship and alternatives have become commonplace in many jurisdictions. Nevertheless, judicial education on these topics, critical in light of rapid changes in laws, policies, and programs, has been sporadic.

Training of other professionals who work regularly with older persons and their families (e.g., health care providers, bankers, social workers, and clergy) also has been rare, although it is perceived as highly important by the network of services for the aging and by elder law practitioners. To illustrate, when the American Bar Association (ABA)

Commission on Legal Problems of the Elderly commenced its Administration on Aging-funded multidisciplinary guardianship alternatives
training project in 1989, 46 states and the District of Columbia requested
training. The training that has been conducted usually has been aimed
only at lawyers. Exceptions have been multidisciplinary in nature and
have not adequately addressed the needs and concerns of specific professions (Stiegel, 1992a).

Public education has not been widespread. Although public and private providers of legal services have educated many older persons and
persons with disabilities, very little has been done to reach out to younger
and middle-aged persons. Yet, the need to plan for possible incapacity
affects everyone. This point is illustrated by the tragic and groundbreak-
ing cases of Karen Quinlan (*In re Quinlan*, 1976) and Nancy Cruzan
(*Cruzan v. Director, Missouri Department of Health*, 1990), young
adults whose families were forced to seek authority from the courts to
make health care decisions for their daughters who had failed to make
and document any planning decisions before losing capacity.

Scenarios such as these have prompted a flurry of coverage in the
popular media about the importance of planning for possible incapacity.
Nevertheless, the information disseminated usually has been incomplete,
and often simply incorrect. For example, following the death of Hillary
Clinton's father, President and Mrs. Clinton began publicly discussing
their desire to sign living wills in order to prevent expensive end-of-life
treatment. An excellent opportunity to use the media to educate the
public about the availability of the more comprehensive and helpful
alternative of health care power of attorney and the benefits of planning
for incapacity was squandered.

AVERSION TO AND TREPIDATION ABOUT PLANNING

Education about guardianship alternatives is only the first step—an individual must be willing to use that knowledge. This means that a person
must think about what decisions he or she would want made and by
whom in the event of incapacity and then complete the necessary documents or other steps that make possible implementation of that strategy.
Yet, many seem afraid or simply unwilling to make these plans, even
those such as elder law attorneys or aging services providers who are

enlightened about the ways to plan for possible incapacity and the consequences of failing to do so.

There seem to be a variety of fears that inhibit planning. Some people are afraid that if they think about and plan for possible incapacity, that contingency will inevitably occur. (These are probably the same people who refuse to make a will because they are convinced that as soon as they sign one, they will be killed in a freak accident.) Others are intimidated by lawyers generally or by the process of finding a lawyer who is knowledgeable about these issues. Still others are afraid of what a lawyer will charge them to make plans for incapacity. Some people are afraid of hurting the feelings of those family members not selected to act as their agent in the event of incapacity. Some people are afraid of their doctor's reaction to plans for health care treatment, concerned either that the doctor will think the patient doubts his or her professional ability or that the doctor will disagree with the advance decision.

Fear is not the only reason why some people refuse to plan for possible incapacity. Some individuals just do not make plans, choosing to live life "by the seat of their pants"; others may not comprehend their human frailty and simply see no reason to plan.

How can the fear of planning and the reluctance to plan be overcome? Americans seem fairly comfortable with the concept of insurance—we have it for our health, life, home, and car—so it may help to shift the focus from "planning for incapacity" to "insuring against the loss of self-control" or "insuring against the appointment of unwanted decision makers." The ABA Commission on Legal Problems of the Elderly did just that in its award-winning legal education video package, *In Your Hands: The Tools for Preserving Personal Autonomy* (ABA, 1988). Nevertheless, enhanced educational efforts and more palatable ways of looking at these issues will never convince everyone to take advantage of the available planning tools, so we need to continue searching for ideas and services that will help people who can not or do not plan to avoid an unnecessary guardianship.

LACK OF CAPACITY TO BENEFIT
FROM GUARDIANSHIP ALTERNATIVES

An individual who is educated about guardianship alternatives and willing to plan for possible incapacity faces another stumbling block; he or she must have the mental capacity to understand and take advantage of the available tools.

As discussed in Charles Sabatino's opening chapter in this volume, the measure of capacity needed to undertake a legal transaction depends on the nature of the transaction. The legal capacity required for one to make a will is fairly low, because it is public policy to encourage the orderly transfer of property among family members and between generations. To make a will, an individual need only have a general understanding of (a) the extent of property owned and (b) the "natural objects of one's bounty" (one must be cognizant of the family members to whom people usually leave their property, although this does not mean that one must leave property to them). To make a contract, an individual must have a higher level of capacity than that required for a will. Unlike a will, which makes a gift from one person at death to another, a contract occurs when one person gives up something in order to get something from another person. The stakes are higher, so the law requires that persons entering into a contract have a more comprehensive understanding of what they are doing.

Legal commentators generally believe that a person must have sufficient capacity to contract in order to execute the legal tools that one can use to plan for possible incapacity, namely durable powers of attorney, health care powers of attorney, living wills, trusts, and joint property arrangements. That level of capacity is also required by money management programs, which generally enter into contracts for services with their clients and also often rely on a durable power of attorney or joint bank account between the client and the program. Professor Kathleen Wilber's research, discussed in the commentary that follows this one, indicates that some of the persons referred to the money management program that she studied lacked sufficient capacity to benefit from its services (Wilber, 1991).

Other guardianship alternatives that do not involve a contract or a quasi-contractual relationship have a lower standard for capacity. Actually, some degree of incapacity is required before these alternatives may be used. For example, in order to appoint a representative payee for an individual, the Social Security Administration must determine that a beneficiary is incapable of handling his or her benefits. A health care surrogate cannot act until an individual is deemed, pursuant to a procedure established by state law or specified in the proxy appointment document, to be incapable of making health care decisions. A limited guardian may be appointed by a court when a person is adjudged incapable of making some, but not all, decisions. But if a person is fully incapable of making decisions, and has not planned for that possibility by the timely naming of substitute decision makers who have ample legal authority to make all necessary decisions, then there may be no choice but to resort to full or plenary guardianship.

Because of the scarcity of education on planning for incapacity and the reluctance of people to make such plans, it is critical for professionals to be aware of these options and to make suggestions or referrals to their clients at the opportune moment. For example, whenever an individual is diagnosed with Alzheimer's disease, the physician should suggest that the patient consider medical and financial planning for incapacity. Those plans must be made while the person still has capacity; when the crisis arrives, it will be too late.

GAPS AND FAILURES IN GUARDIANSHIP ALTERNATIVES

A person who has knowledge about alternatives to guardianship and who is willing and able to take advantage of them may find that good intentions are thwarted by flaws in the alternatives themselves or by breakdowns in his or her plans.

None of the guardianship alternatives is perfect; each has significant disadvantages as well as advantages (Stiegel, 1992b). To enumerate just a few problems: durable powers of attorney and joint bank accounts grant broad authority to an agent or co-owner and may be abused. Trusts usually require a substantial amount of money to establish and may be expensive to maintain. Third parties may refuse to follow a durable power of attorney or a health care power of attorney. In addition, the Social Security Administration may not adequately screen potential representative payees before their appointment or monitor them afterwards (Komlos-Hrobsky, 1989).

Attempts commonly are made to fix these flaws. A number of states have enacted "agency bank accounts," which allow an individual to name on the account an agent who has access to the funds contained therein (e.g., Washington's Financial Institution Individual Account Deposit Act of 1981).[1] Agency bank accounts overcome some of the problems associated with joint bank accounts by restricting the agent's ownership and authority over the funds in the account. Some states have added to their durable power of attorney statutes a mandate that a third party, such as a bank, accept a durable power if it is made in accordance with the state law (e.g., see New York General Obligations Law of 1986).[2] A federal law enacted in 1990 imposed more stringent requirements on the Social Security Administration for its appointment and monitoring of representative payees.[3]

Attempts to use alternatives to guardianship can also fail because of unforeseen circumstances or inadequate planning. A durable power of attorney may prove worthless if, after the principal loses capacity to execute a new durable power, the agent becomes unable to act on the principal's behalf and the document does not name a successor agent. This can also happen with a health care power of attorney, although the more likely problem occurs when the principal fails to discuss future desired health care treatment with his or her agent, family, or health care providers. Likewise, a trust can fail if title to the relevant property is not transferred to the trust or if the trustee loses the capacity to act and the creator has not named a successor trustee and can no longer name a new trustee.

A recent trend in many laws governing guardianship alternatives has been to make it easier for individuals to execute planning devices such as durable and health care powers of attorney without employing a lawyer. There are, of course, benefits from that trend, as persons who can not or do not want to pay for a lawyer may take advantage of the available planning tools. Nonetheless, there are also disadvantages, as people may not receive adequate counseling about the risks that accompany these guardianship alternatives or the ways in which they can draft their documents to address problems and contingencies.

CONCERNS ABOUT MISUSE OR ABUSE OF ALTERNATIVES

The benefit of an alternative to guardianship is that it authorizes someone to make decisions and take actions on behalf of an individual who has lost capacity without the necessity of involving a court in the appointment of a guardian, a process which is usually expensive, time consuming, and often emotionally difficult. That benefit, however, is also a serious weakness; the lack of court involvement may make it easier to misuse or abuse the power granted.

The durable power of attorney is the alternative that seems most subject to abuse, probably because it can be used to grant broad authority with little oversight. Of course, that is precisely what makes it so useful in the first place as an alternative to guardianship. Anecdotal evidence of durable power of attorney abuse is increasing. Nevertheless, the author is aware of only one study of durable power of attorney abuse. Recently completed by two law students at Albany Law School's Government Law Center, this national study questioned approximately 7,000 lawyers, prosecutors, judges, and aging services personnel about their perceptions of and experiences with durable power of attorney abuse (Federman & Reed, 1994). Sixty-six percent of the 410 respondents from 46 states and the District of Columbia had encountered some degree of durable power of attorney abuse. Of those, 72% had encountered abuse three or more times. Despite the low response rate and the exploratory nature of the study, it suggests that abuse is occurring and that further research is necessary.

Other alternatives bear risks as well, with the level of risk depending on factors such as the amount of authority granted to a substitute decision maker and the amount of oversight by some third party. Planning documents, such as durable and health care powers of attorney and trusts, can be drafted so as to lessen the amount of risk or to enhance third-party oversight, but that may mean involving a lawyer and, thus, more expense. Also, the means by which one can lessen the risk may add to third-party reluctance to honor a planning document. While courts have always had authority to review the actions of an agent, a few states have enacted laws giving courts special authority over durable powers of attorney by allowing specified individuals to question or challenge the agent (e.g., see Missouri Durable Power of Attorney Act of 1989[4] and the Illinois Power of Attorney Act of 1987).[5] Some lawyers, aging services personnel and advocates believe that an individual with diminished capacity is always better off having a guardian appointed, in lieu of relying on an alternative, because of the court monitoring that a guardianship entails. Yet, recent studies have indicated that guardianship monitoring is not generally prevalent or, where it does take place, is insufficiently effective (Hurme, 1991). Thus, it is useful for an individual who is contemplating alternatives to guardianship but concerned about risk to learn about the oversight practices followed in whatever court might handle his or her guardianship case.

Concerns about misuse or abuse of alternatives to guardianship are valid, but they must be balanced with concerns about guardianship itself, such as the lack of due process, the statutory definition of incapacity, adequacy of monitoring, and other issues (ABA, 1989). Each individual's different needs and circumstances may necessitate the use of different planning tools or social and legal interventions.

THIRD-PARTY RELUCTANCE OR REFUSAL TO FOLLOW ALTERNATIVES

There remains a final obstacle to the use of guardianship alternatives— third-party reluctance to honor them. The problem can be traced to both the financial and health care planning tools (e.g., the durable power of attorney, the health care power of attorney, and the living will), and to the various third-party entities, including financial institutions, government agencies, schools, businesses, and health care institutions. As Professor Marshall Kapp discusses in this chapter, reluctance to follow these directives may be due in part to concerns about potential liability for relying inappropriately upon them. He also postulates that third-party hesitation may additionally stem from confusion about the law or an unwillingness to spend time assessing a document's validity. Especially with the health care power of attorney and living will, there is also the consideration of whether the third party agrees with the decision of the principal or his or her agent.

To counteract reticence to comply, state laws increasingly provide immunity from liability for a third party who follows a document executed in accordance with state law. Some laws mandate that an individual use the written form set forth in the statute in order to be assured this protection against third-party refusal; such a provision is increasingly found in states that have enacted "short form durable power of attorney" laws that make it easier for persons to execute a durable power without the services of a lawyer (see, for example, the California Uniform Statutory Short Form Power of Attorney Act of 1990).[6]

Widespread public education about these planning documents may help overcome third-party reluctance to accept them. Individuals need education not only on the benefits and disadvantages of these tools, but also on the ways to enhance their successful implementation, should that become necessary. The managers and staff of third-party entities that may be called upon to honor a planning tool also must be educated about the legality of these documents, as well as the reasons for their use, potential liability for acceptance or nonacceptance, and indicators of possible abuse.

CONCLUSIONS

Professor Kapp's research on the fear of liability that impedes the development of alternative-to-guardianship services is of critical importance to the aging network. Education about the law governing liability and about risk management techniques would likely help allay that fear. However, potential providers of alternative-to-guardianship services might be encouraged to defeat their fears, and they might find more funding enabling them to provide those services, if the public would demand available, accessible guardianship alternatives. To help raise that clamor, the public must be educated about the existing mechanisms to plan for or to respond to diminished capacity. The public must also be encouraged to overcome the common fear of planning for incapacity. In addition, to enable the public to use alternatives more easily and with less abuse, problems with existing alternatives should be corrected through legislative action and creative new alternatives should be developed.

NOTES

1. Wash. Rev. Code Ann. §§30.22.010-.900 (West 1986 & Supp. 1991).
2. N.Y. Gen. Oblig. §5-1504 (McKinney 1989).
3. Omnibus Budget Reconciliation Act of 1990, §5105, 42 U.S.C. §§ 405 and 1302 (1990).
4. Mo. Ann. Stat. §404.727(1) (West 1990).
5. Ill. Ann. Stat. §802-10 (West Supp. 1990).
6. Cal. Civil Code §§2475-2484 (West Supp. 1991).

REFERENCES

American Bar Association Commission on Legal Problems of the Elderly. (1989). *Guardianship: An agenda for reform.* Washington, DC: Author.

American Bar Association Commission on Legal Problems of the Elderly. (1988). *In your hands: The tools for preserving personal autonomy* [Videotape]. Washington, DC: Producer.

Cruzan v. Director, Missouri Department of Health, 497 U.S. 261, 110 S. Ct. 2841 (1990).

Federman, J., & Reed, M. (1994). *Abuse and the durable power of attorney.* Albany, NY: Albany Law School Government Law Center.

Hurme, S. (1991). *Steps to enhance guardianship monitoring.* Washington, DC: American Bar Association Commission on Mental and Physical Disability Law.

In re Quinlan, 70 N.J. 10, 355 A.2d 647, cert. denied sub nom. Garger v. New Jersey, 429 U.S. 922, 50 L.Ed.2d 289, 97 S.Ct. 319 (1976).

Komlos-Hrobsky, P. (1989). Representative payee issues in the Social Security and Supplemental Security Income programs. *Clearinghouse Review, 23,* 412–417.

Stiegel, L. (1992a). *Alternatives to guardianship: Development of a training module for professionals working with the elderly* (Final Report, Administration on Aging Grant No. 90-AT-0415). Washington, DC: American Bar Association Commission on Legal Problems of the Elderly.

Stiegel, L. (1992b). *Alternatives to guardianship: Substantive training materials and module for professionals working with the elderly and persons with disabilities.* Washington, DC: American Bar Association Commission on Legal Problems of the Elderly.

Wilber, K. H. (1991). Alternatives to conservatorship: The role of daily money management. *The Gerontologist, 31,* 150–155.

Commentary: Alternatives to Guardianship Revisited: What's Risk Got to Do with It?

Kathleen H. Wilber

Professor Kapp's chapter on alternatives to guardianship addresses two profoundly different issues. First, it explores the role of alternatives in delaying or diverting elders from guardianship. Second, it examines barriers and impediments to the development of alternative-to-guardianship services (AGSs). This commentary focuses primarily on the first area, the effectiveness of identified alternatives as diversions or substitutes for guardianship. Before turning to that discussion, however, it is important to note that, by examining the myths and erroneous assumptions that underlie liability anxiety, Professor Kapp makes an enormously important contribution to the field. Impaired elders are likely to benefit from information that puts legal risks into perspective, thereby encouraging the expansion of protective services such as money management. In addition, the information provided in the chapter should serve as a disincentive for those seeking to initiate petitions for formal guardianship on the assumption that such action will reduce their liability.

The liability discussion relates to at least three other issues that I believe are important to underscore. First, there is anecdotal evidence that at least some administrators of aging services take a "don't ask, don't tell" stance with their staff in terms of financial management assistance. Some service providers readily acknowledge that they operate an informal money management service by managing their clients' checkbooks "out of their desk drawer" at the office (Wilber & Buturain, 1992). Using this approach, bills are paid and clients' accounts are balanced in the absence of a formal program. The assumption seems to be, "no program, no risk." Professor Kapp points to inadequate information about AGSs and lack of industry standards and practice guidelines as contributing to the problem. Perhaps greater recognition of the problems inherent in surreptitious money management practices will encourage the development of explicit daily money management (DMM) services that include provisions for administrative controls, accountability, and employee oversight.

The second issue, addressed briefly in the chapter, is the threat of reputational liability. Experience suggests that providers fear scandal as much as they fear legal liability. Because threats to one's reputation are difficult to protect against and sometimes impossible to diffuse, fear of negative media exposure fosters a conservative approach to service development. I do not have answers for those who wish to address this problem, but I believe that it needs to be more widely recognized.

The final issue is the extent to which institutional requirements drive guardianship decisions. Professor Kapp suggests that third-party resistance to honoring advance directives by health providers, financial institutions, and government agencies results in overuse of legal guardianship. In the battle to cut down on inappropriate guardianship placement, reducing these institutional requirements represents a promising area of intervention.

Turning now to the discussion of AGSs to substitute for guardianship, Professor Kapp clearly identifies the crux of the problem: how to design interventions that balance competing concerns of freedom and safety for persons who have questionable capacity to make "reasoned" decisions. Put another way, what interventions best preserve autonomy and self-determination while protecting vulnerable and dependent adults from harm?

For most, particularly those who have struggled to reform guardianship and ensure that it is used only as an option of last resort, AGSs offer an ideal solution. By offering dependent persons approaches that satisfy both freedom and safety, alternatives imply the best of both worlds. Given such a well-regarded and potentially happy outcome, it is with some discomfort that I take up the mantle of the wet blanket. Unfortunately, evaluations of money management and case management service interventions suggest that such interventions do not necessarily replace guardianship, at least not indefinitely.

The AGS discussion is framed in terms of identifying and employing alternatives to guardianship. The question that is left unanswered here and elsewhere in the literature is the proper role of an alternative. Can an alternative be used in place of a more restrictive option through processes that Schmidt (1990) differentiates as substitution (e.g., DMM is used instead of guardianship) or diversion (if an elder uses DMM, she will not need guardianship now or in the future)? Or, do alternatives represent substantively different options in which the goal is to select the approach that best addresses the needs and preferences of the client? This is a subtle distinction but an important one for the debate on guardianship alternatives. The first definition is implied in the chapter and in the gerontological literature in general. I will argue that, so far, the available empirical evidence does not support this interpretation.

EVALUATIVE RESEARCH ON GUARDIANSHIP ALTERNATIVES

Despite the enthusiastic promotion of guardianship alternatives, only two known evaluations have focused on substitution/diversion. The first, the Guardianship Diversion Project (GDP) (Wilber, 1991), was a study of community-residing persons 60 years of age and older living in Los Angeles County, who had been referred for protective services to the Office of the Public Guardian (OPG) or Adult Protective Services (APS). Approximately two thirds of the subjects had come to these protective services of last resort through the social service delivery system.

After being screened into the study, subjects ($N=63$) were randomly assigned to a DMM intervention or to a control group. Participants in the DMM intervention group were offered the opportunity to take part in a range of services including bill paying, budgeting, accounting, banking, benefits counseling and advocacy, medical insurance billing, credit management, powers of attorney, and representative payee. Control group subjects received customary assessment and follow-up by the Los Angeles County OPG.

Characteristics of the sample indicated high levels of impairment and vulnerability. The majority (66%) showed some degree of cognitive impairment. Referrals indicated that many subjects suffered from severe problems including unsafe living conditions (48%), neglect (46%), and financial exploitation (43%). Although in some instances the problems subjects faced could be addressed with financial management assistance, many were related to other areas such as health and safety concerns, personal care, social support, and mental health.

Follow-up after 12 months indicated a somewhat higher rate of conservatorship (the term used in California for guardianship of persons 18 years of age and older) among those in the intervention group (32.5% versus 17.4%). However, the difference was not statistically significant.

Professor Kapp notes that services such as case management may result in the identification of elders who need guardianship. This casefinding function was an unintended outcome of the GDP study. Ironically, members of the intervention team found themselves in the uncomfortable position of advocating for conservatorship placement. Over the course of the evaluation, 5 treatment subjects were referred back to the OPG for conservatorship after providers became convinced that their problems were beyond the scope of the DMM service intervention.

Although the outcome of the GDP was not what was anticipated, the study suggested several important lessons about the role of daily money management as a substitute for guardianship. One interpretation was that both the timing and the structure of the intervention were problematical. As Schmidt (1990) notes, the low probability of guardianship placement in the general population complicates efforts to study alternatives. Therefore, an important feature of the GDP study was to target persons at high risk of conservatorship by intercepting them at the point of referral to the guardianship system. In analyzing the data, however, it became clear that the crisis situation of some of the participants made substitution unlikely. This interpretation suggests that a preventive model directed toward diverting cognitively impaired elders before they encounter such severe problems as foreclosure, hazardous health conditions or financial exploitation would be more effective.

In addition to the timing of the intervention, concerns were raised about the intervention model itself, which was a freestanding DMM service developed specifically for the study. The multiple problems that characterized many of the participants suggested that a more comprehensive case management service delivery model was needed.

To address these issues, a second study was undertaken (Wilber, 1995) with participants from four existing DMM services in Los Angeles County. These DMM service providers had a proven track record and were committed to the values of client self-determination and community care. Each of the DMM services was embedded in a case management agency, allowing providers to address clients with many needs in a comprehensive fashion. The disadvantage of this design was, of course, that participants could not be randomized to treatment and control conditions. Therefore, the control group from the GDP study was used as a comparison group for the second study.

Treatment subjects for the second study were 36 community-residing participants 60 years of age or older. Treatment and comparison group subjects were similar on demographic characteristics (age, living arrangement, income) and assessment scores (cognition, functional impairment, depression, social support, and service utilization). The second sample had fewer men; however, gender was unrelated to the outcome of guardianship placement. Although their incomes were comparable, the DMM treatment group scored significantly lower on the financial hardship scale (based on problems in purchasing necessary goods and services and the extent that the subject worries about finances). The improved purchasing power and reduced financial anxiety of treatment subjects were believed to be a result of participation in the DMM/case management intervention and therefore part of what was being evaluated.

As with the GDP study, findings at the 12-month follow-up did not support a DMM/case management service diversion effect. Rates of conservatorship placement were 16.7% for the intervention group and 17.4% for the comparison group. The second study also was similar to the earlier study in that cognitive impairment, high risk behavior, and severe health and mental health problems were characteristic of those who were placed under conservatorship.

In interpreting these studies, it is important to note that states differ with respect to the extent that they champion less restrictive decision making options. In California, where both studies were conducted, the probate code discourages inappropriate conservatorship placement through "numerous enlightened" legislative reforms (Heller, 1989,

p. 2–34). In addition, Los Angeles County OPG appears to support the legal presumption of erring on the side of competence. For example, Steinberg (1985) noted that only 10% of the cases referred to the Los Angeles County OPG resulted in conservatorship. Therefore, it could be argued that an evaluation based in Los Angeles does not address the question that Professor Kapp and others (e.g., Schmidt, 1990; Stiegel, 1992) raise concerning substitution in jurisdictions where guardianship is used inappropriately (e.g., as a default bill-paying service) for persons who do meet the legal presumption of competence. In such circumstances, a significant substitution outcome would be more likely to occur.

TOWARD A CONTEXTUAL APPROACH
TO DECISIONAL ALTERVATIVES

Neither of the two available studies supports the hypothesis that AGSs substitute for or divert participants from appropriate guardianship placement. In hindsight, this is not particularly surprising, given that case management and many DMM services are substantially different from legal guardianship in terms of their respective missions, functions, and legal authority. These differences suggest that, rather than selecting the least restrictive option from among services that are assumed to be interchangeable, a contextual approach should be used to guide service selection. Issues to be considered include the individual's capacities, preferences, and needs in the context of the threats, opportunities, and resources in his or her environment.

One of the major drawbacks to plenary guardianship is that it assumes an all or nothing approach to competence. Despite the legislative trend toward limited guardianship, in practice, once an elder crosses the judicial threshold of incompetency, he or she usually loses decisional authority in all realms; contextual variations are seldom considered. Ironically the concept of AGS suffers from a similar problem. Context is ignored. Yet, all alternatives are not created equal. AGSs serve different roles, functions, needs, and capabilities. Therefore, the debate must move from the "alternatives to" assumption that all AGSs will substitute for guardianship to an approach that helps providers, elders, and their family members select the most appropriate decisional interventions given the elder's capabilities, resources, and constraints.

By identifying a spectrum of services that provide assistance with decision making, the current approach to AGSs offers an important first step to the development of a contextual approach. The next step is to identify similarities and differences among decision-making interventions. Professor Kapp begins this task by distinguishing between supportive and surrogate services, between those that are planned and unplanned, and between services offered by the formal service network and an elder's informal support system. Such an approach is helpful for identifying which type of decision-making intervention is likely to be most effective under different assumptions. As I have argued elsewhere (Wilber & Reynolds, 1995), surrogate services (e.g., durable powers of attorney (DPA), representative payee, limited guardianship) are more likely to substitute for plenary guardianship than supportive services (e.g. bill paying, banking, voluntary case management) because, like guardianship, surrogate approaches are designed to serve persons who lack capacity to make reasoned decisions.

Planning with advance directives provides the opportunity to stipulate one's own decisional choices in the event that one loses capacity, thus providing some balance between freedom of choice and protection. And informal services, in which family members and close friends assist an impaired elder with decisions, have several advantages assuming, of course, that the elder's interests are served. Such arrangements are likely to be flexible over time, tailored to the needs of the elder, and grounded in an understanding of the elder's previous preferences. Most elders who lack capacity are able to avoid legal guardianship, not by using less restrictive decisional interventions, but because they can rely on informal support networks.

Where does this leave us? Professor Kapp's chapter offers an important insight: Providers' concern about risk of exposure to liability is a major barrier to the development and provision of AGSs. Ironically, another sort of concern about risk, specifically, AGSs ineffectiveness in addressing certain types of client risk, inhibits the extent to which the less restrictive alternatives that have been developed and implemented are able to replace guardianship.

BEYOND LEGAL LIABILITY: DEFINING CLIENT RISK

Client risk can be conceptualized on two dimensions: first, in terms of threat to the elder's well-being stemming from the interaction of the elder's behavior and his or her environment, and second, the elder's cognitive capacity or ability to understand and evaluate the threat.

Behavior that Threatens the Elder's Well-Being

Paradoxically, the restrictive nature of guardianship, its valuing of safety over freedom, and its authority to act in a surrogate capacity, makes it both the most effective means of managing personal risk and the least desirable. Therefore, in examining the ability of AGSs to substitute for guardianship, it is critical to identify the problems that need to be addressed and the ability of specific AGSs to address them. For example, the 5 subjects from the guardianship diversion study who were referred back to the public guardian for conservatorship were plagued by problems beyond the scope of the DMM service intervention, including inability to avoid financial exploitation, health-threatening self-neglect, and extremely dangerous activities such as wandering into traffic or into high crime areas at night.

While some alternatives such as powers of attorney and representative payee provide decision-making authority to a surrogate to deal with some types of financial risk, few AGSs address personal risk. Thus, when guardianship is precipitated because the elder's behavior threatens his/her well-being, there are few substitutes short of doing nothing.

In evaluating the circumstances in which a less restrictive intervention may be effective, an objective assessment of the threat to the elder is only part of the picture. The critical element is the elder's ability to understand the nature and consequences of the danger. Thus, the elder's competence or capacity to understand the threat is an essential part of the equation that determines whether guardianship may be necessary or if an alternative intervention will suffice.

Capacity to Understand and Evaluate the Threat

The question of capacity is at the center of the alternatives debate. As illustrated by other chapters in this book, the social, psychological, and legal definitions of capacity are still evolving. For the purpose of this commentary, decisional capacity is cognitive and is defined as the ability to make a reasoned decision based on consideration of the nature and consequences of available choices. Capacity does not mean that an individual has to make a conventional choice and is, in fact, more an assessment of the decision-making process (the ability to assess and manipulate information) than the actual choice made (Kapp, 1990). To return to the dangerous behavior discussed earlier, wandering into high crime areas during the night is not by itself an indicator of a need for intervention. Rather, it is the elder's ability to understand the risks and consequences of the behavior that should guide the intervention strategy.

Collopy (1988) and Smyer (1993) distinguish between decisional capacity, or the ability to make a reasoned choice, and executional capacity, the capacity to act on the choice. This distinction is important for the selection of appropriate decisional interventions. For example, an individual may have the reasoning capacity to pay bills but lack the functional ability to execute decisions for a variety of reasons including visual impairment, fatigue, neurological disorders and other health problems. Such persons require assistance to carry out their decisions; they do not need decisions made on their behalf. Conversely, plenary guardianship, as well as other surrogate decision-making interventions such as representative payeeship and limited guardianship, should be based on a finding of at least some areas of decisional incapacity. These surrogate decision-making approaches require consistent evidence that an adult lacks the capacity to reach a reasoned decision and as a result requires a surrogate to manage his or her affairs.

An underlying assumption of supportive or executional services such as DMM is that the client has the capacity to make choices, to decide on her own behalf. Therefore, a critical question in terms of capacity is what type of assistance is needed: help to execute the client's reasoned choices (supportive assistance) or help deciding on behalf of the client (surrogate decision making). Adults who can make their own decisions do not need guardians or other types of involuntary surrogates, although they may need the support of one or more AGSs to execute their decisions.

Of course, not all AGSs are strictly supportive in nature. Some services, such as durable power of attorney and representative payeeship, carry the authority to function in a surrogate capacity for persons who lack decisional capacity. Based on the criterion of capacity, these AGSs can be expected to substitute for guardianship. But, as I have argued elsewhere (Wilber & Reynolds, 1995), they may not substitute on other criteria such as ability to manage complexity, or as discussed earlier, the ability to manage risk. AGSs vary considerably in their scope of authority. While some may be comprehensive (e.g., some trusts), others are quite circumscribed (e.g., representative payee). And, as Professor Kapp points out, some AGSs are limited by institutional practices (e.g., banks that do not accept a DPA). In general, only those services with comparable scope and authority can be expected to provide viable substitution for each other.

CONCLUSIONS

I applaud Professor Kapp's efforts to discourage the overuse of formal guardianship. Guardianship is a highly restrictive decisional intervention that should be used only as a last resort. I am not convinced, however, that most AGSs carry the potential to significantly reduce appropriate use of legal guardianship, particularly in cases involving cognitively impaired persons who are personally at risk, financially exploited, or both. Current research suggests that DMM and case management interventions do not have the authority to ameliorate risk for clients who lack capacity and who have not planned for incapacity. Although AGSs have not demonstrated success at substituting for or diverting elders from guardianship, they provide a variety of other important benefits. These benefits should be recognized and AGSs evaluated on their ability to meet the specific decisional needs for which they were designed, rather than solely on their ability to provide an alternative to a more restrictive option.

Research on decisional interventions is still in its infancy. There is much to learn about the functions, roles, benefits, and risks of these services. Public policies such as the Patient Self-Determination Act and private promoters are championing several types of decisional interventions. More extensive evaluation of the outcomes of these interventions is needed, particularly in the area of advance directives and trusts that plan for incapacity.

We must continue to strive to develop, evaluate, and promote effective decisional interventions that protect dependent persons while safeguarding their basic civil liberties to the greatest extent possible. In doing so, however, we must be clear about what each intervention does and can be expected to do. We also must ensure that whatever course of action is pursued serves the needs, interests, and, to the greatest extent possible, the preferences of functionally and cognitively dependent elders.

ACKNOWLEDGMENT

This commentary is based on research supported by the John Randolph and Dora Haynes Foundation, Los Angeles, California, and the Administration on Aging, Office of Human Development Services, grant number 90-AM-0153. Grantees undertaking projects under government sponsorship are encouraged to express freely their findings and conclusions. Points of view or opinions do not therefore necessarily represent official Administration on Aging policy.

REFERENCES

Collopy, B. (1988). Autonomy in long-term care: Some crucial distinctions. *The Gerontologist, 28* (Suppl.), 10–17.

Heller, J. L. (1989). *Planning ahead: The complete manual on state surrogate financial management legislation.* Washington, DC: American Association of Retired Persons.

Kapp, M. B. (1990). Evaluating decisionmaking capacity in the elderly: A review of recent literature. In E. Dejowski (Ed.), *Protecting judgement impaired adults: Issues, interventions, and policies* (pp. 15–30). New York: Haworth.

Schmidt, W. (1990). Quantitative information about the quality of the guardianship system: Toward the next generation of guardianship research. *Probate Law Journal, 10,* 61–80.

Smyer, M. (1993, Winter/Spring). Aging and decision-making capacity. *Generations,* 51–56.

Steinberg, R. M. (1985). *Alternative approaches to conservatorship and protection of older adults referred to public guardian.* Los Angeles, CA: University of Southern California, Andrus Gerontology Center.

Stiegel, L. (1992). *Alternatives to guardianship: Substantive training materials and module for professionals working with the elderly and persons with disabilities.* Washington, DC: American Bar Association Commission on Legal Problems of the Elderly.

Wilber, K. H. (1991). Alternatives to conservatorship: The role of daily money management. *The Gerontologist, 31,* 150–155.

Wilber, K. H., & Buturain, L. (1992). Daily money management: An emerging service in long- term care. In G. Larue & Bayly (Eds.), *Long-term care in an aging society: Choices and challenges for the 1990s* (pp. 93–117). Buffalo, NY: Prometheus.

Wilber, K. H. (1995). The search for effective alternatives to conservatorship: Lessons from a daily money management diversion study. *Journal of Aging and Social Policy, 7*(1), 39–56.

Wilber, K. H., & Reynolds, S. L. (1995). Rethinking alternatives to guardianship. *The Gerontologist, 35*, 248–257.

CHAPTER 6

Guardianship Reform in the 1980s: A Decade of Substantive and Procedural Change

Penelope A. Hommel

This chapter deviates slightly from the title of the book. Rather than looking at the impact of the law on decision-making capacity of older persons, it examines its impact on their decision-making rights. Specifically, it looks at states' guardianship laws and recent efforts in a number of states to reform those laws to lessen the likelihood that they will unnecessarily or inappropriately deprive older persons of their right to make essential decisions about their lives.

The chapter begins with a brief overview of what guardianship is and how it affects decision making by older adults subjected to it. The chapter then examines the substantial changes that have occurred over the past decade—both in attitudes about, and in the way guardianship laws deal with, the issue of protection versus autonomy. The trend has been away from traditional paternalistic approaches which foster dependency, toward policies and laws focused on maximizing the potential for autonomy and independence among individuals of limited capacity. The chapter emphasizes the issues that reform efforts have focused on, rather than assessing how successful any particular law has been at achieving overall reform.

I will conclude by looking to the future, and suggest that we who are concerned about independent decision making by older persons have a responsibility to be sure that the laws now on the books are followed in practice. Equally important, we have a responsibility to monitor the real impact of these new laws. Are they helping the courts find the delicate but critical balance between providing support, assistance, and even surrogate decision making when it is truly needed, and protecting that most essential right to self-determination?

GUARDIANSHIP AND ITS IMPACT
ON DECISION-MAKING RIGHTS

Guardianship refers to the appointment, by a court, of a third party—the guardian—to assume decision making and to handle the affairs of an individual whom the court has found to be "incompetent" or "incapacitated"—the ward. The terminology varies from state to state. Throughout this chapter, unless otherwise stated, the term *guardian* or *guardianship* is used generically to refer to surrogate decision-makers with authority over personal and/or financial matters.

A guardian may have the right to make decisions only in limited areas, or, as is at present more common, may have full authority to make almost all personal decisions and/or all financial decisions. These include very significant decisions, such as where the individual will live, what medical treatment she or he may receive, how income, bank accounts and other resources will be expended and invested, etc. State statutes and case law, which may vary significantly from state to state, govern the imposition of guardianship.

Full or plenary guardianship is one of the most restrictive and intrusive interventions that can be imposed on an individual, and yet historically, it has been relatively easy to obtain, particularly over older persons. As the term itself indicates, the underlying purpose of guardianship is benevolent: it is intended to assist and protect persons of limited capacity. This is consistent with the beneficent purposes of the *parens patriae* power, which is the power through which the state derives its authority to intervene in the private lives of its citizens and order guardianship over them. *Parens patriae* is distinct from police power, through which the state may intervene to restrict individuals who endanger the health and safety of the community at large, (e.g., criminal law). Because the underlying purpose of the police power is not benevolent and it is used in ways that are manifestly detrimental to individual rights and liberties, strict procedural safeguards and a formal adversarial proceeding always accompany any exercise of the state's police power in order to protect the individual (e.g., presumption of innocence until proven guilty, proof beyond a reasonable doubt, right to counsel, etc).

In contrast, the *parens patriae* power has historically been exercised in an informal setting without strong procedural protections. This has been accepted on the basis that the purpose of state intervention is to protect the individual's best interest (Alexander, 1979). Until recently, guardianship laws and practice throughout the United States were a prime example of this paternalistic approach. This focus on the purpose of state intervention and the notion that guardianship was beneficial to the ward made a judicial determination of incompetence relatively easy to obtain—particularly when the alleged incompetent was an older person (Anderer, 1990). Hearings to determine the need for a guardian were informal, nonadversarial, and lacking in procedural protections.

Beginning in the 1970s, legal scholars concerned about the independence and autonomy of older persons began to focus, not on the purpose of intervention, but on consequences for the individual. Indeed, persons determined to be incompetent and for whom a guardian is appointed suffer very serious negative consequences. First, a determination of incompetence can, by itself, be degrading and stigmatizing. Second, an easily obtained determination of incompetence can lead to significant deprivation of autonomy, reducing an adult to the legal status of a child.[1] A ward under full guardianship typically retains fewer rights than a convicted felon,[2] and suffers almost total deprivation of personal freedom. Full guardianship removes from the ward "probably the most basic civil liberty of all: . . . [the] right to make choices about one's life and to determine where one's own interests lie" (Dudovitz, 1985, p. 77). The ward typically loses such fundamental rights as those of entering into a contract, including a marriage contract; owning property; deciding where to live; consenting to or refusing medical treatment; and even, in some states, voting. The comprehensive loss of rights accompanying guardianship can mean the loss of all control over personal decisions, since state laws generally have not required a guardian to take into account the expressed desires of the ward. Further, the broad power traditionally granted to guardians carries with it great potential for abuse, as was made tragically clear by a nationwide Associated Press study in 1987.[3]

EVOLUTION OF GUARDIANSHIP LAWS AND TRENDS IN LEGISLATIVE REFORM

Over the past two decades, there has been a growing recognition of these negative aspects of guardianship and their detrimental consequences for the individual. At the same time, as the field of gerontology and concern about our older population have grown, there has been a strong push for policies that maximize autonomy and independence for all older persons, including those of limited capacity. Both factors have led, in recent years, to significant legislative reform throughout the country. These reforms have had several aims: preventing unwarranted deprivations of liberty; making available the least restrictive form of intervention, which assists individuals in meeting their needs but maximizes their potential for self-reliance; tailoring the powers of the guardian to particular needs of the individual; and minimizing the potential for abuse of a guardian's power. From 1980–1992, every state in the nation made some revisions in its guardianship law, and a significant number of these were major reforms.

These new statutes generally provide proposed wards[4] with stronger procedural protections and limit the extent of the intervention.[5] The new statutes typically:

- attempt to decrease the stigma attached to guardianship, for example, by changing the term "incompetent" to "incapacitated;"
- give the proposed ward more meaningful procedural protections, such as the right to timely and adequate notice, the right to counsel whose role is to act as an advocate, the right to be present at hearings, and the right to trial by jury;

- require stronger evidence that guardianship is warranted by (a) changing the definition of incapacity to focus on functional abilities and disabilities, not on diagnoses or labels, (b) instituting more stringent procedures for assessing capacity which involve more investigators from different disciplines, and require more detailed support of findings, and (c) placing the burden on the petitioner (the party seeking the appointment of a guardian) to present "clear and convincing" evidence of the need for guardianship, including the inadequacy of less restrictive alternatives;
- state a preference for limited guardianship, and allow the guardian to have power only in those areas where it can be demonstrated that functional disabilities exist;
- limit the power of even full guardians by enumerating certain basic rights that cannot be lost automatically upon a determination of incapacity;
- institute steps to prevent abuse and exploitation by guardians, such as (a) requiring greater scrutiny of the person to be appointed guardian (e.g., checking for conflicts of interest, investigating credit and criminal background), (b) requiring guardians to attend guardian education programs, (c) imposing a duty on guardians to involve wards in decisions to the greatest extent possible, and (d) increasing guardian accountability by, for example, requiring more frequent reports to the court and specifying what information must be provided in those reports;[6]
- specify procedures that make terminating a guardianship easier, and require the court to review, at specified times, whether there is continuing need for guardianships that have been imposed.[7]

Below, a number of substantive and procedural reforms that are harbingers of trends across the country are examined in some depth, drawing examples from a number of states that recently have made major revisions in their statutes. These include the District of Columbia, Florida, Kentucky, Michigan, New Mexico, New York, North Dakota, Pennsylvania, and South Dakota.[8] Substantive reforms that reflect a change in the philosophy underlying guardianship laws are discussed first, followed by an examination of reforms that call for more rigorous assessment of the capacities and limitations of the proposed ward, and reforms aimed at strengthening the procedural protections provided to the proposed ward.

SUBSTANTIVE REFORMS IN GUARDIANSHIP LAW

As noted, recent legislative reforms reflect a fundamental change in philosophy from the paternalism of the *parens patriae* tradition to an appreciation of the "dignity of risk" (McLaughlin, 1988, p. 30). In other words, they place greater value on respecting the individual's right to decide—even when a person's choices may seem foolish to others—than on protecting the "best interests" of the individual. In many of the newer statutes, this is achieved through two major substantive changes: (a) new definitions of incapacity, and (b) an explicit preference for limited guardianship.

The Changing Definition of Incapacity

Most new laws use the term incapacity rather than incompetence, and have made significant changes in its definition. The definition is critical because it provides the framework for guardianship petitions and proceedings—it establishes the basic inquiry regarding a person's need for guardianship.

In this volume, Sabatino thoroughly lays out the categories, and traces the evolution, of substantive definitions of incapacity or incompetence appearing in state guardianship statutes.

For purposes of this chapter, the following types of changes have been most significant. Definitions have moved away from equating conditions or diagnoses with incompetence, including using "old age" as a triggering condition, and have moved away from using value judgments as to whether an individual's actions or decisions are "responsible" or "reasonable." Such definitions are not satisfactory because diagnoses do not necessarily provide any meaningful indication of a person's ability to function on a day-to-day basis, and the use of normative standards such as "responsible decisions" does not promote neutral fact-finding, and increases the risk that an individual might lose *"control over decisions governing his/her own life . . . for mere idiosyncratic behavior."* (Hafemeister & Sales, 1984, p. 338) The newer definitions eliminate the emphasis on conditions and attempt to replace it with objective standards to evaluate the person's ability to manage personal care or financial affairs on a day-to-day basis. In keeping with this emphasis, they use the term incapacity rather than incompetence. They also discourage value judgments as to the "reasonableness" of a person's behavior and focus instead on actual behavior and specific functional abilities to meet essential needs. They typically call for a two-fold investigation, first of whether the person can understand and appreciate the nature and consequences of her/his inabilities and second of whether the person is incapable without the assistance or protection of a guardian of meeting essential health, safety and welfare needs because of the inabilities and lack of understanding of their consequences.

The new definitions should significantly change guardianship proceedings and provide greater protection against inappropriate findings of incapacity by exacting more rigorous, comprehensive assessments of the ability to function in certain essential ways, and requiring stronger evidence of incapacity to be presented at hearings.

Preference for Limited Guardianship

In addition to new definitions, many of the new laws, as well as the Uniform Guardianship and Protective Proceedings Act, now provide that, even if a person is found to be incapacitated, guardianship is to be used only to the extent necessary, allowing protected persons to retain as much control over their own decisions as possible. The statutes state a strong preference for limited guardianship, in which the guardian is granted only those powers and only for that period of time necessary to provide for the demonstrated needs of the ward. The use of limited guardianship should "minimize the invasion of a ward's privacy and fundamental rights and . . . preserve the ward's dignity and self respect."[9] The District of Columbia statute contains a succinct statement of this mandate:

> The court shall exercise the authority conferred in this subchapter so as to encourage the development of maximum self-reliance and independence of the incapacitated individual and make appointive and other orders only to the extent necessitated by the individual's mental and adaptive limitations or other conditions warranting the procedure.[10]

The new statutes require courts to put this preference into practice by directing them to make specific findings regarding the ward's disabilities and to issue specific orders regarding the extent of, and limits on, the guardian's powers. In Pennsylvania, for example, the law directs that the

> . . . court shall enter an order appointing a limited guardian of the person with powers consistent with the court's finding of limitations, which may include:

> (1) general care, maintenance and custody of the incapacitated person.
> (2) Designating the place for the incapacitated person to live.
> (3) Assuring that the incapacitated person receives such training, education, medical and psychological services and social and vocational opportunities as appropriate, as well as assisting the incapacitated person in the development of maximum self-reliance and independence.[11]

In New York's new law, once a person is found to be incapacitated, the court must first determine whether appointment of a guardian is necessary at all. If not, the law provides an alternative. The court is to authorize a transaction or series of transactions necessary to achieve any "security, service or care arrangement to meet the person's needs or accomplish a property transaction."[12] If, however, the court finds there is need for a guardian, the order must be designed to accomplish the least restrictive form of intervention, with powers limited to those the court finds necessary.[13]

To further reinforce limitations on guardianship, a number of the statutes also explicitly provide, as in New Mexico, that "[a]n incapacitated person for whom a guardian has been appointed retains all legal and civil rights except those which have been expressly limited by court order or have been specifically granted to the guardian by court order."[14] The North Dakota law enumerates certain basic rights which the ward may not be deprived of except upon specific findings of the court. These include the rights to vote, to seek to change marital status, to obtain or retain a driver's license, or to testify in judicial or administrative proceedings.[15]

In addition to being a significant substantive reform that will promote the ward's autonomy, the preference for limited guardianship may strengthen the alleged incapacitated person's position in guardianship proceedings by requiring the petitioner to prove specific incapacities and needs for assistance. Like the new definitions, this requirement should encourage more specific, substantiated assessments of capacity and the presentation of stronger evidence at trial.

REFORMS IN METHODS OF ASSESSING CAPACITY

One logical consequence of the new definitions and the preference for limited guardianship is a new approach to the focus and content of assessments of capacity, as well as to who should undertake such assessments. Under the old laws, physicians or psychiatrists were often the key players in assessing the need for guardianship. In some cases, a physician's letter or signature on a preprinted form was the sole basis for a finding of incapacity (Hommel & Lisi, 1989). This situation was probably due to the fact that the terms used in traditional definitions, such as "insanity," belonged to the arcanum of psychiatry, and it fell to the medical profession to identify these conditions (Horstman, 1975, p. 227). The main problem with relying solely on medical opinions is that the information may not be especially useful in evaluating the person's overall capacity to function on a day-to-day basis. Conclusions reached on the need for guardianship, therefore, may not be valid. Many commentators, including physicians, have criticized what they see as a tendency to "abdicat[e] to physicians, the responsibility of making the legal decision on the need for guardianship" (Jost, 1980, p. 1100).

Many have advocated that the law require interdisciplinary teams or specially trained professionals to perform the assessments, and that they be required to base their conclusions on very specific functional criteria (Goodenough, 1988; Hafemeister & Sales, 1984; Scogin and Perry, 1986). Functional evaluations generally seek information regarding the individual's ability to manage essential tasks of daily living, inquiring into such matters as ability to meet basic needs (food, shelter, and clothing), ability to manage financial affairs, and physical and sensory functioning (Kemp & Mitchell, 1992). Another important aspect to investigate is the person's access to helpful resources, such as friends, relatives, transportation, and medical care.

Requiring functional assessments in guardianship proceedings should provide courts with more useful evidence of the proposed ward's capacities and limitations, and is consistent with new statutory definitions and the preference for limited guardianships. The new laws incorporate various approaches by (a) involving professionals other than physicians in assessments, (b) requiring assessments to focus on the subject's functional abilities and produce reports to provide specific support for their conclusions, and (c) supplementing the formal assessments with reports from "visitors" or "court monitors."

The Role of Professionals in Assessments

The new statutes expand the scope of professionals who are to be involved in assessments, and some prefer or require the appointment of a person who has special knowledge of functional impairments. The Florida guardianship law is a good example. Under that law, the court is required to appoint a three-member examining committee to evaluate the person:

> One member must be a psychiatrist or other physician. One of the remaining members must be either a psychologist, another psychiatrist, or other physician, a registered nurse, nurse practitioner or a licensed social worker. The third member need not be any of the above. One of the three members of the committee must have knowledge of the type of incapacity alleged in the petition.[16]

The statute also contains a number of restrictions presumably designed to prevent persons likely to be biased or subject to conflict of interest from sitting on the committee. For example, neither the petitioner nor the attending or family physician may be appointed unless good cause is shown.[17] Also, the members of the committee must not be related to, or associated with, one another, the petitioner, or the proposed ward. A member may not be employed by an agency that has custody of, or furnishes services or subsidies to, the person or the family of the alleged incapacitated person. The Florida statute also requires that members of the committee be able to communicate with the person, either directly or through an interpreter, in the language the person speaks or in a medium understandable to the person.

Some other statutes are not as comprehensive as Florida, but do expand the range of professionals to be appointed to examine the person. New Mexico, for example, requires the appointment of a "qualified health care professional" in every case.[18] "Qualified health care professional" includes a physician or a nurse practitioner with training and expertise in assessment of functional impairment.[19] In Michigan, the court or the respondent may request an independent evaluation by a physician or "mental health professional,"[20] meaning, in this case, a doctor, psychologist, social worker, or registered nurse.[21]

New York law requires the court to appoint a "court evaluator" in every case, unless the court appoints legal counsel. The evaluator must have knowledge of property management, personal care skills, problems of disabilities, and private and public resources available for the type of limitations the person is alleged to have. This role may be filled by an attorney, physician, psychologist, accountant, social worker, nurse, or other, and in some situations, the "mental hygiene legal service."[22]

Focus of the Assessment and Content of the Report

The trend in the new statutes is to require assessment reports to contain more detailed information than in the past and conclusions on both the subject's abilities and limitations; they require evaluators to substantiate their conclusions with specific facts. In addition, standardizing the contents of assessment reports should lessen the danger of "haphazard assessment and fluctuating criteria [that] plague evaluations of older adults potentially in need of guardianship services" (Scogin & Perry, 1986, p. 125).

The Florida statute contains very specific and demanding requirements as to the method of assessment and the contents of assessment reports. It provides that each of the three members of the examining committee examine the proposed ward's ability to exercise those rights which the petitioner has requested be removed. The committee must conduct a comprehensive examination which includes a physical examination, a mental health examination, and a functional assessment. The committee must submit a report which includes an evaluation of the person's ability to retain specific rights (e.g., voting or determining one's place of residence), a description of any matters with respect to which the person lacks the capacity to exercise rights, the extent of the incapacity, and the factual basis of the determination that the person lacks capacity. If the committee decides that the person is incapacitated, it must make a recommendation as to the scope of guardianship services needed.[23]

The statutes in New Mexico, Michigan, and North Dakota also focus on functional abilities, and on how any disabilities interfere with the person's decision-making capacity or ability to handle personal care.[24] The New Mexico law requires that the evaluation contain recommendations and supporting data regarding which aspects of personal care the person can manage (a) without supervision or assistance, (b) with the supervision or assistance of support services and benefits, or (c) not at all without the supervision of a guardian.[25]

New York law lists a number of duties of the court evaluator, including determining whether the alleged incapacitated person wishes legal counsel to be appointed and otherwise evaluating whether legal counsel should be appointed. It also requires a written report and recommendations, with information in response to 17 specific questions set out in the law.[26]

The Appointment of Visitors to Supplement Formal Assessment

A number of the new statutes provide for the appointment of a "visitor,"[27] whose report to the court supplements the formal assessment and provides more information about the proposed ward's living conditions and about changes proposed by the petitioner. The concept of the visitor is not new; a number of the old laws also provided for such an appointment.

Some of the new laws, however, have made the role of the visitor more meaningful and increased the weight to be accorded the visitor's report by, for example, requiring that the visitor be a qualified professional, expanding the visitor's duties, and requiring visitors to submit comprehensive and detailed reports to the court. The duties of a visitor are similar under the old and new statutes. A visitor must visit and interview the alleged incapacitated person, the petitioner, and the person nominated to serve as guardian. Additionally, he or she must visit the residence of the subject and the place where it is proposed that the person reside if a guardian is appointed. A visitor also may be required to investigate or seek other information or to examine documents. In various states, the visitor also has other duties. In the District of Columbia, for example, the visitor is to investigate the existence of a conflict of interest for a person nominated to serve as guardian. If no one has been nominated, then the visitor must nominate a guardian.[28] In North Dakota, the visitor must explain the proceedings to the proposed ward and obtain his or her views, as well as discuss an alternative resource plan "if appropriate."

Visitors are typically required to submit a written report of their findings and recommendations to the Court. North Dakota's specifications for such reports are typical, requiring

1. a description of the nature and degree of any current impairment of the proposed ward's understanding or capacity to make or communicate decisions;
2. a statement of the qualifications and appropriateness of the proposed guardian;
3. recommendations, if any, on the powers to be granted to the proposed guardian, including an evaluation of the proposed ward's capacity to perform [certain enumerated functions];
4. an assessment of the proposed ward's capacity to perform the activities of daily living.[29]

REFORMS TO STRENGTHEN PROCEDURAL SAFEGUARDS

Since guardianship proceedings were traditionally informal and nonadversarial, procedural safeguards to protect the alleged incapacitated person were often seriously lacking. The informality with which guardianship proceedings were conducted created a "substantial possibility that proposed wards [would] be deprived of liberty and property without due process of law." (Horstman, 1975, p. 235) The new statutes address this serious inadequacy by providing more numerous and meaningful procedural protections. These reforms affect all stages of guardianship proceedings, from the filing of the petition to the court's order to either dismiss the petition or appoint a guardian. The reforms should provide proposed wards with the means to participate more fully in the proceedings and to defend against unwarranted guardianship petitions. In combination, these enhanced procedural rights could lead guardianship proceedings to evolve into adversarial trials, which would be a significant change from the traditional model.

The areas of procedural reform to be examined here include (a) the right of the proposed ward to counsel, (b) more stringent requirements for petitions, (c) enhanced notice requirements, (d) formal procedures and rules for guardianship hearings, and (e) requirements regarding findings and orders of the court.

The Right to Counsel as Advocate

A major procedural protection, and one that could make the other procedural rights more meaningful, is the right to representation by counsel.

The traditional role of attorneys in guardianship cases has been limited. Some states did not give proposed wards the right to counsel. Even where this right was guaranteed by statute, wards often were not entitled to court-appointed counsel. Moreover, in cases where attorneys were present, they often were required, or believed they were required, to act as guardians *ad litem* (''GALs''), representing what was, in their judgment, the best interests of the proposed ward, rather than acting as advocates representing the proposed ward's expressed wishes.

As an advocate, the attorney's duty is to promote the proposed ward's desires and defend his or her rights against interference by well-intentioned third parties. The duty to act as an advocate may raise ethical dilemmas for attorneys who suspect that their clients are, in fact, incapacitated (Smith, 1988; Tremblay, 1987) and who may therefore be tempted to advance the perceived best interests, rather than expressed wishes, of the client. These dilemmas, however, are a natural outgrowth of the underlying philosophy of maximizing the individual's potential for independence. If the attorneys for the petitioner and the proposed ward both effectively advocate their positions, then based on a belief in the adversarial system of justice the ''correct'' result will be obtained.

While the right of the proposed ward to representation by an attorney is not new in some states,[30] it is made more meaningful by the requirement that the state bear the expense of representation if the proposed ward is indigent,[31] and by the enumeration of the roles and duties that must be fulfilled by the attorney. Where there is a right to counsel, the trend is to distinguish this from the guardian *ad litem*, and to require counsel to take a more active, adversarial role, representing the proposed ward's wishes. The Florida statute, for example, defines ''counsel for the alleged incapacitated person'' as *''an attorney who represents the expressed wishes of the alleged incapacitated person, rather than acting as a guardian or guardian ad litem who determines the best interests of the person.''*[32]

Some statutes impose on the attorney specific duties related to, and in addition to, representing the person in court. In the District of Columbia, for example, the attorney is to interview the proposed ward, explain the proceedings and their consequences, and inform the proposed ward of his or her rights and of alternatives to guardianship. In addition, the District of Columbia code makes explicit duties which are implicit in the role of a legal advocate: *''The duty of counsel . . . shall include: . . . [s]ecuring and presenting evidence and testimony and offering ar-*

guments to protect the rights of the subject of the guardianship . . . proceeding and further that individual's interests.''[33]

In the New York statute, the Law Revision Commission comments explain:

> The role of counsel . . . is to represent the person alleged to be incapacitated and ensure that the point of view of the person . . . is presented to the court. At a minimum that representation should include conducting personal interviews with the person; explaining . . . his or her rights and counseling the person regarding the nature and consequences of the proceeding, securing and presenting evidence and testimony; providing vigorous cross-examination; and offering arguments to protect the rights of the allegedly incapacitated person.[34]

The new statutes provide attorneys for proposed wards with both procedural and substantive weapons to conduct a true adversarial hearing. The attorney can take advantage of the stringent new definitions of incapacity, the preference for limited as opposed to full guardianship, and the heightened standard of proof (generally, "clear and convincing") to fight the petition. As in any adversarial proceeding, the attorney should be prepared to present objective evidence of the client's capacity to handle personal or financial matters, to present witnesses and cross-examine those of the opposition, and to challenge inadequate assessments and inadmissible evidence. The attorney also has the responsibility of ensuring that the courts follow the new requirements by limiting the powers of the guardian to those areas where there are specific findings of incapacity.

The role of the proposed ward's attorney after the appointment of a guardian is not clear in the new laws, but continuing advocacy on behalf of the ward is clearly desirable. Specifically, the periodic review of the continuing need for guardianship now mandated in several of the new laws, as well as new procedures to facilitate the termination or modification of guardianships, provide the opportunity for continuing intervention on behalf of the ward. In cases of limited guardianship, the ward may desire counsel to ensure that his or her reserved rights are preserved.

While the new statutes provide the right to counsel, the role of the guardian *ad litem* (GAL) has not been eliminated. The specific duties of the GAL, however, vary from state to state. In Michigan and North Dakota, a GAL is the first representative to be appointed for a proposed ward.[35] If the proposed ward wishes to be represented by an advocate, the GAL is to be discharged.[36] The District of Columbia statute permits the court to appoint a GAL in addition to counsel.[37] In New York, the GAL is now known as the court evaluator, whose role is to provide an independent assessment of the alleged incapacitated person, including assessment of the need for counsel.

More Rigorous Requirements with Regard to Petitions

Because statutes traditionally did not contain specific requirements for petitions for guardianship, petitions typically have been vague and worded only in terms of the ultimate issue. The recent trend is to demand that petitions (a) contain specific allegations of incapacity, (b) provide substantiation—or means by which substantiation may be obtained—for their claims, (c) identify the petitioner's interest in the matter, and (d) describe the qualifications of the proposed guardian.

New Mexico's statute, for example, requires that the petition include the nature of the alleged incapacity as it relates to the subject's functional limitations, steps that have been taken to find less restrictive alternatives, and the qualifications of the proposed guardian.[38] If the petitioner seeks to have a conservator (guardian of the estate) appointed, the petitioner must provide information about his or her own interest; reasons why a conservator is necessary, including but not limited to evidence of recent behavior demonstrating gross mismanagement of income and resources; steps taken to find less restrictive alternatives; and the basis for nominating the proposed conservator.[39] Michigan requires the petitioner to state specific facts about the alleged incapacitated person's condition and to cite specific examples of recent conduct that demonstrate the need for the appointment of a guardian.[40]

Florida has a two-step procedure to determine incapacity and appoint a guardian. The petition to determine incapacity must state the facts upon which the petitioner's belief that the person is incapacitated is based, and the names and addresses of persons who have personal knowledge of those facts. The petitioner also must specify which rights the person is allegedly incapable of exercising.[41] The petition for appointment of a guardian must state, among other things, the nature of the proposed ward's incapacity, the extent of guardianship desired, the name of the proposed guardian, the relationship and previous connection of the proposed guardian to the proposed ward, and the reasons that the named person should be appointed guardian.[42]

New York has stringent requirements with respect to the petition. An explanation of the functional level and understanding of the alleged incapacitated person is required. If powers are sought over the person, specific factual allegations must be made to demonstrate the person is likely to suffer harm because of inability to understand and provide for personal needs. If powers are sought over property management, specific factual allegations must be made to demonstrate that the person is likely to suffer harm because of his/her inability to understand and provide for property management. Other information that must be in the petition includes: particular powers and duration of powers sought and their relationship to functional level of the person, the proposed guardian and reasons why the person is suitable, any presumptive heirs of the alleged incapacitated person causing a conflict of interest, and available alternative resources that have been explored.[43]

Requiring petitions to be more informative and specific can provide increased protection for the proposed ward by discouraging unfounded filings and providing defense counsel with a better idea of the allegations against the proposed ward. This knowledge will enable counsel to define the issues, determine what evidence to present, identify potential witnesses, analyze less restrictive alternatives to guardianship, and, thus, better prepare the case.

Enhanced Notice Requirements

The new statutes also strengthen the notice which must be given to the proposed ward and others when a petition is filed. They generally require that notice be personally served on the proposed ward, as well as specified relatives and persons such as the proposed ward's attorney or attorney-in-fact under a power of attorney. Some statutes also provide that the notice to the proposed ward may not be waived unless the person attends the hearing or the waiver is confirmed in an interview with a visitor.[44] The notice must include a copy of the petition, and it must explain the purpose and legal consequences of the proceeding. The notice also must inform the proposed ward of his or her legal rights, such as the right to counsel.[45] Some statutes include very specific provisions to ensure that the ward will be able to read and understand the notice. New

Mexico, for example, requires that the notice be in plain language and large type.[46] The Florida law goes even further, requiring that the notice be read to the allegedly incapacitated person.[47]

The recent New York law is among the most specific. The notice must include the date, time and place of hearing; name, address, and phone number of the court evaluator and court attorney if one has been appointed; a clear and easily readable statement of the rights of the alleged incapacitated person as set forth in the statute, including the right to present evidence, to call witnesses, to cross examine and to be represented by a lawyer of choice; a list of powers the guardian would have if the petition is granted. It must be written in large type, in plain English, and in a language other than English if necessary to inform the alleged incapacitated person of his or her rights. It must also include, on its face, a warning which describes the nature and seriousness of guardianship in "twelve point or larger bold face, double spaced type," containing four separate paragraphs specified in the statute, starting with **"IMPORTANT."** It must be personally delivered to the alleged incapacitated person with a copy of the petition, not less than 14 days prior to the hearing. A broad group of others who must receive notice are also specified.[48]

Formalized Hearing Procedures and Rules

The trend is to make guardianship hearings more formal and adversarial by instituting procedures and rules that have come to be expected in civil and criminal trials. The Florida statute explicitly provides that the hearings be conducted *"in a manner consistent with due process."* [49] Some of the procedural rights are not new to guardianship proceedings, but are made stronger by the new statutes. Some are as straightforward as providing that the hearing be put on the record.[50]

The trend in new statutes is to strongly encourage or require the proposed ward to be present at the hearing.[51] While this right is not new, it has been made more meaningful by the requirement that the proposed ward's presence not be excused in the absence of "good cause."[52] North Dakota provides that physical difficulty to the proposed ward in attending the hearing is not sufficient to constitute "good cause" for his or her absence.[53] In Michigan and New Mexico, the court is required to move the site of the hearing to accommodate the proposed ward's desire to be present.[54] In New York, the alleged incapacitated person must be at the hearing to allow the court to obtain its own impression of the person's capacity. If the alleged incapacitated person physically cannot come or be brought to the courthouse, the hearing must be conducted where the person resides, unless the person is not in the state or all information before the court clearly establishes that the person is completely unable to participate or no meaningful participation will result from the person's presence. Further, if the person is not present at the hearing and the court appoints a guardian, the order must set forth the factual basis for conducting the hearing without the person present.[55]

In keeping with the trend toward adversarial proceedings, the new statutes provide proposed wards with the means necessary to fight their cases—the right to present evidence and the right to cross-examine witnesses.[56] In addition, new legislation removes the lax rules of evidence which prevailed in the past. The New Mexico statute provides that the state's standard rules of evidence apply in guardianship hearings, and that hearsay is generally inadmissible.[57]

In addition to instituting stronger procedural rules, the new statutes also introduce rigorous standards as to the level and quality of proof required before a person may be found incapacitated and a guardian appointed. Several specifically place the burden on the party petitioning for guardianship to present "clear and convincing" evidence to support his or her case.[58] This standard is the most rigorous burden of proof in civil cases. Specification of the clear and convincing standard is significant, because most of the former statutes contained no standard. The court was to pronounce the proposed ward incompetent if it "found" or "was satisfied" that such was the case.[59] Lack of a stated standard permitted courts to apply *any* standard they chose, and meant that the court's finding of incapacity would be very difficult to challenge on appeal if there was any evidence in the record to support it (Mitchell, 1978).

Specificity Required in Court's Findings and Orders

The rigorous standard of proof is accompanied by demands that the court state on the record very specific findings to support the need for a guardian. The new statutes require courts to make some or all of the following findings:

- that the proposed ward is an incapacitated person and the exact nature and scope of the incapacity;[60]
- that no alternative resource plan is available that is suitable to protect the proposed ward's health, safety, or habilitation;[61]
- that the court has considered less restrictive alternatives and that the powers and duties conferred upon the guardian are appropriate as the least restrictive form of intervention consistent with the preservation of the liberties of the proposed ward;[62]
- that appointment of a guardian is necessary as the best means to provide for the continuing care and supervision of the proposed ward;[63]
- that the proposed guardian is qualified, suitable, and willing to serve.[64]

The new laws also place specific requirements on the content of court orders appointing guardians. These requirements enforce the preference for limited guardianship and help to protect the ward from overreaching by the guardian. Many new statutes require that the order of appointment specify the limitations on the guardian's power (i.e., what rights the guardian may and may not exercise and any time limits on the guardianship).[65] North Dakota's statute, for example, provides that the court must state whether the guardian has complete, limited, or no authority in each of the areas of residential, educational, medical, legal, vocational, and financial decision making. If limited authority is granted in any of these areas, the limitations must be specified.[66] Generally, the ward retains all powers not explicitly granted to the guardian.

CONCLUSIONS AND CHALLENGES FOR THE FUTURE

In 1928, Justice Louis Brandeis issued an eloquent warning against allowing benevolent purposes to obscure recognition of government infringement on individual liberty:

> Experience should teach us to be most on our guard to protect liberty when the government's purposes are beneficient. Men born to freedom are naturally alert to repel invasion of their liberty by evil-minded rulers. The greatest dangers to liberty lurk in insidious encroachment by men of zeal, well meaning but without understanding.[67]

The substantive and procedural reforms in the new wave of guardianship laws just described are, in fact, a reflection of this concern that the individual right to autonomous decision making and self-determination be protected from infringement—even infringement by those with beneficient purposes. They are intended to reverse the paternalistic approach of the past and provide strong protection. Two important tasks now before us are to monitor implementation of the new laws to be sure the reforms are translated into practice and to be alert to the real impact of the new laws to be sure they are indeed achieving the intended results.

With respect to translating the written law into practice, there is reason for concern. Recent research in ten states by The Center for Social Gerontology (TCSG) (Lisi et al., 1992) indicates there is substantial discrepancy between what the laws call for and the extent to which those requirements are followed in practice. The data, which were obtained by TCSG from selected courts within each of ten states, included information from the courts' guardianship case files and from observing court hearings. It appears that unless there is an absolute mandate or prohibition in the statute, the statutory language has little effect on practice. Statutory language which only strongly encourages a practice or permits its waiver at the court's discretion does not generally lead to the occurrence of the practice with any more frequency than occurs in states where such statutory language is absent.

In comparing TCSG findings on actual practices with what the laws say should happen, there were significant differences. For example:

- Several states where the law requires legal representation of respondents (Kansas, Minnesota and Florida) were found to have, at best, from 75% to 90% representation.[68] States such as Michigan having statutes that encourage appointment of attorneys but leaving the decision to the discretion of the court show no greater presence of attorneys in court than states without such statutory language. In Michigan, only 8% of the files examined indicated that the respondent had had an attorney appointed. The study also revealed that in 26% of the cases where there was evidence in the file or at the hearing of an objection by the respondent, there was no evidence that the respondent was ever represented by an attorney.
- Although medical evidence of the need for guardianship was in the files or presented in court 63% of the time, independent evalu-

ations were ordered in only 12% of all cases studied. The only states with substantial numbers of independent evaluations were those whose laws mandate them. States with statutory language intended to foster independent evaluations but not requiring them, had no higher rates of such evaluations than states whose statutes do not address this issue at all.

- Data on respondents' attendance at guardianship hearings indicates that statutory provisions have had limited effect. Despite the fact that six of the ten states included in the study have statutory provisions which very strongly encourage the respondent's attendance at the hearing, data indicate that only 28% of respondents did so. There was no discussion of respondent's absence in 55% of the cases, and, even where the absence was discussed, no real reason was provided in 7% of the cases.

- Although many states now strongly encourage use of limited guardianships, very few are actually granted. In four states, California, Indiana, Kansas and Michigan, the percentage of limited guardianships imposed is 3% or less. Only in Minnesota, where the overall system is set up to encourage the use of limited guardianships, is there any substantial use of this alternative (54% are limited). Similarly, five states studied granted limited conservatorships in 7% or fewer of their cases. None of the ten states had limitations on more than 15% of the conservatorships granted, except Minnesota, which placed some limitation on 33% of its conservatorships.

Just as it is important to monitor implementation, it is crucial that we assess the real impact of these new statutes on the older individuals they are intended to protect. As Professor John Regan points out in a paper prepared for a 1985 Elder Abuse Conference, there is a tendency in this country for the pendulum to swing wide between "abandonment and strong intervention." And he points out that these

> opposite responses are symptomatic of the dilemma . . . —the tension between individual autonomy and social paternalism. . . .[S]hould an individual be free to live in whatever lifestyle suits him or her . . . so long as no harm is done to others? Or does a compassionate society have a duty to rescue its victims, . . . regardless of whether or not they want such help? (Regan, 1985)

The trends in legislative reform examined in this chapter are clearly aimed at swinging the pendulum toward individual autonomy and away from paternalism. A number of critics now contend that the pendulum has swung much too far—that in our efforts to undo the problems and deficiencies of the past, we have created a new set of problems and deficiencies. They argue that, in some states, we have set up so many roadblocks (e.g., high costs, time delays, an adversarial process, the need for lawyers, special evaluators, expert witnesses, etc.) that obtaining guardianship is virtually impossible, and this leaves people who are in serious need of assistance with no realistic way of getting it. They also contend that the most serious problem is an inadequate supply of persons willing to serve as guardians and that the added burdens in the new laws will shrink the supply even further.

While there has been no research to support the critics' claims, they cannot be discounted. Therefore, the challenge before us is to seriously examine the criticisms and monitor the impact of the legislative reforms in light of them. And in monitoring that impact, it is important to keep in mind the goal of the reform efforts. They were not intended to preserve autonomy for autonomy's sake or the least restrictive alternative for its own sake. They were intended to establish a process that would—on a case-by-case basis—balance the individual's right to autonomy and independent decision making against the need for some degree of protective intervention. We must take care not to create a system of laws that is ill equipped to address the very real need of some for assistance, and even for surrogate decision making. But at the same time, we must recognize the critical importance of the "dignity of risk" (McLaughlin, 1988, p. 30) and the essential right to make decisions about one's own life, and continue to work toward a system that adequately preserves that dignity and protects that essential right.

NOTES

1. In some states, the guardian was given the power that a parent has with respect to an unemancipated minor child. For example, N.D. Cent. Code §30.1-28-12.1 (1976); Mich. Comp. Laws Ann. §700.455(1) (1980).
2. Preamble to Florida Guardianship Law, Fla. Stat. Ann. §744.101 (1989).

3. Reported in Abuses in Guardianship of the Elderly and Infirm: A National Disgrace, A Report by the Chairman of the Subcommittee on Health and Long-Term Care of the House Select Committee on Aging, House of Representatives, 100th Cong., 1st Sess., (Dec. 1987).

4. In this chapter, the person who is the subject of guardianship proceedings may be referred to as the "proposed ward," "alleged incapacitated person," or "respondent."

5. Many of these reforms parallel the recommendations of the July 1988 National Guardianship Symposium, reported in ABA Commission on the Mentally Disabled and Commission of Legal Problems of the Elderly, Guardianship: An Agenda for Reform (1989).

6. Although these reforms are not specifically addressed in this chapter, they may have important implications, especially, for attorneys for proposed wards.

7. See note 6.

8. These laws may be found, respectively, at: D.C. Code Ann. §21-2001 (Michie Supp. 1993); Fla. Stat. Ann. §744.101 (West 1989); KY Rev. Stat. Ann. §387.510 (Michie Supp. 1992); Mich. Comp. Laws Ann. §700.441 (West Supp. 1989); N.M. Stat. Ann. § 45-5-301 (1989 & Supp. 1993); N.Y. Mental Hyg. Law §81.01 (McKinney Supp. 1993); N.D. Cent. Code §30.1-26-01 (Supp. 1989); 20 PA. Cons. Stat. Ann. §5501 (Purdon Supp. 1993); S.D. Codified Laws §30-36-1 (Supp. 1993).

9. Preamble to the Florida Guardianship Law, Fla. Stat. Ann. §744.101 (1989).

10. D.C. Code Ann. §21-2044 (Michie Supp. 1993). See also Fla. Stat. Ann. §744.1012 (West 1989); Mich. Comp. Laws Ann. §700.444(2),(3) (West Supp. 1989); N.M. Stat. Ann. §45-5-303.1 (1989 & Supp. 1993); N.D. Cent. Code §30.1-28-04.1 (Supp. 1989).

11. 20 PA. Cons. Stat. Ann. §5512.1(b) (Purdon Supp. 1993).

12. N.Y. Mental Hyg. Law §81.16(b) (McKinney Supp. 1993).

13. N.Y. Mental Hyg. Law §81.16(c) (McKinney Supp. 1993).

14. N.M. Stat. Ann. §45-5-301.1 (1989 & Supp. 1993). See also Fla. Stat. Ann. §744.331(5) (West 1989); N.D. Cent. Code §30.1-28-04.5 (Supp. 1989).

15. N.D. Cent. Code §30.1-28-04.3 (Supp. 1989).

16. Fla. Stat. Ann. §744.331(3)(a) (West 1989). The old Florida law

also provided for an examining committee, but it was to be composed of "one responsible citizen and two practicing physicians." Fla. Stat. Ann. §744.331(5)(a) (1984).

17. On the other hand, the committee must consult with the attending or family physician if she or he is available for consultation.

18. N.M. Stat. Ann. §45-5-303.D (1989 & Supp. 1993).

19. N.M. Stat. Ann. §45-5-101.T (1989 & Supp. 1993).

20. Mich. Comp. Laws Ann. §700.443 (3), (4) (West Supp. 1989).

21. Mich. Comp. Laws Ann. §700.8 (4) (West Supp. 1989).

22. N.Y. Mental Hyg. Law §81.09(b) (McKinney Supp. 1993).

23. Fla. Stat. Ann. §744.331(3)(b)-(d) (West 1989). Under the former law, the examining committee was to ascertain the person's "mental and physical condition." If the committee considered the person to be incompetent, it was to "determine his age, whether his condition is acute or chronic, and the apparent cause of the condition." Fla. Stat. Ann. §744.331(5)(b) (1984).

24. N.M. Stat. Ann. §45-5-303.D (1989 & Supp. 1993); Mich. Comp. Laws Ann. §700.443(5) (West Supp. 1989); N.D. Cent. Code §30.1-28-03.5 (Supp. 1989).

25. N.M. Stat. Ann. §45-5-303.D (1989 & Supp. 1993).

26. N.Y. Mental Hyg. Law §81.09(c) (McKinney Supp. 1993).

27. D.C. Code Ann. §21-2041, §21-2054(a) (conservatorship) (Supp. 1993); Fla. Stat. Ann. §744.107 (called "court monitor" rather than "visitor") (West 1989); Mich. Comp. Laws Ann. §700.449 (West Supp. 1989); N.M. Stat. Ann. §45-5-303.E (1989 & Supp. 1993); N.D. Cent. Code §30.1-28-03.3 (Supp. 1989).

28. D.C. Code Ann. §21-2033(c) (Supp. 1993).

29. N.D. Cent. Code §30.1-28-03-6 (Supp. 1989).

30. See, for example, Fla. Stat. Ann. §744.331(4) (1984) (right to appointed counsel); Mich. Comp. Laws Ann. §700.443(2) (1980) (right to counsel).

31. For example, Fla. Stat. Ann. §744.331(6) (West 1989); Mich. Comp. Laws Ann. §700.443a (West Supp. 1989).

32. Fla. Stat. Ann. §744.102(3) (West 1989). See also D.C. Code Ann. §21-2033(b) (Supp. 1993) (duty of counsel is to "represent zealously [the] individual's legitimate interests"); N.M. Stat. Ann. §45-5-303.1 (1989 & Supp. 1993).

33. D.C. Code Ann. §21-2033(b) (Supp. 1993). See also N.M. Stat.

Ann. §45-5-303.1 (1989 & Supp. 1993); N.D. Cent. Code §30.1-28-03.4 (Supp. 1989).

34. N.Y. Mental Hyg. Law §81.11 (McKinney Supp. 1993).
35. Mich. Comp. Laws Ann. §700.443(2) (West Supp. 1989); N.D. Cent. Code §30.1-28-03.3 (Supp. 1989) (attorney is appointed to act as GAL).
36. Mich. Comp. Laws Ann. §700.443a(2)-(4) (West Supp. 1989); N.D. Cent. Code §30.1-28-03.4.C (Supp. 1989).
37. D.C. Code Ann. §21-2033(a) (Supp. 1993).
38. N.M. Stat. Ann. §45-5-303.A (1989 & Supp. 1993).
39. N.M. Stat. Ann. §45-5-404.B (1989 & Supp. 1993).
40. Mich. Comp. Laws Ann. §700.443(1) (West Supp. 1989).
41. Fla. Stat. Ann. §744.320 (West 1989).
42. Fla. Stat. Ann. §744.334 (West 1989).
43. N.Y. Mental Hyg. Law §81.08 (McKinney Supp. 1993).
44. For example, Mich. Comp. Laws Ann. §700.451(2) West Supp. 1989); N.D. Cent. Code §30.1-28-09.2 (Supp. 1989).
45. Generally, D.C. Code Ann. §21-2031 (Supp. 1993); Fla. Stat. Ann. §744.331(1) (West 1989); Mich. Comp. Laws Ann. §700.451 (West Supp. 1989); N.M. Stat. Ann. §45-5-309 (1989 & Supp. 1993); N.D. Cent. Code §30.1-28-09 (Supp. 1989).
46. N.M. Stat. Ann. §§45-5-309.C (1989 & Supp. 1993). See also N.D. Cent. Code §30.1-28-09.3 (Supp. 1989) (not less than double-spaced 12-point type).
47. Fla. Stat. Ann. §744.331(1) (West 1989). Although the statute does not specify who is to read the notice to the person, it implies that it must be read when it is served. Many of the other statutes further ensure that the proposed ward will understand the nature of the proceedings by requiring that court-appointed guardians ad litem explain the hearing procedure, as well as the purpose and effects of the appointment of a guardian. For example, Mich. Comp. Laws Ann. §700.443a(1) (West Supp. 1989).
48. N.Y. Mental Hyg. Law §81.07 (McKinney Supp. 1993).
49. Fla. Stat. Ann. §744.331(4)(a) (West 1989). This statement contrasts with the provision in the former statute that "hearings shall be conducted in as informal a manner as may be consistent with orderly procedure . . . " Fla. Stat. Ann. §744.331(4) (1984). The new Florida statute lists a litany of rights to which the proposed

ward is entitled. Some of these rights resemble the rights of criminal defendants. See §744.1095.

50. For example, Fla. Stat. Ann. §744.109 (West 1989) (mandatory; if appeal is taken, transcript must be furnished to indigent ward at public expense); N.M. Stat. Ann. §45-5-303.I (1898 & Supp. 1993) (if requested by proposed ward or counsel or ordered by court).

51. D.C. Code Ann. §21-2041(h) (Supp. 1993); Fla. Stat. Ann. §744.331(4)(b) (West 1989); Mich. Comp. Laws Ann. §700.443(6) (West Supp. 1989); N.M. Stat. Ann. §45-5-303.F (1989 & Supp. 1993); N.D. Cent. Code §30.1-28-03.7 (Supp. 1989).

52. For example, D.C. Code Ann. §§21-2041(h), 21-2054(e) (Supp. 1993); N.D. Cent. Code §30.1-28-03.7 (Supp. 1989).

53. N.D. Cent. Code §30.1-28-03.7 (Supp. 1989).

54. Mich. Comp. Laws Ann. §700.443(6) (West Supp. 1989); N.M. Stat. Ann. §45-5-303.G (1989 & Supp. 1993). See also N.D. Cent. Code §30.1-28-03.8 (Supp. 1989).

55. N.Y. Mental Hyg. Law §81.11(c),(d) (McKinney Supp. 1993).

56. D.C. Code Ann. §21-2041(h) (Supp. 1993); Fla. Stat. Ann. §744.1095(2)-(5) (West 1989); Mich. Comp. Laws Ann. §700.443(7) (West Supp. 1989).

57. N.M. Stat. Ann. §45-5-303.H (1989 & Supp. 1993).

58. D.C. Code Ann. §21-2003 (Supp. 1993); Fla. Stat. Ann. §744.331(4)(c) (West 1989); Mich. Comp. Laws Ann. §700.444(1) (West Supp. 1989); N.M. Stat. Ann. §45-5-303.H (1989 & Supp. 1993); N.D. Cent. Code §30.1-28-04.2.b (Supp. 1989).

59. See Fla. Stat. Ann. §744.331(7) (1984); N.M. Stat. Ann. §45-5-304 (1978); N.D. Cent. Code §30.1-28-04 (1976).

60. Fla. Stat. Ann. §744.331(5)(a) (West 1989); N.M. Stat. Ann. §45-5-304.C(1) (1989 & Supp. 1993); N.D. Cent. Code §30.1-28-04.2.b(1) (Supp. 1989). See D.C. Code Ann. §21-2044(b) (Supp. 1993); Mich. Comp. Laws Ann. §700.444(1) (West Supp. 1989).

61. N.M. Stat. Ann. §45-5-304.C(3) (1989 & Supp. 1993); N.D. Cent. Code §30.1-28-04.2.b(2) (Supp. 1989).

62. Fla. Stat. Ann. §744.331(5)(b) (West 1989); N.M. Stat. Ann. §45-5-304.C(4) (1989 & Supp. 1993); N.D. Cent. Code §30.1-28-04.2.b(4) (Supp. 1989).

63. N.M. Stat. Ann. §45-5-304.C(2) (1989 & Supp. 1993); N.D. Cent. Code §30.1-28-04.2.b(3) (Supp. 1989).

64. N.M. Stat. Ann. §45-5-304.C(5) (1989 & Supp. 1993).

65. D.C. Code Ann. §21-2044(c) (Supp. 1993); Fla. Stat. Ann. §744.344 (West 1989); Mich. Comp. Laws Ann. §700.444(2) (West Supp. 1989); N.M. Stat. Ann. §45-5-304.C (1989 & Supp. 1993); N.D. Cent. Code §30.1-28-04.2-5 (Supp. 1989).
66. N.D. Cent. Code §30.1-28-04.5 (Supp. 1989).
67. *Olmstead v United States*, 227 US 438, 479 (1928) (Brandeis dissenting).
68. These figures include both court appointed attorneys and private attorneys retained by the respondent.

REFERENCES

Alexander, G. J. (1979). Premature probate: A different perspective on guardianship for the elderly. *Stanford Law Review 31,* 1003–1033.

Anderer, S. J. (1990). *Determining competency in guardianship proceedings.* Washington, DC: American Bar Association.

Dudovitz, N. (1985). Protective services and guardianships: Legal services and the role of the advocate. In *Representing older persons: An advocates' manual* (pp. 77–88). Washington, DC: National Senior Citizens Law Center.

Goodenough, G. K. (1988). The lack of objectivity of physician evaluations in geriatric guardianship cases. *Journal of Contemporary Law, 14,* 53–60.

Hafemeister, T. L., & Sales, B. D. (1984). Interdisciplinary evaluations for guardianships and conservatorships. *Law & Human Behavior, 8,* 335–354.

Hommel, P. A., & Lisi, L. B. (1989). Model standards for guardianship: Ensuring quality surrogate decision making services. *Clearinghouse Review, 23,* 433–443.

Horstman, P. M. (1975). Protective services for the elderly: The limits of parens patriae. *Missouri Law Review 40 (II),* 215–278.

Jost, T. D. (1980). The Illinois guardianship for disabled adults legislation of 1978 and 1979: Protecting the disabled from their zealous protectors. *Chicago Kent Law Review, 56,* 1087–1105.

Kemp, B. J., & Mitchell, J. M. (1992). Functional assessment in geriatric mental health. In J. E. Birren, R. B. Sloane & G. D. Cohen (Eds.), *Handbook of mental health and aging* (2nd ed.) (pp. 671–697). San Diego, CA: Academic.

Lisi, L. B., Burns, A. M., Hommel, P.A., Baird, K. B., Lindgren, C., Roe, E., & Brewster, S. (1992). *Final report: National study of guardianship system and feasibility of implementing expert systems.* Ann Arbor, MI: The Center for Social Gerontology.

McLaughlin, C. (1988). Doing good: A worker's perspective. *Public welfare 46 (II)*, 29–32.

Mitchell, A. M. (1978). Involuntary guardianship for incompetents: A strategy for legal services advocates. *Clearinghouse Review, 12*, 451–468.

Regan, J. J. (1985). *The discovery of elder abuse: Learning to live in the brave new world of mandatory reporting, protective services and public guardianship.* Paper presented at Elder Abuse Prevention and Intervention Policy: A Working Conference, Chicago, July, 1985. (Available from the Center for Social Gerontology, 2307 Shelby Ave., Ann Arbor, MI)

Scogin, F., & Perry, J. (1986). The role of functional assessment and gerontologists. *Law & Psychology Review, 10*, 123–132.

Smith, L. F. (1988). Representing the elderly client and addressing the question of competence. *Journal of Contemporary Law, 14*, 61–70.

Tremblay, P. R. (1987). On persuasion and paternalism: Lawyer decisionmaking and the questionably competent client. *Utah Law Review, 3*, 515–22.

Commentary: The More Things Change: Principles and Practices of Reformed Guardianship

Alison P. Barnes

In the closing observations in Penelope Hommel's chapter, she sketches the limited implementation of guardianship reforms despite the passage of extensive legislation. The unavoidable conclusion is that guardianship reform has largely failed to achieve its goals of (a) establishing individualized, less stigmatizing court-supervised assistance for all incapacitated persons, (b) causing more petitions to be modified or denied as inappropriate intrusions, and (c) assuring that only those in greatest need become wards. Extensive anecdotal evidence and limited research data show that such effects are not widespread (Keith & Wacker, 1992; Kritzer & Dicks, 1992). Further, there is no reason to expect improved results with the passage of time, for reasons that are the focus of this commentary.

The implementation has failed despite energetic information dissemination and careful thought on the part of reform proponents. Indeed, five years ago I was preparing state-specific judicial training materials, which the State Justice Institute (the funding agency) intended to adapt as each successive jurisdiction enacted reforms. State by state, other

254

advocates, with zeal for improved status for impaired elderly people and repugnance at the careless cruelties perpetrated in recent decades under traditional guardianship, imagined and worked for more humane substitute decision-making processes.

The failure of guardianship reform for the elderly—or limited success, if you prefer, since examples of some good effects are undeniable—lies in a simple, if not obvious, cause. Specifically, the impetus for statutory reform originated outside the system of guardianship adjudication for the elderly, which sought to manage assets rather than to promote human rights. Advocates for the elderly came almost exclusively from legal and social service agencies which only recently mobilized around guardianship for indigent persons, rather than from the private bar which serves elderly people with any significant assets. For more affluent elderly people who are the traditional subjects of such private assistance, human rights and dignity are not threatened by the harsh realities of poverty, and property issues loom relatively important. Reform procedures prove to be a poor fit for persons with significant assets. Also, many reformers were concerned with developmentally disabled persons, for whom diagnosis is secondary to functional assessment as an indicator of need for assistance. The functional definition of incapacity in many reformed statutes is, therefore, inappropriate for the aged, for whom the diagnosis and prognosis separate incapacity from knowing, if eccentric, choice.

Because the purposes of guardianship reform are complex and somewhat muddled, legislative mandates have neither forced on the legal system the principles and values of reform nor persuaded the majority of participants of the reforms' moral or practical value. In short, we reformers did not understand fully the nature of guardianships for the elderly, so reform proposals are incompatible with some fundamental aims of guardianship. The questions now are ''What aims?'' and ''Why incompatible?'' The answers may show how the genuine problems motivating reformers can be effectively addressed.

I propose three principal impediments to guardianship reform as envisioned in the 1980s. First, intensive procedural due process and oversight are too rigidly legalistic for the guardianship transaction, and particularly for most people—family, guardians, and the elderly—who seek help from guardianship. Second, the limited guardianship model, which requires that the guardian's powers be tailored to the ward's incapacities, conflicts with the law's need for uncompromised authority to deal in property, and fails to respond to the practical reality of changing capacity over time. One might say limited guardianship is "not legal enough" for the courts to use effectively. Last, I assert that society has not resolved fundamental ambivalence about the aged and property control.

THE LEGALIZATION OF GUARDIANSHIP

Reformed, or "legalized," guardianship statutes poorly fit society's needs and values because they are burdened with the rhetoric of rights. Discussion of rights is fundamental to American thinking on individual autonomy and liberty, so it may be inevitable and proper that legal reforms begin there. However, our concept of individual rights as a shield against oppressive authority originated in 18th century political philosophy (Glendon, 1991). The paradigm is not the relationship between individuals, but rather the relationship between the individual and the sovereign. Rights are the trump card accorded the individual, to play when political leaders abuse their powers.

The rights concept is an ill fit for the relationships of most individuals who use the guardianship system, for whom the giving and receiving of care is based on love, need and duty. Such relationships are complex, ongoing exchanges, characterized by negotiation and compromise of each others' personal desires. The values system of caregiving, rather than being rights-based, has been called an "ethics of accommodation" (Collopy, Dubler, & Zuckerman, 1990).

The trump card of rights, instead of clarifying issues and easing decision making, might be seen as tantamount to taking a machete to a baseball game. Rather than observing the rules of the game (i.e., the rules of interpersonal relationships inherent in the caregiving relationship) a machete- armed player can stop a runner on third, or assure that no opponent will impede a home run (i.e., force an elderly care recipient into a nursing home for convenience' sake, or perhaps bring charges of abuse against a noncriminal but inadequate caregiver). None would say the machete wielder (or the wielder of rights) has won the real game, however, which is securing loving, or at least decent and respectful, care from chosen, willing friend or kin.

"Rights talk" poses a serious problem in all aspects of care for the vulnerable. An alarming and offensive outgrowth of rights rhetoric is the characterization of caregiving as an adversarial relationship. Consider, for example, the elder abuse laws described by Elias Cohen in chapter 4 of this volume. For legislators' purpose of defining a social ill amenable to solution, flimsy data were inflated into national statistics on abuse of the frail elderly and transformed into the accusation that overburdened principal care providers are the most likely abusers (U.S. Congress, House Select Committee on Aging, 1981, 1985, 1990). The impact of such generalizations on social workers and other direct service providers subject to the resulting mandatory abuse reporting statutes (Lee, 1986) is frightening; loving homes all become potential chambers of horror.

The observation that most guardians are good guardians does not deny or trivialize the findings of the press which sparked the 1980's wave of reform (Bayles & McCartney, 1987; Good & King, 1986). Nor does it deny the incidence of emotional, physical, sexual, and financial abuse of the elderly by their caregivers, whether by family members or others. Sad to say, while in home care administration this author saw unforgettable instances of each of these.

However, we must distinguish between the failure of a system to identify, correct, and prevent ongoing abuses, on one hand, and poisoning the entire system with ill-conceived mistrust for caregivers, on the other. A pervasive rights orientation is worse for the great majority than haphazard traditional guardianship standards.

Can we monitor family guardianships without destructive effect? Oversight based on rights and legal process is not only intrusive and potentially destructive, but largely ineffective in policing the quality of family care. In truth, it is very difficult for government, in the form of police or social services, to provide effective protection against persons in one's family circle. This is due not just to shortages in funding or poor training of public service workers, but also to the very healthy force of private life to shut out public intervention (Bok, 1982).

From a legal view, intervenors in America require the consent of any competent elderly person before intervention can proceed, regardless of the egregious nature of the abuse.[1] Sad to say, in even the worst conditions, vulnerable persons will protest vehemently and coherently any action against a caregiver, out of fear either of change or retribution. As we gain insight into the thinking of hostages and battered spouses, such an observation should surprise no one. Even criminal charges, which strictly speaking do not require a complaint by the victim, are often precluded because of the difficulty of proceeding without the victim's participation. Thus, the mandate for intervention is seldom clear when the victim of abuse or exploitation is a person whose incompetence has not been established.

The legal rhetoric of guardianship reform, then, is designed to intercede in the worst caregiving relationships, those that exploit, injure, or demean the vulnerable member, providing at best only a tortured remnant of the impulse to give care. It might also be employed when the guardian–ward relationship is an ''arm's length transaction'', in which society does not assume the caregiver's good behavior (a ''worst case'' only in the sense that the ward has no friend able to give assistance). In particular, reformed guardianship is appropriate to constrain a government entity which serves as guardian, recognizing that such powers might extend not only to seriously incapacitated persons, but ultimately to all citizens. Who can say, after all, that there is no one more competent to make our financial or personal choices, to guard against our own follies? Thus, reformed guardianship is a good model when the guardian is a stranger to the ward, particularly one affiliated with the state. This is an appropriate use of a rights claim, this being the weakest moral claim for care, when love and honor are insufficient.

If this is so, many guardianships created under reform statutes should include government action either as petitioner or guardian, or both. Logically, the number of public guardianships should be growing as states acknowledge a service responsibility; however, data are sketchy. A Wisconsin study of reform guardianship cases found, for example, that 54% of petitions were filed by social service agencies (Kritzer & Dicks, 1992). Under traditional guardianship law, it was estimated that more than 80% of petitions were filed by family members and friends (Bayles & McCartney, 1987). Public guardians such as New Hampshire's, established under a revised, functional guardianship statute, have been vocal in support of the rights of wards and proposed wards (Casananto, Saunders, & Simon, 1986).

Evidence that more affluent persons, particularly those with responsible relatives, avoid guardianship is anecdotal. Within a year after reforms were enacted in Florida, this author heard from several people with elderly relatives about their extreme reluctance to initiate guardianship proceedings, though they needed legal authority to make pressing decisions about an elderly person's situation. One correspondent, a law school dean, reported that his attorney strongly advised against guardianship for his mother-in-law because of the new requirements. Some articles warn of the expense (e.g., Fultermeyer, 1991). This response is not surprising. Why incur costs for procedures and oversight that are potentially destructive and largely ineffective?

Revisions of focus and policy with regard to guardianship will help make sense of the mixed results of reform. First, we must accept that guardianship after reform is seldom a tool for the middle class (i.e., persons with property and access to legal counsel to plan less intrusive means of substitute decision making). Rather, it provides protection for poor, uneducated and/or isolated persons inherently lacking power to advocate for themselves, by equalizing their status with that of the stranger serving as guardian. The law should not and will not acknowledge this fact, since it is neither desirable nor constitutionally acceptable to restrict guardianship to the most likely users. As a result, however, family (i.e., private) responsibility is as important as ever for impaired elderly persons who are not poor.

Second, acknowledging that some abuse exists in unsupervised family caregiving relationships among all economic classes, we must develop better ways to identify and respond to mistreatment. One aspect, already implemented in a few states and in England, is registration of durable (or enduring) powers of attorney, the middle-class alternative to guardianship powers.[2] Caregivers who need legal authority to make pressing decisions seek sympathetic legal counsel to execute durable powers of attorney authorizing financial and personal decisions for the impaired old. The law's requirement that the elderly individual be competent to execute such a power, and free from duress, is neatly (or sometimes, not so neatly) brushed under the rug. A growing body of evidence of abuses of durable powers of attorney suggests that guardianship's problems have merely moved to a new legal address (Law Commission, 1991).

Creating an administrative system for durable powers is likely to be criticized as ineffective, a bureaucratic inconvenience without deterrent value. Undeniably, a careful plan to spend assets without authorization can evade detection. On the other hand, a carefully maintained register requires the reporting party to lie, plausibly and consistently. In addition to providing a basis for detecting inconsistent and untrue responses, it serves to confirm that the exercise of a durable power is a transaction in which society has a significant interest. Basically honest, but lax or corruptible, caregivers would be deterred from filing false information about the ward's health, finances or general well-being. Traditional guardianship failed in its responsibility to wards when courts failed to require filing of basic reports or failed to read them.

An essential step toward quality guardianship is improving education for caregivers about the nature of good and respectful care, the types of formal assistance available to supplement family care, and the psychological impact of caregiving in the family. Educational programs are mandated, if less often provided, for new guardians under many reformed statutes. Such programs need more development, however, and should be required and conveniently available to all caregivers, not only court-appointed guardians. A very significant corollary is development of effective respite care, still a knotty problem and beyond the scope of this chapter.

Next, we must admit that no amount of education or assistance will improve all relationships that are not grounded in the values of loving caregiving. When the impaired elder is willing, then, we must be ready with effective protective services, including homes where displaced, impaired persons can live and receive assistance during the painful break from a family caregiver, and some choice of secure places to live after the intensive transition. To date, protective services remain a rudimentary exercise in legal procedure, informed by widely varied capabilities in emergency response workers. The ways to make the possibility of change less awful for the elder to contemplate than continued familiar abuse is a subject for study by government and social scientists.

Finally, we must acknowledge there are some things the law just won't do. Intervening in family caregiving over the objection of all participants simply does not happen until someone, presumably the impaired person, is hospitalized or murdered. The responsibility lies, even in legally oriented American society, with neighbors, friends, and professional "friends" from churches and social service agencies, to inquire about the well-being of disabled elderly persons, to visit, and to be aware of their quality of life. Sometimes, those tasks require living with the knowledge that a good person lives with risk, sorrow, and disrespect; not everything is immediately remedied by the law. The continual presence of outsiders can prevent a stressful relationship from deteriorating into abuse, however. It is the only way to increase the likelihood that an elderly person can imagine a life without abuse, and take the risks necessary to achieve it.

For the longer term, we might create a family tribunal to consider specific problems of deteriorated family relations of all types. Family courts already exist in some (primarily urban, high volume) jurisdictions, to deal with child and spouse abuse and truancy. (Guardianship matters by contrast, are considered appropriate for probate courts, which settle estates of the dead.) An alternative tribunal might be developed which strikes the right balance among administrative efficiency, investigative potential, and social services expertise. Such a new body might be justified by the growing numbers of very elderly persons in the next century. Indeed, unless the numbers of very elderly, incapacitated persons are limited by new treatments for Alzheimers' disease, stroke, and other disorders of reasoning or communication, the very effectiveness of medical technology is likely to produce an even larger contingent of impaired survivors (Barnes, 1992).

LIMITED GUARDIANSHIP

Reformed guardianship, with its limited guardianship paradigm, requires the courts to search for the holy grail of the perfect match between guardian's authority and ward's abilities—and judges reasonably have been reluctant to pursue it. While limited guardianship is an admirable attempt to reflect the dynamics of a healthy caregiving relationship, it is legal quicksand which swallows the main task of the law, namely, assigning responsibilities among the parties.

Limited guardianship is not a new concept, and a historical review is enlightening. Limited guardianship refines the traditional division of a persons's capabilities into management of property and personal affairs—a model originally based in the jurisdiction of the early English King's Courts over real property, while church courts heard issues of equity and personal property (Holdsworth, 1966; Barnes, 1992). The division of personal and property powers is gross enough for the courts to utilize. The principal objection to this dichotomy is that, as it is presently applied, many wards may be deprived of rights to make decisions about which they feel strongly concerning living conditions and caregivers.

A somewhat different division of decision-making authority appears more useful. An incapacitated individual should be given the greatest authority and latitude to make very personal decisions, such as medical choices, where to reside, and who should be a caregiver, regardless of the objective impact of the choice. Such decisions can and should be delayed until a lucid interval occurs, and any input from the individual should be taken seriously even when comprehension is doubtful. On the other hand, it is more useful to commit financial management decisions to another for a less-than- competent owner. Financial decisions with important lifestyle ramifications (such as whether to move, or with whom to live) should be recognized as personal decisions, regardless of their financial impact, provided impoverishment is not a foreseeable result. Since guardianships for the elderly are created to make specific decisions (Iris, 1988), balancing the public interest opposing welfare versus private lifestyle choice can assist the courts in determining the scope of guardians' powers and appropriate oversight.

Is that shift in focus sufficient? Finer divisions of a person's powers can pose serious problems for the courts. Such distinctions have been considered from time to time in the context of voluntary guardianship, a device that allows an individual (usually elderly) to petition the court to appoint and supervise a guardian for specific purposes, such as financial management. Problems arise when a voluntary guardian takes actions to which the ward objects, the ward's acts conflict with the guardian's, or third parties refuse to accept the authority of either (*Reed v. Bryan and Century National Bank*, 1986). Courts have been confused quite consistently about whose powers or acts control, and who is responsible for any harm which results to guardian, ward, or third parties. Though the finer divisions of voluntary and limited guardianship satisfy theorists, practitioners are virtually unanimous in recommending alternatives.

The subdivision of powers is confusing not only at the point of exercise, but also in the definition of legal incapacity which is the basis for appointing a guardian in the first place. A person might take action without having the ability to make a decision, or might act in self-destructive ways for reasons others fail to grasp. Yet courts are ill prepared to distinguish the act from the decision-making capability, to make the diagnostic distinctions necessary to anything more than a rudimentary division of powers and capabilities. Although some tests have been developed to assess decision-making capacity, they are not tailored to the needs and deliberations of courts of law (Altman & Parmalee, 1990). Rather, the inquiry invites battles of expert psychologists' opinions, derived from careers in evaluation development and implementation. Until the test results are better tailored to the evaluation required by the law, there is no hope of going forward to define the nature and degrees of human comprehension for the purposes of appointing a substitute decision maker. This volume just begins to explore this rich field for multi-disciplinary research.

A third, related difficulty with limited guardianship determinations is their transitoriness. Even if decision-making capacities could be more reliably identified, results of such an evaluation could be presumed valid only for the time of testing, since many elderly people have greatly varying capacity over the course of a day or sometimes much longer cycles. The meaning of the test result is therefore problematic. If the test results identify capacity in specific decision-making capabilities during 10% of the subject's day (e.g., the subject is lucid from 8:00 to 10:30 in the morning), should a guardian be appointed to make all decisions the individual cannot make during the 90 percent period, only those which arise outside of the lucid interval, or must all the affected decisions wait for the individual's most capable hour?

Many would advocate holding all decisions for the most lucid interval, but the question becomes trickier still. What if the individual makes potentially destructive choices during the rest of the day? Can an individual effectively consent to recommended surgery at noon, while protesting vehemently into the evening? Can one contract to sell property one day, only to deny the transaction the next? A court's judgment about legal capacity is meaningless if the guardian's authority is too limited to protect and assist the ward.

In addition, some limited guardianship statutes introduced a purely functional definition of capacity,[3] considered by proponents to be a more objective standard, free from the stigma of diagnostic labels (Green, 1944; Leifer, 1984; Murphy, 1991). Functional statutes require only detailed proof of an individual's ability to meet basic needs. The redefinition of incapacity was most acceptable to advocates for developmentally disabled persons who have never had legal capacity and for whom capabilities are relatively stable.

The results for the elderly can be disastrous. Without a diagnosis of the cause of mental incapacity, the alleged incapacity can consist of intentionally chosen antisocial or self-destructive choices. The test for legal capacity could become whether one has made the socially approved choices, rather than whether one can make a choice at all (Mitchell, 1979). Further, without the diagnosis of the cause of the decision-making "failure," the findings are limited to the time of testing. Neither result is acceptable in determining the capacity of an elderly person. Rather, "pure" functional capacity statutes must be changed to require a well-documented diagnosis and prognosis for future behavior.

In summary, the difficult case is the ward who is neither wholly capable nor completely incapable of decision making. The property/personal decision model has proven to overburden the elderly, because the right to spend is typically the right to choose where and how to live. The typical limited guardianship "laundry list" of 15 or 20 powers that might be transferred by the court from ward to guardian is impractical because the ability to make similar decisions is difficult to pin down and impossible to generalize over time for many incapacitated elderly. New standards for substitute decision making must include a presumption that the individual is capable of making very personal decisions, as well as a presumption that another person is more likely to carry out effective property management for persons with limited capacity, particularly that which varies over time. In addition, functional definitions of incapacity must be replaced by definitions that require a diagnosis of the cause of the incapacity, the functional deficits which result from the diagnosed illness, and proof of a causal link between them.

PROPERTY RIGHTS FOR THE LIVING

One must ask why we continue to debate the rights of impaired elderly, when the movements for rights of younger physically, mentally, and developmentally disabled persons have had greater and quicker impact on society in terms of education and social programs (Barnes, 1992, pp. 645–650). The expense of elderly autonomy is not limited to the cost of procedural reforms. Rather, it is the social cost of property control by persons reasonably expected to die sooner than most, when they manage their assets in ways that do not promote social order or reinforce family expectations. That is, elderly people may become a threat to conventional social order when they choose to spend their assets in ways that do not benefit their heirs or other socially approved causes, though their purposes are neither illegal nor, for other age groups, subject to criticism or constraint.

It is useful to recall that guardianship in early modern English law was concerned with managing property, not personal affairs, and that the sovereign who had responsibility for the impaired most often gave management of the lands to the family, reserving only some receipts for costs. The property orientation of guardianship persisted through the centuries. At the end of the 19th century, several states passed new legislation authorizing a less formal procedure for guardianship of property, often called conservatorship, to assist caregivers of elderly persons without extensive court process. The statutes did not apply to incapacitated persons who were not old.

Case law in the 20th century on guardianship appeals and will contests (when the elderly person makes a new will not invalidated by a determination of incompetency) provides insight into the conflict over property control between the generations. In one typical scenario, an elderly man meets a much younger woman (often of perceived inferior socioeconomic circumstances) and begins spending assets on gifts, travel, or a new home (*In re* Benjamin F. Roll, 1971; *In re* Josiah Oakes, 1945; *In re* Ver Vaecke's Estate, 1923). He may propose or make a will in favor of his new companion, over the objections of his adult children (*Hoffman v. Kohns*, 1988). Courts are often willing to find incapacity or, in the case of wills, undue influence or duress, in order to redistribute assets along more conventional lines. Older woman/younger man scenarios are also found in the reported cases, which often need even less evidence of an unconventional relationship to spark disruptive disapproval (e.g., *In re* Will of Moses, 1969).

Without implying that the decisions cited have done justice, there is a certain visceral logic arising from the fact that the elderly will reach a natural conclusion to their lives sooner than younger family members. Faced with hard decisions, courts are not without reason to favor the social structure represented by a traditional family, implicitly supporting the physical care of the old by the financial powers or/and vitality of the young. That is, under the cloak of individual case adjudications courts render decisions in favor of social and family stability.

Family inheritance is fundamental to the law. Though its rules are less rigid in the United States than in the United Kingdom, and younger Americans increasingly express doubts about the right to inherited wealth, there is no reasonable expectation that inheritance will disappear from American society. Arguments in favor of inheritance cite its influence for saving rather than spending throughout a lifetime, and for motivating the young to care for the old. Whether or not such ideas are persuasive as social planning, it remains true that each person must die, and that a greater proportion and far larger absolute number of individuals than in times past leave accumulated assets. Some system must distribute the assets of the dead to ownership by the living.

Yet, it is grossly unfair that courts cannot articulate their reasoning without offending our most fundamental rights to freedom from unequal treatment and unwarranted intrusion. Lawyers and policy makers need to respond with new rules that divide property rights with more discernment, neither leaving all discretion to the ''competent'' elderly person to spend as desired, nor giving all control to the younger generation upon a judgment of incapacity or undue influence. Anthropologists and social psychologists are called upon for studies of our real values and attitudes, which are presently obscured by guilt and ill-fitting behavioral norms.

The rights orientation of reformed guardianship has said too little about the property rights of the elderly to provide any useful guide for defining the role of the elderly in a society with scarce resources, but the issues remain in the public sphere. The right to pass on property, for example, is critical in debates on Medicaid long-term care eligibility guidelines, which determine how much of an elderly person's own assets must be committed to pay for nursing home care. The health care reform debates are likely to provide further insight into our assumptions about the allocation of resources for limited returns. We may hope, however, that the conversation among disciplines reflected in this volume will enable us not simply to make decisions, but to understand the consequences of our own policies.

NOTES

1. Fla. Stat. §415.105(5) (1993).
2. English law: Enduring Powers of Attorney Ch. 29 (1985) Mental Health Act; Fla. Stat. §709.08 et seq. (1987).
3. Mo. Re. Stat §475.010 et seq. (1993); N.H. Rev. Stat. Ann. §464-A:2 (XI) (1993).

REFERENCES

Altman, W. M., & Parmalee, P. A. (1990). Discrimination based on age: The special case of the institutionalized aged. In *The handbook of psychology and law*. New York: Springer Publishing Co.

Barnes, A. P. (1992). Beyond guardianship reform: A reevaluation of autonomy and beneficence for a system of principled decision-making in long term care. *Emory Law Journal, 41*, 635.

Bayles, F., & McCartney, S. (1987, September 22). Six-part series prepared for Associated Press. *Tampa Tribune*, p. 1F ff.

Bok, Sisela. (1982). *Secrets*. New York: Pantheon.

Casananto, M. D., Saunders, A. G., Jr., & Simon, M. S. (1986, Fall). Individual functional assessment: A guide to determining the need for guardianship under the New Hampshire law. *New Hampshire Bar Journal, 28*, 13.

Collopy, B., Dubler, N., & Zuckerman, C. (1991, December). The ethics of home care: Autonomy, and accommodation. *Hastings Center Report, 20*, 31.

Fultermeyer, E. (1991, February 25). The perfect death. *Fortune*, 131.

Glendon, M. A. (1991). *Rights talk: The impoverishment of political discourse*. Maxwell McMillan, NY: Free Press.

Good, J., & King, L. (1986, December 14). Wards of the court. *St. Petersburg Times*, p. A1.

Green, M. D. (1944). Proof of mental incompetency and the unexpressed major premise. *Yale Law Journal, 53*, 271- 276-278.

Hoffman v. Kohns, 385 So.2d 1964 (Fla. 2d D.C.A. 1980).

Holdsworth, W. S. (1966). *A history of English law* (7th ed., rev.). Oxford, England: Claredon.

In re Benjamin F. Roll, 117, N.J. Super, 122, 283 A.2d 764 (1971).

In re Josiah Oakes, 8 Law Rptr. 122 (Mass. 1845).

In re Ver Vaecke's Estate, 223 Mich. 419, 194 N.W. 135 (1923).

In re Will of Moses, 227 So. 2d 829 (MS 1969).

Iris, M. A. (1988). Guardianship and the elderly: A multiperspective view of the decision-making process. *The Gerontologist, 28* (Suppl.), 39.

Keith, P. M., & Wacker, R. R. (1992). Guardianship reform: Does revised legislation make a difference in outcomes for proposed wards? *Journal of Aging and Social Policy, 4*, 139.

Kritzer, H., & Dicks, H. (1992, January). *Adult guardianships in Wisconsin: An empirical assessment*. Report for the Center for Public Representation and the Elder Law Center Coalition of Wisconsin Aging Groups.

Law Commission. (1991). *Mentally incapacitated adults and decision-making: An overview* (Consultation Paper No. 19). London: Her Majesty's Stationary Office.

Lee, D. (1986). Mandatory reporting of elder abuse: A cheap but ineffective solution to the problem [Note]. *Fordham Urban Law Journal, 14,* 723.

Leifer, R. (1984). The competence of the psychiatrist to assist in the determination of competency: A skeptical *(sic)* inquiry into the courtroom functions of psychiatrist. *Syracuse Law Review, 14,* 564, 570.

Mitchell, A. (1979). The objects of our wisdom and our coercion: Involuntary guardianship for incompetency. *Southern California Law Review, 52,* 1405.

Murphy, J. R. (1991). Older clients of questionable competency: Making accurate competency determinations through the utilization of medical professionals. *Georgetown Journal of Legal Ethics, 4,* 899.

Reed v. Bryan and Century National Bank, 498 So. 2d 868 (Fla. 1986).

U.S. Congress, House Select Committee on Aging. (1981). *Elder abuse: An examination of a hidden problem* (H. 277, 97th Cong., 1st sess.) Washington, DC: Government Printing Office.

U.S. Congress, House Select Committee on Aging, Subcommittee on Health and Long-term Care (1985). *Elder abuse: A national disgrace* (H. 83, 99th Cong., 1st sess.) Washington, DC: Government Printing Office.

U.S. Congress, House Select Committee on Aging, Subcommittee on Health and Long-term Care (1990). *Elder abuse: A decade of shame and inaction* (H. 997, 101st Cong., 2d sess.) Washington, DC: Government Printing Office.

Commentary: Revising Revisionism in Guardianship: An Assessment of Legal Reform of Decisional Incapacity

Winsor C. Schmidt

The decade of the 1980s saw examples of significant procedural and substantive change in guardianship law. Many of the statutory changes from 1989 to 1993 for the District of Columbia, Florida, Kentucky, Michigan, New Mexico, New York, North Dakota, Pennsylvania, and South Dakota are catalogued by Hommel in this volume. These changes reportedly represent a guardianship trend away from paternalism and dependence toward maximization of independence and autonomy.

After summarizing the reforms, Hommel identifies several challenges for the future: (a) monitoring implementation to see that the new laws are translated into practice, (b) assessing the impact of the new statutes, and (c) establishing and maintaining a balance between individual independence and autonomy on the one hand, and the need for protective intervention on the other. The challenges are conveyed in such a way that they offer Barnes (in the preceding commentary) the opportunity to venture the "unavoidable conclusion . . . that guardianship reform has largely failed. . . ." (p. 254).

Barnes asserts three impediments to successful guardianship reform. First, "legalization" of guardianship is too rigid. Second, the limited guardianship concept is impractical and *"not legal enough"* [emphasis mine] (p. 256). Third, and, most fatal to reform, "society has not resolved fundamental ambivalence about the aged and property control" (p. 256). The third point refers to the idea that too much protection for older persons' autonomy threatens a notion of social order and stability.

> That is, elderly people may become a liability for conventional social order when they choose to spend their assets in ways which do not benefit their heirs or other socially-approved causes, though their purposes are neither illegal nor, for other age groups, subject to criticism or constraint. (p. 264)

I propose that Barnes' three impediments are not impediments but revisionism, and that they demonstrate that reform of the law regarding older adults' decision-making capacity has not gone far enough. I suggest that implementation of reforms can be facilitated by heeding Hommel's observation that statutory language is effective when in the form of "absolute mandate or prohibition" (p. 245). I suggest that assessment of the new statutes' impact must include a determination of the extent to which wards' interests are served, or whether third-party interests are served instead. I also suggest that balancing autonomy against protective intervention is not appropriate in the current guardianship environment, but rather that maximizing autonomy should continue and expand. The risks of too much paternalism are greater than the risks of too much autonomy.

RIGHTS AND GUARDIANSHIP

At the outset, one should recognize that Barnes is not only quite provocative, but also does a significant service to guardianship literature. As Hommel observes, there is little or no research supporting reform critics' claims that the pendulum has swung too far from paternalism to autonomy. There is also little, if any, antireform analysis in the guardianship literature. Barnes' hammering on the guardianship anvil can strengthen the sword of reform.

Barnes argues that the rights paradigm underlying guardianship reform is not appropriate for the relationship between individuals in guardianship, but rather applies to the relationship between individual and sovereign. I disagree and argue that guardianship is a very appropriate area for the application of the rights paradigm.

The research on guardianship practice (e.g. Lisi et al., 1992; Schmidt, 1981, 1990; Schmidt, Miller, Bell & New, 1981) demonstrates that guardianship is a contemporary example of oppressive authority necessitating application and implementation of a rights shield. Private relationships between individuals in law are governed first by contract, and by contract law. Private substitute decision making for living adults is carried out in the law through such mechanisms as power of attorney, durable power of attorney, and living wills. When private legal relationships are unsuccessful, resort to courts (public dispute resolution forums) and public law occurs. When private decision-making and caregiving relationships are unsuccessful, resort to probate court (public decision-dispute resolution forums) and guardianship law occurs.

Law and lawyers would be more loved if loving decision making and empathic caregiving could be legislated. But there is no legal duty to rescue precisely because such things cannot be legislated, implemented, and enforced as mandates. As James Madison indicated, there would be no need for law or government if people were angels. Rights protect us from individuals, authorities, and organizations that are not angelic. Protection is admittedly costly and inefficient to good guardians, decision makers, and caregivers, but this is the price paid to maximize autonomy and freedom.

Barnes asserts, " 'Rights talk' poses a serious problem in all aspects of care for the vulnerable. An alarming and offensive outgrowth of rights rhetoric is the characterization of caregiving as an adversarial relationship." (p. 256) This complaint continues Glendon's (1991) lament over the alleged contemporary tendency to frame social controversies as a clash of rights. Instead of anxiety over the implementation of American law's adversarial model, one could identify a golden age of American law, especially for the vulnerable, with greatly exaggerated reports of litigiousness (e.g., Galanter, 1983). In the Kuhnian (Kuhn, 1970) sense of paradigm, the accumulation of casebooks, treatises, and other curriculum material (e.g., Frolik & Barnes, 1992; Kapp, 1992; Perlin, 1989–1993; Reisner & Slobogin, 1990) chronicling the federal and state statutes and cases devoted to rights of the vulnerable heralds the arrival of a rights revolution for the vulnerable and less able. What other society has a better legal environment for the vulnerable?

Barnes suggests that guardianship reform's apparent mistrust of guardianship caregivers and the "pervasive rights orientation" (p. 257 poisons the system. She observes that such vulnerable persons as hostages and battered spouses sometimes protest action against caregivers, and that the intervention mandate is seldom clear and largely ineffective. One can agree that paternalism's goals in guardianship are mixed, confused, and easily abused. Some of this, however, may be a function of misunderstanding and failure to do legal triage.

A hostage or battered spouse is a victim of kidnapping, as well as assault and battery. The first remedy is criminal justice, the intervenor is the state, the victim's psychological dependence is largely irrelevant to the crime, and the state's interest is in protecting and enforcing public wrongs against its citizens. The victim then has the opportunity of self-care in the private market through private contract. If the victim is incompetent, guardianship may be appropriate to facilitate decision making about needs. The state's role here is determining incompetence and providing a public guardian if a private guardian is unwilling, irresponsible, or unaffordable. Neither the criminal justice system nor the incompetence justice system is perfect, but they have comparatively clear purposes. The first won't care for the victim, and the second won't punish or deter the caregiver.

The guardianship system is being " 'legalized' " (Barnes, p. 256). Barnes cites an inconvenienced law school dean and the cost objections of the private bar and of the relatively affluent families the private bar represents. The inconvenience and cost suggest that reform is having an effect. Guardianship is like intestate succession in that, if one makes a will, he or she decides; if not, then the court decides. If one establishes a durable power of attorney and living will, that person decides; if not, guardianship court decides. Cost and inconvenience are the price of not planning. Procedure encourages planning, negotiation, and settlement; it deters failure to plan. The private bar and its clients will find private agreements and remedies. The more difficult problem addressed by guardianship reform is substitute decision making for the state's clients, people for whom no one else will care and who do not have private agreements and remedies. Failure of private markets necessitates government intervention, regulation, and procedure. If the state doesn't offer care, who will? And if the state offers care and substitute decision making, there must be rights protection against the bear hug of the sovereign.

There is also support for application of the rights paradigm to guardianship in constitutional analysis. A finding of legal incompetence in most states limits or takes away

> the right to make contracts; sell, purchase, mortgage, or lease property; make gifts; travel, or decide where to live; vote, or hold elected office; initiate or defend against suits; make a will, or revoke one; engage in certain professions; lend or borrow money; appoint agents; divorce, or marry; refuse medical treatment; keep and care for children; serve on a jury; be a witness to any legal document; drive a car; pay or collect debts; manage or run a business. (Brown, 1979, p. 286)

When such protectible property and liberty interests are identified, state procedures regarding these interests are assessed in constitutional due process claims according to three factors:

> First, the private interest that will be affected by the official action; second, the risk of an erroneous deprivation of such interest through the procedures used, and the probable value, if any, of additional or substitute procedural safeguards; and finally, the Government's interest, including the function involved and the fiscal and administrative burdens that the additional or substitute procedural requirement would entail. (*Mathews v. Eldridge*, 1976, p. 335)

In the official sovereign or government action of guardianship, the alleged incompetent faces loss or restriction of some or all of the enumerated private property and liberty interests. The guardianship literature (e.g. Lisi et al., 1992; Schmidt, 1981; Schmidt, 1990; Schmidt, Miller, Bell & New, 1981) is replete with evidence of the risks of erroneous deprivation of these interests through the prereform procedures. The probable value of additional and substitute procedures is demonstrated by the reported inconvenience and deterrence of reform procedures, and the accumulating evidence about the efficacy of procedure. In the context of the family court, cited by Barnes, and in estate settlement, research shows that adversary procedures produce greater participant satisfaction with personal custody outcomes, and enhance perceptions of fairness (Martin, 1980; Melton & Lind, 1982).

The government's interests include substitute decision making for legal incompetents about their person and property, efficient fiscal and administrative practice, participant satisfaction that one has been heard, and fairness. Efficient fiscal and administrative practice considers not just economic efficiency, but also efficiency in a federalist, democratic government that values justice and equity and that understands their financial cost (e.g., Rosenbloom, 1986).

The United States Supreme Court has not ruled on whether procedural due process applies to guardianship, although former Chief Justice Burger's concurring opinion in *O'Connor v. Donaldson* (1975) suggests that it does:

> Of course, an inevitable consequence of exercising the *parens patriae* power is that the ward's personal freedom will be substantially restrained, whether a guardian is appointed to control his property, he is placed in the custody of a private third party, or committed to an institution. Thus, however the power is implemented, due process requires that it not be revoked indiscriminately. (p. 583)

One federal appeals court failed to find a constitutional right to appointment of a guardian *ad litem* in guardianship (*Rud v. Dahl*, 1978). But another federal appeals court more recently recognized a liberty interest in controlling one's lawsuit and in avoiding the stigma of an incompetency declaration. That court identified a due process right to a hearing before a guardian *ad litem* can be appointed (*Thomas v. Humfield*, 1990).

Notwithstanding Barnes's arguably misplaced critique of the rights paradigm in guardianship, her recommended focus and policy revisions are salutary and endorsable. The revisions are ironically legalistic, regulatory, and rights oriented. Barnes first recommends acceptance of reform protection "for poor, uneducated and/or isolated persons inherently lacking power to advocate for themselves, by equalizing their status with a stranger serving as guardian." (p. 259) Second, Barnes advocates registration of durable powers of attorney. This would provide public oversight to unregulated private transactions that increasingly are subject to reports of abuse and exploitation. We should not be sanguine, however, about the alleged deterrent effect of registration on the filing of false information by irresponsible caregivers. Statutory mandates for filing annual reports in guardianship without court reviews and audits have been unsuccessful in accomplishing accountability (e.g., Schmidt, 1984).

Barnes's next focus and policy revisions include improving caregiver education and values, respite care, and protective services (e.g., Blenkner, Bloom, Nielson & Weber, 1974; Schmidt, 1986; Schmidt & Miller, 1984). These points are understated but important.

Finally, Barnes suggests the establishment of a new "family tribunal" to address "deteriorated family relations," especially for the growing proportion of elderly persons (p. 261). The creation of what might be called an "elder court" is temptingly analogous to juvenile court. But the juvenile court institution has arguably failed to realize its paternalistic rehabilitation mission and is itself increasingly legalistic. There is also an infantilization inherent in the juvenile court analogy that is arguably ageist. Functional jurisdiction (for example, probate court to deal with matters of legal disability and death) may ultimately prove a less problematic division of judicial labor.

LIMITED GUARDIANSHIP PARADIGM

In addition to the rights paradigm in guardianship, Barnes also challenges the limited guardianship paradigm. She identifies three principal difficulties: First, tailoring the guardian's authority to the extent of the ward's disability is too confusing legally and too difficult to exercise in practice. Second, tailoring the guardian's authority to the extent of the ward's disability is too confusing in the legal definition of incapacity "for the purposes of appointing a substitute decision maker" (p. 263). Finally, limited guardianship distinctions are too transitory to be legally meaningful.

The theory of the limited guardianship paradigm is essentially that the law's requirement of a bright line, where one is either wholly incompetent or wholly competent, is excessively simplistic. Some slight functioning is retained by most legal incompetents. Total incompetence is, for the most part, limited to persistent vegetative states, if not death. To protect against adjudication of excessive and inappropriate incompetence, limited guardianship only adjudicates the precise extent of incompetence. A person may be competent to balance a checkbook but incapable of managing a stock portfolio. A person may be competent to take appropriate medications, but incapable of making a nursing home placement decision.

Unfortunately, this humanizing theory of limited guardianship is little utilized in practice, even when it is available. The judicial attitude seems to be that it is preferable that a guardian be given full powers now, rather than to create a situation where everyone will be back in court in a few months asking for more authority. Limited guardianship also has the potential to expand the net of inappropriate guardianships. Limited incompetence is an easier threshold to prove than total incompetence, and there is no indication that procedural protections are greater for limited legal incompetence than for more easily evaluated total incompetence.

However, it may be premature to abandon the limited guardianship paradigm. One fundamental difficulty is ambiguity in the conceptualization of guardianship. Executional incapacity is too easily confused with decisional incapacity. Guardianship is most clearly about decisional incapacity and legal substitute decision making. A guardian is a surrogate decision maker and services broker, not a services provider (other than providing decision-making services). A guardian lives the decisional life of another, the ward, who is incompetent to make decisions.

The characterization that "courts are ill prepared to distinguish the [incapable] act from the decision-making capability" (p. 262) is too well demonstrated in much contemporary guardianship practice (e.g., Schmidt, 1987). However, the notion that courts and the law are institutionally incapable of distinguishing act from mental capability, or of assessing the extent of decision-making capacity, is not reflected in other judicial activities and areas of the law. Criminal law goes to great lengths to distinguish *actus reus* from *mens rea*, and to denominate the gradations of criminal mental intent, in the course of assessing whether or not there is criminal responsibility, as well as in assessing the precise extent of criminal responsibility. There are a few criminal law scholars who advocate strict liability, focusing only on whether the defendant did the deed, just as there are advocates of no-fault strict liability in automobile accident behavior, divorce, and medical malpractice. But the predominant paradigm in law is free will (autonomy) and individual responsibility, even if they are only legal fictions upheld for moral and policy reasons. There is preliminary research on tests for legal competence (Lidz et al.,

1984; Roth, Meisel & Lidz, 1977), but the field is largely undeveloped and merits substantial attention.

Barnes' third difficulty with the limited guardianship paradigm is the transitoriness of some decision-making competencies. This may be more of a problem in theory than in practice. As previously indicated, courts in practice underutilize limited guardianship and tend to award too much authority, rather than too little. A professionally competent guardian will have decision-making authority, but will also negotiate with a ward to the extent possible and defer as much as possible to the ward's choices.

Barnes endorses others' advocacy of changing functional capacity statutes to include mandated reporting of diagnosis, functional deficits, causation, and prognosis of disability. Functional capacity guardianship statutes were originally designed for the developmentally disabled. But Barnes concludes that such a test of decision making gets too easily implemented as a test of whether a socially approved choice has been made. Barnes' diagnosis of the potential abuse is astute, but the remedy may go too far. A prognosis is a prediction, and predictions in the mental disability area are notoriously problematic. Focusing on current decision-making ability as evidenced by recent behavior may be an approach more amenable to judicial assessment.

LIVING RIGHTS FOR THE LIVING

In asserting "that society has not resolved fundamental ambivalence about the aged and property control" (p. 256), Barnes gives voice to "a certain visceral logic" (p. 265) that unconventional relationships, like older man/younger woman or older woman/younger man, threaten the "conventional social order" (p. 264) and "social and family stability" (p. 265).

The history of guardianship is indeed a history of the management of property. Law generally is concerned that property, and titles to property, are kept in circulation in the market. An incapacitated property owner impedes commerce in the property. Similarly, the law is concerned that a citizen's decisions are kept in circulation through agreements and contracts. Guardianship serves the function of keeping property, and titles to property, on active, available status in the market. Guardianship also provides a substitute decision-making mechanism for individuals incapable of legally deciding for themselves; guardianship keeps decisional capacity in circulation. With these functions in mind, then, the following conclusion is not much of a surprise:

> Under the present system of "Estate Management by Preemption" we divest the incompetent of control of his property upon the finding of the existence of serious mental illness whenever divestiture is in the interest of some third person or institution. The theory of incompetency is to protect the debilitated from their own financial foolishness or from the fraud of others who would prey upon their mental weaknesses. In practice, however, we seek to protect the interests of others. The state hospital commences incompetency proceedings to facilitate reimbursement for costs incurred in the care, treatment and maintenance of its patients. Dependents institute proceedings to secure their needs. Co-owners of property find incompetency proceedings convenient ways to secure the sale of realty. Heirs institute actions to preserve their dwindling inheritances. Beneficiaries of trusts or estates seek incompetency as an expedient method of removing as trustee one who is managing the trust or estate in a manner adverse to their interests. All of these motives may be honest and without any intent to cheat the aged, but none of the proceedings are commenced to assist the debilitated. (Alexander & Lewin, 1972, p. 135)

Acknowledging that guardianship serves the interests of third persons and institutions rather than the legal incompetent is not to congratulate cleverness. Rather, guardianship for older adults amounts to an insidious and ageist effort at social control. The common variable to older man/younger woman and older woman/younger man relationships is age not unconventionality. Lineal inheritance may motivate some of the young to care for the old, but dependence on such motivation encourages caregiving premised on preserving inheritances and seeking recognition in a will rather than on maintaining the elder as a matter of "love, need and duty" (Barnes, p. 256), or as a matter of the elder's right.

In 1982, the California Law Revision commission recommended to the legislature changes in intestate succession to conform to public survey preferences (Monahan & Walker, 1985). Empirical studies demonstrated that most people want all of their estate distributed to their surviving spouse rather than to their children, parents, and brothers and sisters (Fellows, Simon, & Rau, 1978; Niles, 1979). This recommendation was eliminated from the final bill, however, because of the unanimous opposition of the Estate Planning, Trust, and Probate Section of the State Bar of California. The lawyers argued that "it was their 'gut feeling', from talking to their clients who made wills that these recommendations were 'not what people wanted' " (Monahan & Walker, 1985, p. 282). In contrast to the "visceral logic" and "gut feeling" of probate lawyers, the surveyed public seems to prefer elder and generational autonomy and self-sufficiency.

A rights paradigm says to the elder: "Enjoy your money now if you want; you earned it." This approach is probably good for the contemporary economy and provides employment for families. The notion that "society's interest is the transfer of family property so as to maintain the family as a secure unit" (Kossow, 1976, pp. 238–239), rather than society's interest being "the average intestate's intent" (Kossow, 1976, pp. 238–239), is a social myth and legal fiction for which there is little evidence now or in history.

Reality is not a private sector or a private market, but an encompassing larger market of private and public organizations, institutions, and individuals interactively seeking the fairest and most efficient means of providing services like substitute decision making and long-term care. Reality is a dynamic, mobile, aging society where the aggregation and juxtaposition of individual rights, choices, and interests constitute social order and the social interest.

A NEW, ALTERNATIVE MECHANISM FOR ADDRESSING DECISIONAL INCAPACITY

When an individual dies without a will (which would have reflected the individual's choice about disposition of property and person), the state decides disposition according to its intestate succession statute. When an individual becomes incompetent without a living will and durable power of attorney, there should be an analogous alternative to the state deciding disposition according to the guardianship process and system.

I propose the design and adoption of an incompetence succession statute. As with intestate succession, the scheme would identify a line of succession for substitute decision makers,[1] as well as a designation of property allocation. The line of succession and property allocation could mimic intestate succession. Guardianship tends to be triggered by the most interested third party or institution. Incompetence succession would be triggered by incompetence combined with the absence of choices expressed by a living will and durable power of attorney. It would change the focus of attention from third parties' interests to the individual's decision-making capacity, and would accomplish living rights for the living, rather than "property rights for the living" (Barnes, p. 264).

CONCLUSIONS

Guardianship reform has proceeded on the basis of a rights paradigm. This is not inappropriate. But guardianship continues to serve primarily third-party interests and social control purposes. The ultimate realization of guardianship reform may lie in adoption of an incompetence succession statute. Incompetence succession offers the opportunity to bypass guardianship and focus on the decision making capacity and needs of the person who is incompetent.

NOTE

1. Thirty-three jurisdictions have surrogate health care devolution decision-making statutes providing for family consent (Sabatino, 1994). They are Arizona, Arkansas, California, Colorado, Connecticut, District of Columbia, Florida, Georgia, Idaho, Illinois, Indiana, Iowa, Louisiana, Maine, Maryland, Mississippi, Missouri, Montana, Nebraska, Nevada, New Mexico, New York, North Carolina, North Dakota, Oregon, South Carolina, South Dakota, Texas, Utah, Virginia, Washington, West Virginia, and Wyoming.

REFERENCES

Alexander, G. J., & Lewin, T. H. D. (1972). *The aged and the need for surrogate management*. Syracuse, NY: Syracuse University Press.

Blenkner, M., Bloom, M., Nielson, M., & Weber, R. (1974). *Final report: Protective services for older people, Findings from the Benjamin Rose Institute study*. Cleveland: Benjamin Rose Institute.

Brown, R. (1979). *The rights of older persons.* New York: Avon.

Fellows, M., Simon, R., & Rau, W. (1978). Public attitudes about property distribution at death and intestate succession laws in the United States. *American Bar Foundation Research Journal, 1978,* 319–391.

Frolik, L., & Barnes, A. (1992). *Elderlaw: Cases and materials.* Charlottesville, VA: Michie.

Galanter, M. (1983). Reading the landscape of disputes: What we know and don't know (and think we know) about our allegedly contentious and litigious society. *UCLA Law Review, 31,* 4–71.

Glendon, M. (1991). *Rights talk: The impoverishment of political discourse.* New York: Free Press.

Kapp, M. (1992). *Geriatrics and the law: Patient rights and professional responsibilities* (2nd ed.). New York: Springer.

Kossow, J. (1976). The New York law of intestate succession compared with the Uniform Probate Code: Where there's no will there's a way. *Fordham Urban Law Journal, 4,* 233–262.

Kuhn, T. (1970). *The structure of scientific revolutions* (2nd ed.). Chicago: University of Chicago Press.

Lidz, C., Meisel, A., Zerubauel, E., Carter, M., Sestak, R., & Roth, L. (1984). *Informed consent: A study of decisionmaking in psychiatry.* New York: Guilford.

Lisi, L. B., Burns, A., Hommel, P., Baird, K. B., Lindgren, C., Roe, E., & Brewster, S. (1992). *National study of guardianship system and feasibility of implementing expert systems.* Ann Arbor, MI: Center for Social Gerontology.

Martin, J. (1980). Justice and efficiency under a model of estate settlement. *Virginia Law Review, 66,* 727–775.

Mathews v. Eldridge, 424 U.S. 319 (1976).

Melton, G., & Lind, E. (1982). Procedural justice in family court: Does the adversarial model make sense? *Children & Youth Services, 5* (1/2), 65–83.

Monahan, J., & Walker, L. (1985). *Social science in law: Cases and materials.* Mineola, NY: Foundation.

Niles, R. (1979). Probate reform in California. *Hastings Law Journal, 31,* 185–220.

O'Connor v. Donaldson, 422 U.S. 563, 583 (1975) (Burger, C.J., concurring).

Perlin, M. (1989-1993). *Mental disability law: Civil and criminal* (Vols. 1–3). Charlottesville, VA: Michie.

Reisner, R., & Slobogin, C. (1990). *Law and the mental health system: Civil and criminal aspects* (2nd ed.). St. Paul, MN: West.

Rosenbloom, D. (1986). *Public administration: Understanding management, politics, and law in the public sector.* NY: Random House.

Roth, L., Meisel, A., & Lidz, C. (1977). Tests of competency to consent to treatment. *American Journal of Psychiatry, 134,* 279–284.

Rud v. Dahl, 578 F.2d 674 (7th Cir. 1978).

Sabatino, C. (1994). Pathways of health care surrogate decisionmaking. *Bioethics Bulletin, 3* (1), 27.

Schmidt, W. (1981). Guardianship of the elderly in Florida: Social bankruptcy and the need for reform. *Florida Bar Journal, 55,* 189–195.

Schmidt, W. (1984). The evolution of a public guardianship program. *Journal of Psychiatry & Law, 12,* 349–372.

Schmidt, W. (1986). Adult protective services and the therapeutic state. *Law and Psychology Review, 10,* 101–121.

Schmidt, W. (1987). Recommended judicial practices in guardianship proceedings for the elderly. *Florida Bar Journal, 61,* 35–40.

Schmidt, W. (1990). Quantitative information about the quality of the guardianship system: Toward a next generation of guardianship research. *Probate Law Journal, 10,* 61-80.

Schmidt, W., & Miller, K. (1984). Improving the social treatment model in protective services for the elderly: False needs in the therapeutic state. *Journal of International and Comparative Social Welfare, 1,* 90–106.

Schmidt, W., Miller, K., Bell, W., & New, E. (1981). *Public guardianship and the elderly.* Cambridge, MA: Ballinger.

Thomas v. Humfield, 916 F.2d 1032 (5th Cir. 1990).

Afterword: Decision-Making Capacity Among Older Adults: Person, Process, and Context

Michael A. Smyer

Alyce Mary Utsey's husband brought her to the Valley View Home, after caring for her at home for 4 years. She had become increasingly disoriented; she had also become incontinent. Her lifelong problems with arthritis had gotten much worse, so that she was now confined either to her wheelchair or to her bed. She had been on a regimen of low doses of pain killers and a tranquilizer to help her sleep.

When she got to Valley View, Mrs. Utsey was confused, but pleasant. Because she had been a nurse 50 years earlier, she was comfortable in the nursing environment. She thought she was a supervisor—not a new resident. The staff went along with this view of the world—an easy accommodation to help Mrs. U (as they quickly came to call her) adjust.

Everyone was pleased with the first week. Mrs. U seemed to adapt very easily to the unit. She couldn't remember any of the staff members' names, but she covered for this deficit by calling each one

"Honey." She couldn't quite remember the directions to her room, but she got help by asking staff members to "walk me home."

All in all, Mrs. U was getting along nicely until the social worker, Ms. McGraw, approached her about advance directives. She gave Mrs. U the leaflet that Valley View had developed to comply with the federal Patient Self-Determination Act. Ms. McGraw then tried to assess Mrs. U's ability to be involved in specifying her wishes about advanced directives:

"Do you know what an advance directive is?" Ms. McGraw thought she'd start with the basics.

"Advanced directions? Honey, I don't worry about those things." Mrs. U was having none of it.

"If you knew you had a fatal illness, would you want to be kept alive using heroic measures?" Ms. McGraw wanted to get some sense of Mrs. U's own values and preferences.

"My heroes have always been the First Ladies. I especially liked Mamie Eisenhower." Mrs. U may have been commenting on the heroic nature of marital commitment, but she was not focusing on advanced directives.

Ms. McGraw was willing to give it one more try: "If you knew you were going to die without special medical treatment, would you want us to do anything we could to keep you alive?"

Mrs. U. stared at her for a moment. Then, in a low but clear voice she answered: "I am pro-life. I think you shouldn't die until your time comes, so you'd better do what it takes to keep life alive."

"So you'd want us to do whatever it takes to keep you alive?" Ms. McGraw felt that she was closing in on a decision. "Alive, alive, o. . . ." Mrs. U's lucidity had vanished as quickly as it had come.

Exchanges like this one represent the intersection of public policy, clinical practice, and ethical choices in the everyday lives of older people (Kane & Caplan, 1990). Is Mrs. Utsey capable of specifying an advanced directive? Is she capable of engaging in the decision-making process? How would *you* decide?

PERSON-PROCESS-CONTEXT: A FRAMEWORK

The answer to this question may depend upon the assumptions you make regarding three interacting elements: the person, the process, and the context. Bronfenbrenner (1989) reminds us that behavior and development are a function of these three, a perspective that is a direct descendant of Lewin's work (1935, 1951).

The contributions in this book represent reports from the front lines in the battle to understand older adults' capacity for being involved in decision making, to respect their abilities and limitations, and to engage them to the fullest extent possible. These chapters also allow us to reflect on our changing understanding of older adults, the processes we use to assess their capacity for decision making and the impact of contexts on decision making.

Person

Assessing a person's decision-making capacity requires an evaluation (Langer & Park, 1990; Sternberg, 1990). As Sabatino notes in chapter 1 of this volume, we are witnessing a transformation in our "legal fiction" of the elderly person with questionable decision-making capacity. In an earlier time, age itself was equated with incapacity. Now, states are refining their legal fictions to encompass some combination of three elements: presence or absence of a disability or disabling condition, a functional impairment, and some indication of an impairment in either making or communicating a decision (Anderer, 1990). Just as our legal fiction is changing, so, too is our assessment of the elements that comprise it. Our social understanding of frailty (and, by extension, of disability) increasingly focuses on the biomedical aspects (Kaufman & Becker, this volume), while the ethical dilemmas of autonomy are also increasing.

Is Mrs. Utsey capable of making a decision regarding end-of-life care? In part, our answer depends upon our assumptions regarding her capacity as an individual. In part, our answer depends upon our assumptions regarding the process necessary to make a decision.

Process

In his commentary to chapter 1, Salthouse has highlighted the importance of focusing on the process of decision making for older adults. For example, the ways in which we provide information (e.g., reading level, structure of the information, etc.) can directly affect what the older person will comprehend. Willis, in chapter 3, noted that the fit between the individual's capacity and the demands of the setting should be the subjects of assessment. Her emphasis on everyday problem solving, for example, links the general concern for capacity to specific adaptation processes that directly affect an older person's ability to remain in the community, care for herself, and be involved in her treatment decisions. Similarly, Dellasega and her colleagues, in their commentary to Willis, provide useful information on the effects of altering the way in which information is given to older adults in acute care settings (hospitals). Building on earlier work by Appelbaum and Grisso (1988), they document that the process can directly facilitate or impede an older adult's capacity for decision making.

At the same time, however, Kapp reminds us in chapter 5 that these processes are developed within a larger context—a context that can directly affect the process of assessing decision-making capacity and the implications of the decision.

Context

The context regarding legal, ethical, and clinical issues of older adults' decision making is changing rapidly, as Hommel, Barnes, and Schmidt point out in chapter 6. McFarlane, in chapter 2, describes a medico-legal system in Great Britain that paternalistically makes many decisions for impaired older adults. In contrast, contemporary American efforts are focusing on engaging the impaired older adult to the greatest extent possible. Thus, Stiegel and Wilber commenting in chapter 5, document attempts at developing alternatives to guardianship, alternatives to acting on behalf of older adults.

ETHICAL CONCERNS

Throughout our discussion, ethical issues have been both implicit and explicit. There is a healthy tension between our concerns for beneficence and the individual's autonomy. On one hand, we want to protect the individual from harm, even self-inflicted harm. On the other hand, we want to allow the individual as great a freedom as possible—even the freedom to make bad judgments. Cohen's suggestion (chapter 4) that we should be concerned with protecting the inchoate estate of the individual's rights strikes a responsive chord. However, the theoreotical issues still must be resolved the old-fashioned way: one case at a time.

Is Mrs. Utsey capable of specifying advance directives? The answer might depend on our assessment of her individual capacity, her history and previous values, the process we develop for assessing and sharing information, and the legal and political context for our decision. The purpose of this volume has been to enrich our understanding of the person, the process, and the context of older adults' decision-making capacity. If we have been successful, then we might view Mrs. Utsey's situation from a different vantage point: What are the optimal conditions for engaging Mrs. Utsey's capacity for decision-making?

REFERENCES

Anderer, S. J. (1990). *Determining competency in guardianship proceedings.* Washington, DC: American Bar Association.

Appelbaum, P. S. & Grisso, T. (1988). Assessing patients' capacities to consent to treatment. *New England Journal of Medicine, 319,* 1635–1638.

Bronfenbrenner, U. (1989). Ecological systems theory. In R. Vasta (Ed.), *Six theories of child development* (pp. 185–246). Greenwich, CT: JAI Press.

Kane, R. A., & Caplan, A. L. (Eds.). (1990). *Everyday ethics: Resolving dilemmas in nursing home life.* New York: Springer Publishing Co.

Langer, E. J., & Park, K. (1990). Incompetence: A conceptual reconsideration. In R. J. Sternberg & J. Kolligian, Jr. (Eds.), *Competence considered* (pp. 149–166). New Haven, CT: Yale University Press.

Lewin, K. (1935). *A dynamic theory of personality.* New York: McGraw-Hill.

Lewin, K. (1951). *Field theory in social science.* New York: Harper & Brothers.

Sternberg, R. J. (1990). Prototypes of competence and incompetence. In R. J. Sternberg & J. Kolligian, Jr. (Eds.). *Competence considered* (pp. 117–145). New Haven, CT: Yale University Press.

Author Index

Subject Index

Activities of Daily Living (ADLs), 51, 90, 92–93, 113, 128, 130, 136, 237

Adult Protective Services (APS) 80, 184–187, 215

Advanced (health care) directives, 13, 15, 42, 82, 146–147, 150, 153, 156, 158, 165, 168–169, 171, 214, 219, 222, 284, 287

Alternatives-to-Guardianship Services (AGSs), 184,–185, 188–189, 191, 193–195, 197–199, 202–209, 211, 213–215, 217–222

Alzheimer's Disease, 17, 73, 100, 102–104, 106, 136, 207, 261

Assessment(s), 2, 15, 19, 24–25, 29–30, 37–38, 51–53, 56–59, 61, 74, 88, 90, 96–97, 99, 105–106, 108–110, 114–118, 129, 131, 135, 143, 145, 157, 170–171, 182, 186, 215, 217, 220–221, 227, 231–237, 239–240, 261, 270, 278, 285–287

tools (instruments), 88, 129, 139–140

Assisted suidicdes, 83–84

Behavioral, 12, 44, 62,
  change, 60–61
  impairment test, 12–13, 15, 18, 25, 44
Bioethics, 62–63

Caregiver(s), 53–55, 61, 154, 168, 170, 188, 190, 257–258, 260, 262, 265, 271–275

Caregiving, 117, 256,–257, 259, 261, 271–272, 274, 278

Care plan(s), 52, 186

Case mnager/management, 57–58, 61, 184–186, 192, 215–219, 222

Cognitive,
  function(ing), 12–13, 15, 17, 24, 37, 91, 103, 136, 146, 152, 156

impairment(s), 17, 36–37, 53, 88, 100, 114, 151, 158, 184, 192, 194–195, 198–199, 216–217, 222, 234

test(ing), 13, 15–18, 25, 45–46

Cognitively impaired persons, 88, 114, 184, 192, 194–195, 199–199, 216, 222

Community Competence Scale, 113–114

Conservator(ship) (see also guardianship), 12, 22–2487, 91–92, 99, 108, 130, 138, 164–165, 183, 193, 196, 216–218, 220, 240, 246 265

Construct validity, 115, 120

Court(s),
  evalulator, 20, 80–81, 137, 234–239, 240–245,
  investigators, 21, 79–80, 99, 131–132, 137, 139
  monitoring, 135–136, 209, 233
  visitors, 21–23, 80, 137, 233, 236, 241

Court of Protection, 71–72, 74, 76

Daily Money Management (DMM), 188, 214–218, 220–222
  case management intervention, 217
  least restrictive option, 217
  preventative model, 215
  service delivery model, 217
  service intervention, 216–217, 220

De Praeroativa Regis, 5, 72

Decision maker(s) see guardianshp

Decision making process(es), 97, 150, 181, 221

Decisional intervention, 219, 221–222

Dementia(s), 36, 38, 43–44, 75–76, 91, 97, 99–100, 102–103, 119, 131, 135, 167, 187

Dependence, 49, 51–54, 63, 65, 80, 96–97, 176, 189, 196, 214–215, 222–223, 226, 268, 272